INSIDE

Network Security Assessment

Guarding Your IT Infrastructure

Michael Gregg
David Kim

SAMS

Sams Publishing, 800 East 96th Street. Indianapolis, Indiana 46240 USA

Inside Network Security Assessment: Guarding Your IT Infrastructure

Copyright © 2006 by Sams Publishing

International Standard Book Number: 0-672-32809-7

Library of Congress Catalog Card Number: 2005902139

Printed in the United States of America

First Printing: December 2005

08   07   06   05   4   3   2   1

Trademarks

All terms mentioned in this book that are known to be trademarks or service marks have been appropriately capitalized. Sams Publishing cannot attest to the accuracy of this information. Use of a term in this book should not be regarded as affecting the validity of any trademark or service mark.

Warning and Disclaimer

Every effort has been made to make this book as complete and as accurate as possible, but no warranty or fitness is implied. The information provided is on an "as is" basis. The authors and the publisher shall have neither liability nor responsibility to any person or entity with respect to any loss or damages arising from the information contained in this book.

Bulk Sales

Sams Publishing offers excellent discounts on this book when ordered in quantity for bulk purchases or special sales. For more information, please contact

> **U.S. Corporate and Government Sales**
> **1-800-382-3419**
> **corpsales@pearsontechgroup.com**

For sales outside of the U.S., please contact

> **International Sales**
> **international@pearsoned.com**

Acquisitions Editor
Linda Bump Harrison

Development Editor
Songlin Qiu

Managing Editor
Charlotte Clapp

Senior Project Editor
Matthew Purcell

Copy Editor
Barbara Hacha

Indexer
Bill Meyers

Proofreader
Leslie Joseph

Technical Editor
Guy Bruneau

Publishing Coordinator
Vanessa Evans

Designer
Gary Adair

Page Layout
Eric S. Miller

Contents at a Glance

Table of Contents

About the Authors

Michael Gregg is the president of Superior Solutions, Inc., a Houston-based security assessment and training firm. He has more than 20 years of experience in the IT field. He holds two associate's degrees, a bachelor's degree, and a master's degree. Some of the certifications he maintains are the following: CISSP, MCSE, CCNA, CTT+, A+, N+, Security+, CIW Security Analyst, CEH, NSA IAM, SCNP, DCNP, CCE, and TICSA.

He has consulted and taught for many Fortune 500 companies. Although consulting consumes the bulk of Michael's time, he enjoys teaching. Michael has a proven reputation as both a dynamic and influential speaker. His delivery style is considered energetic and entertaining, yet insightful. Michael has written articles for various magazines and is a frequent contributor to IT websites. He is also the author and technical editor of other books, including *CISSP Exam Cram 2*. Michael led the development of Villanova University's Online Security curriculum.

He is a member of the American College of Forensic Examiners and of the Texas Association for Educational Technology. When not working, Michael enjoys traveling and restoring muscle cars.

David Kim, B.S.E.E., is the senior vice president and chief operating officer of Security Evolutions, Inc. (SEI), and former chief operating officer of (ISC)² Institute. SEI specializes in IT security training, IT security consulting services, and IT security development. David is responsible for leading the vision of SEI's information security products and services portfolio and managing the day-to-day operations for SEI's P&L Business Units.

David's IT and IT security experience encompasses more than 20 years of technical engineering and management in the IT field. This experience includes LAN/WAN, internetworking, enterprise network management, and IT security. Currently, he is an active IT security consultant, trainer, and developer and is instrumental in defining SEI's products and service portfolio. David also program manages large-scale risk and vulnerability assessment projects for large commercial, government, and higher-education clients throughout the world. In addition, he works with large service organizations developing risk and vulnerability assessment professional services, all based on the same foundational elements found in this book.

Dedications

Michael Gregg: I would like to dedicate this book to my brother, Gary D. Gregg, because he helped spark my interest in all things technical including phonevs, circuits, and computers.

David Kim: In memory of Dr. Charles W. Kim.

Acknowledgments

Michael Gregg: I would like to offer a big "thank you" to Christine, Curly, Betty, Elvira, Alice, Gen, and all my family. I would also like to acknowledge David Kim for helping create this book. A special thanks to the people of Sams who helped make this project a reality, including Linda Harrison, Songlin Qiu, and Matt Purcell.

David Kim: In recognition of my colleagues at (ISC)^2 Institute, the training arm of the International Information Systems Security Certification Consortium, Inc., and Security Evolutions, Inc., I would like to thank them for the inspiration they provide me to secure the world's IT and network infrastructures.

In the interest of my children Annie, Janis, Christina, and Alex, and my wife, MiYoung, who stands beside me wherever I go, I want to thank you for providing me with the motivation to work hard.

We Want to Hear from You!

As the reader of this book, *you* are our most important critic and commentator. We value your opinion and want to know what we're doing right, what we could do better, what areas you'd like to see us publish in, and any other words of wisdom you're willing to pass our way.

You can email or write me directly to let me know what you did or didn't like about this book—as well as what we can do to make our books stronger.

Please note that I cannot help you with technical problems related to the topic of this book, and that due to the high volume of mail I receive, I might not be able to reply to every message.

When you write, please be sure to include this book's title and author as well as your name and phone or email address. I will carefully review your comments and share them with the author and editors who worked on the book.

Email: networking@samspublishing.com

Mail: Mark Taber
Associate Publisher
Sams Publishing
800 East 96th Street
Indianapolis, IN 46240 USA

Reader Services

For more information about this book or another Sams Publishing title, visit our website at www.samspublishing.com. Type the ISBN (excluding hyphens) or the title of a book in the Search field to find the page you're looking for.

Introduction

WELCOME, AND THANK YOU FOR PURCHASING *Inside Network Security Assessment*. Our goal was to create a practical guide for planning, performing, and reporting on the risk and vulnerability assessment process. This is a critical topic for IT professionals given that a security assessment provides the necessary information and data for organizations to form the foundation for a reliable and secure IT infrastructure.

This book takes a look inside the network vulnerability assessment process. Its purpose is to teach individuals a methodology for network security assessments. For those of you who must manage or outsource these duties, this book will provide you with tips, pointers, and insight into what a vulnerability assessment is all about. This book is broken up into 10 chapters that follow the vulnerability assessment process from creation to finish. It also discusses, in brief, basic risk assessment methodologies. So even if you are not ready for a full-blown vulnerability assessment, you should be able to start adding basic risk assessment methodologies to new projects and the change control process.

The security assessment process incorporates both risk assessment and vulnerability assessment, which includes the science, tools, methodology, and practices involved in finding, analyzing, and assessing risk for known or unknown vulnerabilities and exposures in a given Information Technology (IT) infrastructure. This book examines the entire IT infrastructure, which encompasses all the IT assets commonly found in an IT environment, such as the data, applications, servers, workstations, and network infrastructure (LANs, WANs, and LAN-to-WAN). The term *IT infrastructure* is generally used to describe the entire landscape of IT assets and elements. The term *IT assets* is generally used to describe the individual IT assets or elements commonly found in an IT environment.

All organizations need to assess, identify, define, and confirm the minimum level of acceptable security for their organization and IT assets. Until now, organizations needed to spend thousands of dollars on high-priced consultants to perform a variety of assessments. With *Inside Network Security Assessment*, readers will receive a collection of tools, utilities, templates, and a step-by-step approach for conducting a security assessment process that incorporates both risk assessment and vulnerability assessment.

Who Should Read This Book

This is an intermediate-level book for IT security professionals and system and network administrators who need to learn more about the security assessment process. *Inside Network Security Assessment* provides a step-by-step approach for assessing security, from paperwork to penetration testing to ethical hacking. This book is a valuable reference for individuals who are interested in creating their own methodology for conducting a comprehensive security assessment and in expanding their knowledge of network security tools and techniques to perform such evaluations. Almost every organization needs to evaluate the security of its IT infrastructure and IT assets.

Depending on the scope of the IT infrastructure and the scope of the security assessment, organizations can spend tens or hundreds of thousands of dollars to conduct a security assessment. With proper controls and objectivity, conducting a security assessment with internal IT security staff is a viable solution. To do this, the IT security staff must create their own methodology and implement it in-house.

Why We Created This Book

The world of information security continually evolves. More tools are available to attackers and defenders than ever before. There has also been an onslaught of books, classes, and seminars focused on security testing, tools, and techniques. But we as authors felt that something was missing. Among the wealth of information on tools and the how-to of security testing, very little was being discussed about the mechanics of security testing; therefore, we created this book to inform readers that the creation of a methodology and approach for conducting a security assessment is the critical missing piece. Unlike other books that focus on hacking tools or small segments of the assessment process, this book was designed to offer the reader a comprehensive step-by-step approach for guiding them through the security assessment process.

Overview of the Book's Contents

We would like to introduce this book from a 50,000-foot view. The first two chapters, "Introduction to Assessing Network Vulnerabilities" and "Foundations and Principles of Security," serve as a foundation for later chapters. These chapters introduce basic concepts of everything we will talk about throughout the book. Chapter 3, "Why Risk Assessment," and Chapter 4, "Risk Assessment Methodologies," deal specifically with risk. We examine risk terminology, quantitative risk assessment, qualitative risk assessment, and how risk is analyzed in real life.

Chapters 5 through 10 are designed to guide you through the security assessment process. Chapter 5, "Scoping the Project," presents a discussion of the scoping phase. Topics such as the forces driving the assessment are introduced. Chapter 6, "Understanding the Attacker," discusses who the real threat is. Both inside and outside attacks typically follow a given pattern. These stages of attack are discussed, as are ways to reduce the threat. If the assessment you are performing is being driven because of an attack, you'll find this a particularly valuable chapter.

Chapter 7, "Performing the Assessment," introduces the activities performed during the actual assessment. This might be only a policy review or may involve extensive hands-on testing. If hands-on testing is required, you will need a variety of tools, which are discussed in Chapter 8, "Tools Used for Assessments and Evaluations." Chapter 9, "Preparing the Final Report," introduces you to the report-writing phase. Everything you have done must be documented, and this chapter discusses ways to write a successful report. Finally, Chapter 10, "Post-Assessment Activities," describes what happens next. Post-assessment activities typically involve change. So this chapter delves into the topics of policy change, hardware implementation, and user training.

We have also outfitted the book with five appendixes. Here we provide security assessment resources, sample forms, and information on how to deal with outside consultants should you feel the need to outsource part of this process. Performing a security assessment is a challenging journey, and we hope that our approach to guarding your IT infrastructure makes your path more comfortable.

Conventions Used in This Book

This book follows a few typographical and stylistic conventions:

- New terms are set in *italic* the first time they are introduced.
- Each chapter concludes with key terms that have been introduced within the chapter.
- Whenever possible, we reference the Common Vulnerabilities and Exposures (CVE) database to enable you to obtain additional information about the vulnerabilities; for example, `http://cve.mitre.org/cgi-bin/cvename.cgi?name=CAN-2004-0965`.
- This book also contains the following elements for additional information, such as notes, tips, cautions, and sidebars.

Note

Notes provide additional information about a topic.

Tip

Tips provide information that can make a task easier or ease an administrative burden.

Caution

Cautions are items you need to be aware of that may pose a problem or need to be carefully considered.

A Sidebar Looks Like This

We often use sidebars to present illustrative examples or add greater depth to the material.

1

Introduction to Assessing
Network Vulnerabilities

THIS CHAPTER INTRODUCES SOME BASIC SECURITY CONCEPTS, such as what security really is. It also starts the discussion of risk assessment as a process. *Risk* is all around us, and good Information Technology (IT) governance requires us to assess its potential dangers. Finally, this chapter will provide an overview of the network vulnerability assessment. Understanding how the network vulnerability assessment fits into the overall security program will help as we go through the entire process in subsequent chapters.

What Security Is and Isn't

Computer security is unlike other forms of security. Products such as locks, safes, and steel doors give clear ratings on what types of attacks they can withstand and how long they can withstand them. Most IT security products do not come configured in such a manner. These devices state only that they will prevent, block, drop, or protect from specific risks. Technology has failed to offer one complete perfect solution. Sure, you will find vast quantities of security technologies advertised in all the latest glossy security magazines and at security trade shows, but simply throwing money at products isn't the real solution. Security is not technology.

Misconfiguration, improper installation, and poor management are other causes of poor security. I have seen IT workers and managers involved in poor practices. I'll never forget the time a government agency showed me a *firewall* that was supposed to be protecting the internal network. The problem was that it wasn't even hooked to the network. It was configured in loop back mode. Security is not the administration.

Policies are another item pointed to when someone speaks of security. Many organizations don't have a well-defined security policy. Others have policies but they are poorly written or no one follows them because there are no consequences built in to the policy. After all, it's just a paper document. Policies are not security.

By now, you may be wondering what I think security is. Security is a process. Yes, security requires technology, people, and policies; however, that is not enough. Security is a process that requires input from the entire organization to be effective. It involves work on a proactive basis, such as patching vulnerable systems and monitoring audit files and IDS systems' activity logs. Security also requires support from senior management; it includes risk analysis, good implementation, employee training, patch management, and periodic vulnerability assessments. Figure 1.1 outlines the flow of this process.

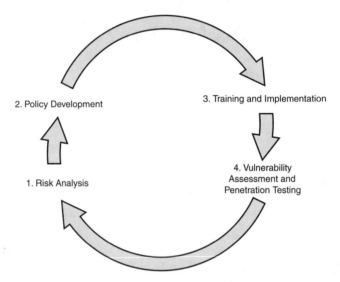

Figure 1.1   The risk assessment process.

Process for Assessing Risk

Assessing risk is a process and as such, is something that must be periodically repeated. It's really not much different from the automated patch-management tools you are probably using. True security requires ongoing effort. There is never a wrong time to assess risk and examine network vulnerabilities. There are three key points at which assessments should be considered:

1. When a new program is developed, a risk analysis should be performed to establish the security state of the system. An analysis performed early on like this helps establish whether security problems exist. This is beneficial when new code or applications are developed for which problems can be found and fixed early on.

2. An analysis of risk should be performed whenever changes are made to systems, processes, or programs. A risk analysis performed during this time is instrumental in uncovering vulnerabilities that occur as a possible side effect from the change.

3. A vulnerability assessment should be performed periodically to examine the controls that have been implemented. It's also advisable anytime there has been a breach in security, an intrusion, or an attack. At this point, the assessment is critical because it can help uncover how the breach occurred and discover what problem in policy or system vulnerability allowed the event to occur.

Note

In Chapter 4, "Risk Assessment Methodologies," you learn more about the methodologies that can be used to assess and analyze risk.

What is important to note at this point is why developing a risk assessment process is so important. A primary reason is to show *due care* and *due diligence*. Other reasons include the following:

- Maintain customer confidence.
- Protect confidentiality.
- Prevent inappropriate disclosure.
- Ensure the integrity of the organization's informational *assets*.
- Ensure that the organization's resources are not misused or wasted.
- Comply with state, provincial, and federal laws and regulations.
- Avoid a hostile workplace atmosphere.

Four Ways in Which You Can Respond to Risk

So is finding and identifying risk enough? No, not really. After you have found and identified risk, your job is not yet over. You will have to determine how you are going to handle the potential risk. There are four ways in which you can respond to risk: *avoidance*, *transference*, *mitigation*, and *acceptance*:

- Avoiding a risk can be accomplished by taking steps to change your plans, go with different technologies, or hire employees that are skilled in dealing with the problems you are facing. Consider the example of your daughter's wedding. She has made up her mind that it should be this summer on the beach in the Bahamas. You have explained to her that there is always the chance that a hurricane could occur on that same week as the wedding. To avoid the risk, you have suggested that it be moved to Hawaii.

- Transferring a risk is another valid approach. To transfer the risk, you will move ownership to a third party. Insurance is one way to transfer risk. They assume the risk, but we are saddled with the cost of the insurance. In our example of the wedding, we could transfer the risk by buying hurricane insurance.

- Mitigating a risk is the third possible approach. Mitigation is an active attempt to reduce the effect of the risk even before it happens. For a software project this might mean spending more time in development, adding security features, or incurring the cost of a longer, more thorough, beta test. For the future bride, a potential mitigation strategy might consist of securing tents on the beach to protect the attendees from sun or rain and possibly moving the reception inside the hotel to a more sheltered area.

- Accepting the risk is the final option and only when no other options are available or the potential loss is small when compared to the project's benefits. If this is the chosen path, it is important to prepare contingency plans to make sure you will be able to deal with the risk if it occurs. To use the wedding analogy one final time, we can see that if the bride has her heart set on this wedding on the beach, it may be best just to go along. Although what she doesn't know is that the hotel has agreed to allow them to hold the event indoors should the weather turn bad. Knowing that there's a contingency plan eases the worries.

Network Vulnerability Assessment

How does a network vulnerability assessment fit into the risk assessment process previously discussed? The network vulnerability assessment is a tool that looks at the existing security program and analyzes it to see if it meets the organization's needs. The network vulnerability assessment seeks to answer the following questions:

- What are the organization's most important assets?
- Should more or fewer security countermeasures be implemented to protect them?
- What is the organization's true security posture?
- What would be the effect of a security breach?

Types of Network Vulnerability Assessments

Network vulnerability assessments are also known as vulnerability testing, network evaluations, red-team exercises, penetration testing, host vulnerability assessment, and vulnerability assessment and management. No matter what they are called, the assessment is a systematic examination of an organization's network, policies, and controls. Its purpose is to determine the adequacy of security measures, identify security deficiencies, provide data from which to predict the effectiveness of potential security measures, and confirm the adequacy of such measures after implementation. In the course of this book, an assessment will be addressed in one of three terms. Each of these terms has a specific meaning and includes high-level assessments, network evaluations, and penetration tests.

- **Policy assessments**—We will call this a level I assessment. It is a top-down look at the organization's policies, procedures, and guidelines. This type of vulnerability assessment does not include any hands-on testing. The purpose of a top-down policy assessment is to answer three questions:

- Do the applicable policies exist?
- Are they being followed?
- Is there content sufficient to guard against potential risk?

- **Network evaluations**—We will call this a level II assessment. It has all the elements specified in a level I assessment plus hands-on activities. These hands-on activities include information gathering, vulnerability assessment scanning, and so on.

- **Penetration tests**—Unlike assessments and evaluations, penetration tests are adversarial in nature. We will refer to penetration tests as level III assessments. These events typically take on an adversarial role and look to see what the outsider can access and control. Penetration tests are much less concerned with policies and procedures and are more focused on finding "low-hanging fruit" and seeing what a hacker can compromise on this network. We almost always recommend that organizations complete an assessment and evaluation before beginning a penetration test, because a company with adequate policies and procedures can't implement real security without documented controls. Figure 1.2 shows the three types of assessments.

Note

The U.S. government has been performing penetration tests on their own networks since the 1970s. These individuals were referred to as *red teams* and were given permission to hack into government systems.

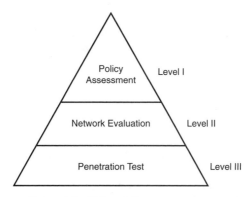

Figure 1.2   Vulnerability assessment types.

Pen Testing in Real Life

During the late 1990s, the U.S. government initiated an intensive penetration test code named Eligible Receiver. The penetration test used red teams of hackers who were dispersed throughout the United States with orders to infiltrate Pentagon systems. Much of this project is still classified. What is known is that the red teams were allowed to use only publicly available systems and tools. Even without specialized tools available to the NSA and other government agencies, these individuals were able to infiltrate the Pacific command center's computers and take control of power grids and 911 systems in nine major U.S. cities.

What Procedures Govern the Vulnerability Assessment?

There is not one single document that anyone preparing for a vulnerability assessment can point to as the true and correct method. Industries such as accounting have clearly defined rules, procedures, and regulations that govern that profession's activities. Generally Accepted Accounting Principles (GAAP) is an example, because it dictates the actions and approaches an accountant must abide by.

In the world of security, several sets of principles and procedures have been developed over the years. Some look inward, such as the *Information Technology Security Evaluation Criteria (ITSEC)* and the *Trusted Computer System Evaluation Criteria (TCSEC)* and examine items such as trust and assurance. Others look outward and examine policies, procedures, and external controls. One of these is the *Generally Accepted System Security Principles (GASSP)*. The intention of GASSP was to create an infrastructure that mirrored the GAAP principles that underwrite the accounting profession. GASSP embodies information security concepts and incorporates them into the following hierarchy of nine high-level items:

1. **Accountability**—The responsibility for security must be clearly defined and acknowledged.
2. **Awareness**—Knowledge of applicable threats should be known.
3. **Ethics**—Ethical behavior is an important issue and as such, information should always be used and handled in an ethical manner.
4. **Multidisciplinary**—Security should address the viewpoints of everyone within the organization.
5. **Proportionality**—Security should be proportionate to the potential risks.
6. **Integration**—Organizational policies should be integrated with the security goals of the organization.
7. **Timeliness**—Responds to potential threats in a timely manner.
8. **Assessment**—Periodic assessment should be performed.
9. **Equity**—The rights and dignity of individuals should be respected by management.

Other such documents include *ISO 17799* and Control Objectives for Information and Related Technology (COBIT). Even the government got in the game back in 1998. The then president of the United States, Bill Clinton, enacted PDD 63. This presidential policy required that specific measures be taken to protect the nation's critical infrastructure. PDD 63 required that the federal government address the cyber and physical infrastructure vulnerabilities of the federal government. Each department and agency is required to work to reduce its exposure to new threats and to perform periodic assessments.

NIST's Role in Security

The National Institute of Standards and Technology (NIST) is one department that works closely with governmental agencies to help them improve security. NIST has developed many documents and procedures that address security. In just one year—2003—NIST created 1,200 pages of security controls. One of the NIST standards that is worth looking at is NIST 800-26, the Security Self-Assessment Guide for IT Systems. Although these documents are written to help federal agencies meet governmental security standards, they can easily be adopted by commercial organizations. NIST 800-26 is a good approach to adapt to measure information technology security assurance. Used as a basis of a network vulnerability assessment, NIST 800-26 can provide a degree of confidence in the administrative, technical, and operational security measures.

The Role of Policies in the Vulnerability Assessment

A level I or II assessment focuses on the policies and procedures that have been developed to protect an organization. To a large extent, the policy framework will determine the level of security of an organization. Policies set the tone and inform employees as to what is and is not permissible. The extent to which individuals abide by and implement their standards will play a large part in the security stance of the organization. There are a multitude of ways in which the policies can be categorized and examined. Two well-known ways are shown here. First is ISO 17799. This document divides policies and procedures into 10 major sections. These 10 sections cover all aspects of IT infrastructure policies and procedures:

1. Business continuity planning

2. System access control

3. System development and maintenance

4. Compliance

5. Physical and environmental security

6. Personnel security

7. Security organization

8. Computer and network management

9. Security policy

10. Asset classification and control

Tip

To determine how closely your organization is complying with ISO 17799, take Human Firewall Council's ISO 17799 survey, the Security Management Index (SMI). It's a quick test that asks 35 questions that are divided over the 10 domains. It's available at www.humanfirewall.org.

The second method that can be used to categorize and assess the organization's policies is NIST 800-26. It's a little more granular because it divides policies and procedures into

17 categories. Another advantage is that it is broadly available to all security professionals and is free of charge. These categories are shown next:

1. Risk management
2. Review of security controls
3. Life cycle
4. Authorize processing (certification and accreditation)
5. System security plan
6. Personnel security
7. Physical and environmental protection
8. Production, input/output controls
9. Contingency planning
10. Hardware and system software maintenance
11. Data integrity
12. Documentation
13. Security awareness, training, and education
14. Incident response capability
15. Identification and authentication
16. Logical access controls
17. Audit controls

What Drives the Assessment?

Most of the time, a network vulnerability assessment is not performed in a vacuum. Usually, some type of catalyst drives the process. Although it is wise to periodically perform assessments, they are usually performed for one of three reasons:

- To show due diligence.
- To comply with state, provincial, or federal law.
- Because of a breach in security.

Due Diligence

Due care and due diligence are related terms but do not have the same meaning. For example, *due care* could be used to describe the process of implementing policies to protect the security of an organization. *Due diligence* could be described as the process of ensuring that these policies are enforced. When senior management decides to perform a network vulnerability assessment because of due diligence, they are seeking to ensure that the control mechanisms that have been put in place are being followed. A failure of due diligence can be seen in the failure to follow security protocols when George Bush made a quick stop in May 2005 to the former Soviet Republic of Georgia. After the president made a quick speech and left the country, Georgian authorities reported that a hand grenade had been thrown within 100 feet of Bush's location during the speech. A Georgian security officer picked up the device, removed it, and only later informed the U.S. Secret Service.

Note

When companies implement standards that far exceed due care and due diligence, it's commonly referred to as a *gold standard*.

Compliance with Federal Laws

The second reason why network vulnerability assessments are performed is to verify compliance with governmental regulations such as the Health Insurance Portability and Accountability Act (HIPAA), Gramm-Leach-Bliley Act, Sarbanes-Oxley (SOX), and others. For example, the HIPAA security rule requires that any health care organization that stores or transmits health information electronically assess potential risks and vulnerabilities to the individual's health data in its possession in electronic form. These organizations are also required to develop, implement, and maintain appropriate security measures. Wrongful disclosure of information could cost companies up to $50,000. Other federal laws such as Sarbanes-Oxley have stiff criminal penalties for those who violate their mandates. These offer ample reasons to perform regular network vulnerability assessments.

Breaches in Security

Consider the fact that the Computer Emergency Response Team (CERT) reports that there has been a 3,600% increase in reported computer security incidents since 1998. This should give you ample reason to see why many network vulnerability assessments are performed. Although it's unfortunate that assessments aren't performed until after the fact, there is still hope. Because an organization has decided to perform an assessment, problems can be found, vulnerabilities that lead to the initial problem can be uncovered, and solutions can be proposed.

CardSystem Solutions Discovers the Cost of Poor Policy Implementation

CardSystems Solutions found out about the cost of poor policy implementation the hard way—after a hacker successfully stole details about 40 million credit card users from their database. An assessment after the attack revealed a software vulnerability that was quickly patched. It was also discovered that even though CardSystems Solutions had policies in place that stated this information was not supposed to be retained in their databases, it had been. CardSystems allegedly broke Visa and MasterCard policies that prohibit storing confidential consumer information. They now face a class-action lawsuit. Among other things, the suit claims that the company violated policy and practiced unlawful and deceptive business practices under California's Unfair Competition Law.

Managing a Vulnerability Assessment

Regardless of the reason, a network vulnerability assessment will rarely be performed without the approval and leadership of senior management. After all, these are the individuals in charge and are ultimately responsible. Although you shouldn't expect to see them running the assessment team, reports, feedback, results, and recommendations will be forwarded up the managerial structure for their ultimate review.

The day-to-day management of the network vulnerability assessment will probably be handled by the chief security officer or one of his representatives. This individual should have a mix of technical and managerial skills. He does not have to be an *uber hacker* but will need to be able to interpret and extrapolate the test results.

Building Cooperation with Other Departments

We should make it clear from the beginning that an assessment is not an audit. The goal here is not to hold anyone responsible or point fingers. However, you will be expected to identify risks and suggest solutions. Even though you'll be trying to improve things, don't expect everyone to be happy to see you. Consider the following as an example. Your duties may lead you to discover problems with account management. Consider that IDC, a leading information technology market intelligence and advisory firm, has found that up to 60% of the access profiles in the average corporation are not valid. Your assessment may find that when employees in critical positions leave the organization, their accounts are not disabled and passwords are not changed. This process may be the culmination of factors from several departments, including IT management, human resources, and those in charge of policy. Reporting on this issue and suggesting changes probably won't put people in the best of moods. Therefore, it is critical that senior management is driving the process so that needed changes will be implemented.

Importance of Setting and Maintaining a Schedule for Assessments

Setting and maintaining a schedule is an important part of the assessment process. Things change so quickly in this business that information that's six months old may no longer be considered valid. This is why the entire assessment process should run no more than 90 days. Not all organizations are going to need this much time. Much of the schedule will depend on the size of the organization and the type of assessment performed. No matter what type of assessment, level I, II, or III, the process should conclude with a written report that starts with an executive summary and then details the positive and negative findings. This should include data and resource vulnerabilities.

A sample timeline is shown in Figure 1.3. It details the following steps:

1. **Scope the project**—This portion of the assessment will require you to establish a timeline, determine the scope of the assessment, and build your team. It's covered in detail in Chapter 5.

2. **Perform the assessment**—This portion of the assessment is where the real work begins; onsite assessments will take place, interviews and demonstrations will occur, and you'll be examining physical, technical, and administrative controls. It's covered in detail in Chapter 7.

3. **Prepare the final report**—By this time, you will be done with most of the hands-on testing, although you'll still need to compile your report and make some solid recommendations. This portion of the methodology is covered in detail in Chapter 9.

4. **Post assessment activities**—At the conclusion of the assessment activities you'll still need to compile your report and make some solid recommendations. This portion of the methodology is covered in detail in Chapter 9, "Preparing the Final Report." Management will most likely expect to see some of the recommendations implemented. You may or may not be involved in these activities. Implementation and training are two key activities. They are discussed in detail in Chapter 10, "Post-Assessment Activities."

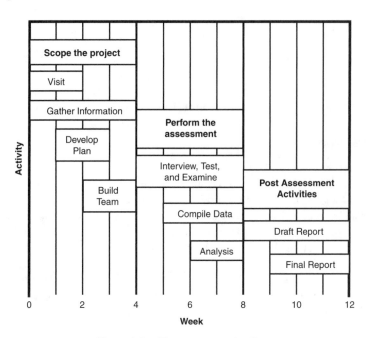

Figure 1.3   The assessment timeline.

Summary

Building real security is not an easy task. It is a continuous process that is made up of much more than equipment and policies. Real security is much like a living, breathing organism. Just like a living organism, security requires care and maintenance; otherwise, its useful value will diminish over time. Senior management plays a big part in this process. They have inherited this leading role because real security is possible only when senior management demands it. Many organizations don't take security seriously and simply reject risk. This foolish attitude is based on the hope that it just won't happen to them. Fortunately, many other organizations do take security seriously—some so much so that they have developed gold standards. These gold standards go far above and beyond what could be seen as a minimum standard and actually set a benchmark for others to strive for.

No matter where your company resides along the security continuum, there is always room for improvement. One of the best ways to improve security is to build it in to every aspect of the organization, assess risk when new ventures or processes are considered, and perform periodic vulnerability assessments to benchmark where the organization really falls between written policy and actual practice. These goals are made easier because there is a multitude of written documentation to help us meet this challenge. These include ISO 17799, COBIT, and NIST documents. Just remember that change usually doesn't happen in a vacuum. Make sure you know what the catalyst for change is in your organization. It may be because of a need to demonstrate due diligence, to comply with state, provincial, or federal laws, or because of a breach in security.

Key Terms

The following acronyms and terms are used in this chapter. For the explanation and definition purpose of this chapter, these acronyms and terms are defined as follows:

Asset   Anything of value owned or possessed by an individual or business.

Due care   The standard of conduct taken by a reasonable and prudent person. When you see the term *due care*, think of the first letter of each word and remember "do correct," because due care is about the actions that you take to reduce risk and keep it at that level.

Due diligence   The execution of due care over time. When you see the term *due diligence*, think of the first letter of each word and remember "do detect," because due diligence is about finding the threats an organization faces. This is accomplished by using standards, best practices, and checklists.

Firewall   A hardware or software security system that is intended to protect an organization's network against external threats, such as attackers, coming from another network or the Internet.

Generally Accepted System Security Principles (GASSP)   A NIST special publication 800-14 that is designed to help organizations improve their operation and management security controls.

Gold standard   Generally regarded as practices and procedures that are the best of the best.

Information Technology Security Evaluation Criteria (ITSEC)   A European standard that was developed in the 1980s to evaluate confidentiality, integrity, and availability of an entire system.

ISO 17799   A comprehensive security standard that is divided into 10 sections. It is considered a leading standard and a code of practice for information security management.

Red team   A group of ethical hackers who help organizations explore network and system vulnerabilities by means of penetration testing.

Risk   The exposure or potential for loss or damage to IT assets within that IT infrastructure.

Risk acceptance   An informed decision to suffer the consequences of likely events.

Risk assessment   A process for evaluating the exposure or potential loss or damage to the IT and data assets for an organization.

Risk avoidance   A decision to take action to avoid the risk.

Risk mitigation   Taking action to reduce the effect of potential risk.

Risk transference   Shifting the responsibility or burden to another party or individual.

Trusted Computer System Evaluation Criteria (TCSEC)   U.S. DoD Trusted Computer System Evaluation Criteria, also called the Orange Book. TCSEC is a system designed to evaluate standalone systems and place them into one of four levels: A, B, C, and D. Its basis of measurement is confidentiality.

Uber hacker   An expert and dedicated computer hacker.

2

Foundations and Principles
of Security

THIS CHAPTER DISCUSSES SOME OF THE BASIC PRINCIPLES and theories of security. Some of you are probably very familiar with the methodologies discussed in this chapter and if that is so, let this serve as a quick review. Others may be looking for a complete, holistic approach to understanding risk assessment. If so, this chapter will serve as a good basis. In the end, security is not one item, technology, or tool. It is an ongoing process that includes assessing risk, building good policies, implementing protections for key informational assets, training employees, and designing true defense in depth.

By the time you finish reading this chapter, you will understand these basic components and how they contribute to security. So, let's start our journey by discussing some basic security principles.

Basic Security Principles

Security can be achieved in many ways, but it's pretty well universally agreed that *confidentiality, integrity, and availability* (CIA) form the basic building blocks of any good security initiative. Although the acronym of CIA, used for the security triad, may not be as intriguing as the governmental agency with the same name, it most likely fits the priorities of security professionals better.

The concept of availability provides that information and systems are available when needed. Although many may think of availability only in electronic terms, it also applies to physical access. If you need access at 2 a.m. to backup tapes that are stored in a facility that allows access only from 8 a.m. to 5 p.m., you definitely have an availability problem.

Availability in the world of electronics can also manifest itself in many ways. Having access to a backup facility 24/7 does little good if there are no updated backups to restore from or if backups haven't been tested to ensure that they work. Backups are the simplest way to ensure availability. Backups provide a copy of critical information should files and data be destroyed or equipment fail. Failover equipment is another way to ensure availability. Systems such as *redundant array of inexpensive disks* (RAID) and redundant sites (hot, cold, and warm) are two examples. Disaster recovery is tied closely to availability because it's all about getting critical systems up and running quickly. Availability is attacked by denial-of-service (DoS) attacks.

Russian Mob Targets Companies for DoS

Criminal gangs from the former Soviet Union have been quite active in targeting random companies for extortion. The victim is typically contacted and asked for protection money to prevent the victim from being targeted for DoS. Those that don't pay are targeted for attack. One such site, multibet.com, refused to pay and was brought under DoS attack for more than 20 days. After the company paid the extortion, the DoS attack was lifted. Companies targeted for attack have two possible choices: pay up and hope they're not targeted again or install protective measures to negate the damage the DoS may have done.

Integrity is the second piece of the security triad. Integrity provides for the correctness of information and allows users of information to have confidence in its correctness. Integrity can apply to paper documents as well as electronic ones. We have all seen some of the checks and balances used to protect the integrity of paper documents. It is much easier to verify the integrity of a paper document than an electronic one. For a good example, look no further than the 2004 election. Some sources claimed to have documents that placed the president's military service in an unfavorable light. Typography experts quickly raised questions about the integrity of the memos, stating that they appeared to be computer generated in a way that wasn't even available in the early 1970s. Certainly, forgers can copy and create fake paper documents, but it is not a skill easily learned. Protecting and verifying the integrity of electronic documents and data is much more difficult. Integrity must be protected in two modes: storage and transit.

Information in storage can be protected by using access and audit controls. Cryptography can also protect information in storage through the use of *hashing algorithms*. Real-life examples of this technology can be seen in programs such as Tripwire, MD5Sum, and Windows File Protection (WFP). Integrity in transit can be ensured primarily by the protocols used to transport the data. These security controls include checksums, hashing, and cryptography.

Confidentiality addresses the secrecy and privacy of information. Even today, we can see a number of controls used in the real world to protect the confidentiality of information. Items such as locked doors, armed guards, and fences are but three such examples. Others include information-classification systems, such as the commercial and military data classification systems. Just as with integrity, confidentiality must be protected in storage and in transit. For an example, let's return our attention to backups. News reports have detailed several large-scale breaches in confidentiality, such as corporations misplacing or losing backup tapes with customer account, name, and credit information. The simple act of encrypting the backup tapes could have prevented or mitigated the damage.

Cryptography is also a useful tool to protect the confidentiality of information in transit. By sending information in an encrypted form, attackers are denied the opportunity to sniff clear-text information. Just because they cannot understand the information does not mean that it doesn't have any value to the attacker. Some military agencies set up channels that transmit a constant flow of traffic, thereby preventing attackers from performing *inference* attacks. Inference occurs anytime an attack may notice a spike in activity and infer there is some pending event. It may be hard to believe, but some news agencies actually monitor the White House for pizza deliveries. The belief is that a spike in pizza deliveries indicates that officials are working overtime and that there is a pending event of importance.

Note

The new standard for cryptographic protection became *Advanced Encryption Standard* (AES), also known as Rijndael, in November 2001. This came after the U.S. government spent five years studying what would replace the aging *Data Encryption Standard* (DES). Rijndael can be implemented in one of three key sizes: 128, 192, and 256 bits. It is considered a fast, simple, and robust symmetric encryption mechanism.

Security Requires Information Classification

All companies should take steps to protect the integrity and confidentiality of their information assets. An information classification system is one big step toward accomplishing this goal. If you are not sure that an information classification system is needed in your organization, consider the following:

- Government regulations such as Health Insurance Portability and Accountability Acts (HIPAA) and the Gramm-Leach-Bliley Act hold corporations accountable for the privacy, integrity, and security of information.
- Industry is more dependent than ever on the Internet. Many organizations use it for critical and sensitive communications.
- Identity theft and loss of personal information is at an all-time reported high.

An information classification system will help meet these risks. It will also help the organization determine what information is most critical and how its release may damage or affect the organization. Finally, it demonstrates the organization's commitment to security.

Now, if you're wondering if there is more than one way to categorize information, the answer is yes. The governmental information classification system is one widely used method. Another is the commercial information classification system.

Governmental Information Classification System

The governmental system is most concerned with protecting the confidentiality of information; therefore, it is divided into categories of Unclassified, Confidential, Secret, and Top Secret.

- **Unclassified**—Information is not sensitive and need not be protected. Its loss or disclosure would not cause damage.
- **Confidential**—Its disclosure could cause damage to national security and should be safeguarded against disclosure.
- **Secret**—Its disclosure would be expected to cause serious damage to national security and may divulge significant scientific or technological developments.
- **Top Secret**—Its disclosure would cause grave damage to national security. This information requires the highest level of control.

Note

Information classifications and access control are closely related. A good example of this can be seen by examining the *Bell-LaPadula* model. This access control model was developed out of the U.S. Department of Defense multilevel security policy. It's considered a need-to-know confidentiality model.

Commercial Information Classification System

The nongovernmental private sector also has established information classification standards. These standards address integrity, availability, and confidentiality. The commercial system is categorized as public, sensitive, private, and confidential.

- **Public**—Similar to unclassified information in that its disclosure or release would cause no damage to the corporation.
- **Sensitive**—This information requires controls to prevent its release to unauthorized parties. Damage could result from its loss of confidentiality or its loss of integrity.
- **Private**—This category of restricted information is considered personal in nature and might include medical records or human resource information.
- **Confidential**—This is the most sensitive rating. This is the information that keeps a company competitive. Not only is this information for internal use only, but its release or alteration could seriously affect or damage the corporation.

Note

Access control models such as *Clark-Wilson* and *Biba* more closely align with commercial information classification systems because they are focused on integrity.

Classification Criteria

After a decision has been reached to implement an information classification system, you will need to develop some type of criteria to determine how to categorize your information. Following are some of the items an organization will want to consider to determine what information goes into which category:

- Laws
- Useful life of data
- Value
- Age
- Damage of disclosure
- Damage of modification

Even with the data placed into its proper category, there will still need to be controls to prevent the loss of integrity and the confidentiality of the information. The seven steps shown next can help ensure that there is the infrastructure needed to protect the information.

1. Identify the administrator or custodian who will be in charge of maintaining the data.
2. Specify the criteria that will be used to identify how the data will be classified and labeled.
3. The data owner must indicate and acknowledge the classification of the data.
4. Specify and document any exceptions that are allowed to the classification policy.
5. Indicate the security controls that will be implemented to protect each classification level.
6. Specify the end-of-life (EOF) procedures for declassifying the information and procedures for transferring custody of the information to another entity.
7. Integrate these issues into an employee awareness program so that individuals understand and acknowledge the classification controls.

Classification is one big step toward securing your information assets; however, you'll also need a policy framework to further categorize and manage the documentation system. This is discussed next.

The Policy Framework

Establishing security policies, guidelines, and procedures is a critical step in securing an infrastructure and its information. The lack of well-designed viable security policies and documents is one of the biggest vulnerabilities many organizations have. Policies put everyone on the same page and make it clear where senior management stands on policy issues. They also set the overall tone and define how security is perceived by those within an organization. Policy must flow from the top. Bill Gates gave us a good example of this when he wrote a memo addressed to all employees in 2002. In this memo, Bill Gates spoke about how security was to become Microsoft's number one priority. What's most important about this story is that Bill Gates did more than just state that security was an objective; he provided a strategic roadmap that detailed how these goals would be met.

Building a policy framework is not easy. Some surveys show that only 40% of companies have written and implemented security policies. Those that haven't stated that their failure to do so was because of not knowing where to start, worries that the policies wouldn't work, and a fear that the policies wouldn't be enforceable. Therefore, the following sections will discuss the types of security policies, how to define appropriate policies, how to deploy policies, and the policy life cycle. After all, nothing lasts forever.

Types of Policies

Policies come in many shapes and sizes. With so many types of policies, how can you keep track of them all? The National Institute of Standards and Technology (NIST) special publication 800-12, the Computer Security Handbook, breaks policies into three broad categories:

- **Management**—These policies define security roles and responsibilities within an organization. They also define how policies are created, revised, and retired.

- **Operational**—These policies deal with operational aspects of an organization. Examples of operational controls include physical security and employee training and awareness.

- **Technical**—These policies address all things that are technical. These are the policies that IT employees are familiar with. These types of policies cover such things as identification, authentication, and account management.

Within these categories of policies are many individual policies. Combined, these policies control every aspect of security within an organization. Policies are not technology specific. This type of control is left for lower-level documents such as procedures.

Note
Although the term *policies* is used generically here, the types of security documents that an organization maintains include policies, standards, baselines, guidelines, and procedures.

Policies should do six things for a company:

- Protect confidential, proprietary, and sensitive information from unauthorized disclosure, modification, theft, or destruction.

- Define appropriate and inappropriate activities of employees and include consequences.

- Reduce or eliminate legal liability to employees and outsiders.

- Prevent waste of company IT resources.

- Comply with federal, state, provincial, local, and regulatory requirements.

- Demonstrate due diligence and due care.

It should be noted that most of the preceding items deal with preventing or reducing risk. Therefore, some type of risk assessment is usually performed before policies are created. Nothing happens in a void.

Defining Appropriate Policy

Before beginning the drafting of an actual policy, you'll need to clearly define what the objective of the policy is. You must also determine who the policy applies to, and finally, you must determine who is responsible for the policy. These three key sections are shown next:

- **Purpose**—Articulates why the policy was created, what is its purpose, and what the organization will gain from its creation. Policies can be created because of regulatory requirements, to be informative, or to advise if certain required activities or behaviors are allowed.

- **Scope**—Specifies who the policy applies to. It may address all users who telecommute, it may apply to those who have computer access, or it may address only those individuals who have access to the server room.

- **Responsibility**—Defines who is responsible. Someone must be in charge of the policy and verify that it is properly implemented, that employees are aware of its requirements, and that they have received adequate training.

When the draft policy is developed, it must be approved by upper management and evaluated to ascertain that the objectives that drove the policy development have been met or exceeded. Following are questions that can be asked to verify this:

- Is the policy enforceable—will it work?
- Does the policy comply with all pertinent laws?
- Will the policy compromise the interest of any group, such as employees, stakeholders, or customers?
- Has it been presented to and agreed upon by senior management?

> **Tip**
> SANS has a great collection of policies templates at www.sans.org/resources/policies. These can help ease the burden of policy creation.

Finally, you will want to build in some means to update and change the policy as needed. This revision history provides a mechanism to control the change process. Policies are like everything else in the world and will require periodic change.

Deploying Policy

After the policies have been created, you will need the help of the entire organization to get them deployed and put in place. Three critical items are needed for success: implementation, employee awareness, and employee buy-in.

Implementation

Rolling out new policy may seem to be no more difficult than dictating the date of expected compliance, but that is not the case. Consider a major change to the authentication and authorization policy. You mandate that everyone must change to complex passwords on the first day of the next month. So, on Monday morning, all your employees attempt to change passwords and many experience problems. The result is that the help desk is flooded with calls and many individuals experience an unproductive morning, waiting to log in and begin work. Policies should be implemented in such a way that the change is gradual, staged, or piloted. Many individuals already have the belief that security policies inhibit work and slow things down, so you want to make sure that any change you make does not contribute to that sentiment.

Employee Awareness

Employees need to know about policy changes and how the changes affect them. Depending on the policy, they may also require training. Human resources and training can help, but it's also up to the security department. Take, for example, a policy that dictates how the Internet is to be used by employees. HR can make employees sign an acceptable use policy, provide training to inform employees on what type of Internet activities are acceptable and unacceptable, and/or place a warning banner on all user computers that make them click through or agree to usage rights each time they access the Internet. This type of control goes a long way in ensuring compliance.

Don't fall into the trap of just writing policies and forgetting about them, because that won't build real security. Also, never think that employees don't watch the actions of management. Policies that have the "do as I say, not as I do" look and feel will never be successful. Management must not only support security policies, but also follow them. Otherwise, don't expect the employees to.

Employee Buy-In

Employee buy-in is another important piece of deploying policy. The individual department heads who are affected by the policy and their employees must buy in to the process. Think of it this way: senior management has determined that strong access control should be used to prevent unauthorized individuals from accessing critical parts of the organization. Therefore, an iris scanner is installed. Because some employees are uncomfortable with having their eyes scanned, and others feel the system is too close to "big brother," these individuals figure out that it's possible to piggyback into the areas by following an authenticated person in while the door is open. So, the zeal of implementing stronger security has actually led to a situation that is not good for the organization and may have opened it up to more potential risk than it originally faced.

By implementing systems that employees will accept and gaining the support of mid-management, companies can implement stronger security. These policies go a long way toward showing due care. Due care is the act of analyzing the risks an organization faces and responding to those risks by developing policies and procedures to counter those risks.

Policy Life Cycle

After policy has been implemented, you may think that the job is done, but unfortunately, it is not. The final piece to the policy framework is periodic maintenance, change management, and disposal. Even a good policy won't last forever. Therefore, policies need to be monitored and periodically reviewed. The goal is to make sure the policy is still relevant and applicable. The policy written 10 years ago that prohibited employees from attaching modems to internal computers may still be applicable, but it may need to be updated to include wireless access points (WAPs). Many organizations use some type of change review to examine changes and make sure that they don't cause more problems than they cure. This may be no more than a single meeting that has representatives from those groups affected. After an agreement is reached that the change is needed, the process starts anew because you must again deploy the updated policy, get employee buy-in, and complete awareness training.

The Role Authentication, Authorization, and Accountability Play in a Secure Organization

Authentication, authorization, and accounting are three terms sometimes referred to as "AAA." Together, these items represent a framework for enforcing policy, controlling access, and auditing user activities. These three items are critical for security.

Authentication

At most, basic authentication is a method of identification. It grants access to physical or logical resources based on someone's identification. Individuals typically identify and authenticate themselves in one of these methods: something you know, something you have, or something you are.

Passwords—Something You Know

The use of computer passwords goes back to the early days of computing. Way back then, passwords were short, typically seven characters or fewer. Passwords were kept short to make it easier for people to remember and because they were easier to enter. Over time, short passwords presented a series of problems, such as users using words that were easy to guess and using repeating letters or numbers such as 411. Short passwords are vulnerable to shoulder-surfing attacks because they are easy to memorize and steal.

Over time, these insecurities led to the implementation of more robust passwords. Controls were implemented that forced users to change passwords at regular intervals, and new passwords were checked to make sure they were different. Passwords that didn't meet complex requirements could be screened and rejected. The goal of these changes was admirable, but usually, the end effect was that users would write down their passwords, put them under the keyboard, or place them on a Post-it note attached to the monitor. So, although password security has increased, passwords remain the weakest form of authentication.

What Is Your Password Worth?

Maybe you thought with so much emphasis placed on security over the past few years that people are doing more to secure and protect their passwords. A survey performed at a security conference in Europe found that 71% of those polled were willing to give up their passwords for a piece of chocolate. Although most stated that they would not give their passwords to someone calling on the phone, others said they would give their passwords to their bosses. For more on this story check out www.securitypipeline.com/news/18902074.

Tokens—Something You Have

Tokens come in two basic types: *synchronous password tokens* or *asynchronous password tokens*. Password tokens can be purchased as smart cards, USB plugs, key fobs, or keypad-based units. These devices generate authentication credentials that can be used as *one-time passwords* (OTPs) and for *two-factor authentication*.

Tokens are a great way to implement one time passwords. One-time passwords are used only once and are valid for only a short period of time. One-time passwords are implemented by using tokens that display the time-limited password on an LCD screen.

By combining tokens with passwords, strong authentication can be achieved. Just think of it—two-factor authentication makes it much more difficult for unauthorized individuals to gain access. Anyone who has a safety deposit box can attest to this. The bank will require you to authenticate yourself with a driver's license or account number, and you'll also be required to possess a key. Both forms of authentication will be required to access the safety deposit box.

Synchronous

Tokens that are said to be synchronous are synchronized to an authentication server. Each individual pass-code is valid only for a very short period of time. Even if someone is able to sniff the token-based password, it would be valid only for a very short period of time. After that small window of opportunity, it would have no value to an attacker. RSA's SecurID and VeriSign's authentication token are both considered synchronous tokens.

Asynchronous

Asynchronous token devices are not synchronized to an authentication server. These devices use a challenge-response mechanism. CiscoSecure ACS can function in asynchronous mode. These devices work as follows:

1. Server sends the user a value.

2. The value is entered into the token.

3. The token performs a hashing process on the entered value.

4. The new value is displayed on the LCD screen of the token device.

5. The user enters the displayed value into the computer for authentication.

802.1x Port Authentication

802.1x is a good example to show how many organizations are now implementing stricter authentication. Although 802.1x can be used on wired networks, it's widely used on wireless networks. It has been implemented to address some of the inadequacies of *wired equivalent protection* (WEP). 802.1x provides a framework for port-based authentication.

To provide a standard authentication mechanism for IEEE 802.1X, the Extensible Authentication Protocol (EAP) was chosen. EAP is defined in RFC 2284. When used with wireless devices, it's referred to as EAP over LAN (EAPOL). With 802.1x implemented, EAPOL traffic passes through the switch. After the client has been authenticated, normal traffic can pass through the switch. Port-based authentication is great because no one can access your network until they have been authenticated.

Biometrics—Something You Are

Biometric systems identify individuals by measuring some part of a person's physiology or anatomy. Biometric systems are known to be the most accurate of all types of authentication. Although biometrics may sound difficult, these systems have made a lot of progress in the past decade. There are many types of biometric systems, including iris scan, voice recognition, fingerprint, and signature dynamics—just to name a few. Regardless of which method is used, they all work basically the same way. Users must first enroll in the system. Enrollment is not much more than allowing the system to take one or more samples for later comparison. Then, at a later time when a user requests to be authenticated, the sample is used to compare to the user's authentication request. A match allows the user access but a discrepancy between the two causes the user to be denied access.

Two important factors that must be examined when considering various biometric devices is the *false acceptance rate* (FAR) and the *false rejection rate* (FRR). The FAR, which is also called a type II error, is when the biometric system accepts users who should be rejected. The FRR, which is also called a type I, occurs when the biometric system rejects legitimate users. The point at which the FRR and FAR meet is known as the *crossover error rate* (CER). Although there are many things to consider when deploying a biometric device, this is one of the more critical items. The lower the CER, the more accurate the system. Besides accuracy, the big advantage of a biometric system is that you cannot loan a fingerprint to someone else, you cannot forget it, and it makes it hard for someone to steal your authentication.

Authorization

Authorization is the next natural step following authentication. Authorization should be tied to policies as a control of what commands and processes a user is authorized to run and perform. Three ways in which authorization is commonly controlled are *mandatory access control* (MAC), *discretionary access control* (DAC), and *role-based access control* (RBAC).

Until the early 1990s, most systems used either MAC or DAC. Both models are defined in the *Trusted Computer Security Evaluation Criteria* (TCSEC). The MAC model is static and based on a predetermined list of access privileges; therefore, in a MAC-based system, access is determined by the system rather than by the user. The MAC model is typically used by organizations that handle highly sensitive data (such as the DoD, NSA, CIA, and FBI). Systems based on the MAC model use sensitivity labels. Labels such as top secret, secret, or sensitive are assigned to objects. When a user attempts to access an object, the label is examined for a match to the subject's level of clearance. If no match is found, access is denied.

The DAC model is widely used commercially. Microsoft Windows NT, Windows 2000, and Windows XP all have DAC capabilities. You're probably familiar with DAC because it is similar to the control you see in a peer-to-peer computer network. Each of the users is left in control. The owner is left to determine whether other users have access to files and resources. DAC is a highly decentralized approach to access control management. It functions by means of access control. If you've ever assigned read, write, or full control privileges on a folder or drive, you've seen DAC at work.

RBAC is the newest of the three models. It wasn't developed until 1992. RBAC is unlike DAC and MAC because everything centers on the role of individual users. Rights are assigned to users based on their roles in the organization. The roles almost always map to the organization's structure. Role-based access control models are used extensively by banks and other organizations that have very defined roles. Windows 2003 has moved aggressively toward RBAC because it maps better to the administrative model used for access control that most organizations use. By assigning access rights and privileges to a group rather than to an individual, the burden on administration is reduced.

Accountability

Accountability gives administrators the capability to track what activities users performed at specific times. It's also the primary way to see what services were used and how much system resources were consumed by individual users. Accountability is carried out by performing auditing and developing systems to create and store audit trails.

Audit trails help reconstruct events in case of problems, intrusion detection, or incident response. Audit trails are of little value without individual accountability. Sufficient authentication must be used to make sure that individuals are held accountable for their actions. Auditing and monitoring must be performed in a way that is consistent with applicable laws and regulations. For example, *Computer Emergency Response Team* (CERT) recommends that all users be informed by means of an acceptable use policy or login banner as to what is or is not acceptable use for the computer system. If you fail to inform users and then determine inappropriate activity, it may be difficult to prosecute violators. Legal cases have occurred in which defendants have been acquitted of charges for tampering with computer systems because no explicit notice was given prohibiting unauthorized use of the computer systems involved. Other cases have occurred where organizations have been taken to court and sued for allegedly violating an individual's privacy because no notice was given regarding authorized monitoring of the user's activities on a computer system.

Encryption

Encryption is the process of encoding information in such a way that unauthorized individuals cannot view it. Encryption is needed because there is plenty of information that organizations must ensure is kept private and confidential. Some of this information includes the following:

- Bank-account information
- Credit-card information
- Private correspondence
- Personal details
- Privileged information
- Sensitive company information
- Social Security numbers
- Trade secrets

Encryption is performed by using the science of cryptography. Cryptography is a vast and complex subject. An in-depth understanding of it is beyond the scope of this book. Therefore, this section does not discuss how encryption works. What is important to know is that just about all organizations need to use encryption. Many are already using encryption, but others will wait until they suffer through a bad experience or have to comply with new laws that mandate the protection of personal data. Encryption's role in the organization includes the following:

- **Authentication**—Services such as Challenge Handshake Authentication Protocol (CHAP) and Extensible Authentication Protocol (EAP) make use of authentication.

- **Data encryption**—Information in storage can be encrypted to protect it from prying eyes. Microsoft's Encrypted File System (EFS) is one such example.

- **IPSec**—IPSec can be used to provide confidentiality and/or integrity to information in transit. It is widely used to help implement virtual private networks (VPNs).

- **Public Key Infrastructure (PKI)**—This is a widely used system to verify and authenticate the validity of each individual involved in an Internet transaction.

- **Pretty Good Privacy (PGP)**—PGP is as close to military-grade encryption as a private individual can get, and it works well at securing email. Unlike public key infrastructure (PKI), PGP works by using a web of trust. Users distribute and sign their own public keys. It can be used to encrypt information in storage or in transit.

- **Secure Shell (SSH)**—This application-layer protocol can provide secure communications and is a good replacement for Telnet and FTP.

- **Secure Sockets Layer (SSL)**—An application-independent protocol that was developed to encrypt information in transit.
- **Transport Layer Security (TLS)**—A protocol that guarantees privacy and data integrity between client/server applications.

As shown in the preceding list, encryption can be used at all levels of a security infrastructure—from protection to network communications over the Internet to encrypting data on a drive. Encryption can provide confidentiality, authentication, integrity, and nonrepudiation for information in storage or in transit.

Security and the Employee (Social Engineering)

In the end, no security control in the world will be its most effective without the support and compliance of all employees. With each of the items discussed in the chapter, employees must be informed and trained. Organizations can have the best technological controls in the world and still suffer debilitating attacks.

Social engineering is the act of obtaining or attempting to obtain otherwise secure information or access by conning an individual into revealing secure information. Social engineering attacks are hard to protect. The best means of protection is through security awareness training. Only by educating everyone in the enterprise on the company's security policies and procedures can you begin to reduce this threat. Employees must be trained and know what information needs to be protected and how to protect it. Only then are employees in a much better position to recognize social engineering when it occurs. Social engineers, or con artists, have been studied for many years. Robert Cialdini developed a list of six basic techniques that social engineers use to attempt to gain compliance of a victim:

- **Authority**—This form of attack attempts to use authority or power to gain compliance.
- **Liking**—This attack works by making the victims believe that they are similar to the attacker, have common beliefs, or like him.
- **Consistency**—This attack is made possible by the victim's attempt to remain consistent. We all tend to follow through or want to do what seems acceptable.
- **Reciprocation**—This attack relies on the fact that after you have been given something, behavior dictates that something must be given in return.
- **Social validation**—This attack functions on the premise that it is the right thing to do. It seems to be what anyone else would do.
- **Scarcity**—This attack feeds on the action that people respond when they believe time or quantities are limited.

> **Phishing, a Most Successful Form of Social Engineering**
>
> *Phishing* is a type of social engineering that attempts to lure the victim into revealing information of a sensitive or personal nature, including passwords and credit card details. In such an attack, the victim is approached by email from someone of authority, typically a bank or credit institution.
>
> Zachary Hill is one of the individuals that practiced this scam until he was caught and sentenced to four years in prison. According to the criminal information to which Hill has entered his plea of guilty, Hill used the scheme to access 473 credit card numbers, 152 sets of bank account numbers and routing numbers, and 566 sets of usernames and passwords for Internet services accounts. The information also charges that Hill used the fraudulently obtained credit card numbers to obtain goods and services valued at more than $47,000.

Summary

Nothing works right 100% of the time. That is one reason why each of the pieces previously discussed are needed. Each of these items helps build a security infrastructure that supplies *defense in depth*. Defense in depth is about building security in layers. If one layer is breached, you have multiple layers beneath it to continue protecting your organization's assets. Defense in depth is about finding a balance between the protection cost and the value of the informational asset. For example, you have an information classification system but have also encrypted this data. Strong controls have also been placed on who has access to the information; the physical devices the information is located on have been secured; and when it is in transit, it is transmitted only in a encrypted form. Now, it's not that this information cannot be attacked or disclosed, but you have implemented several items to prevent its release. Someone targeting this information will have to successfully overcome one or more of these barriers to be successful.

Key Terms

The following acronyms and terms are used in this chapter. For the explanation and definition purpose of this chapter, these acronyms and terms are defined as follows:

Accountability   The traceability of actions performed on a system to a specific system entity or user.

Advanced Encryption Standard (AES)   The new U.S. standard for encrypting sensitive but unclassified data. Also known as Rijndael, this symmetric encryption standard can be implemented in one of three key sizes: 128, 192, and 256 bits. It is considered a fast, simple, robust encryption mechanism.

Authentication   A method that enables you to identify someone. Authentication verifies the identity and legitimacy of the individual to access the system and its resources. Common authentication methods include passwords, tokens, and biometric systems.

Authorization   The process of granting or denying access to a network resource based on the user's credentials.

Availability   Ensures that the systems responsible for delivering, storing, and processing data are available and accessible as needed by individuals who are authorized to use the resources.

Bell–LaPadula   This access control model was actually the first formal model developed to protect confidentiality. This is a state machine that enforces confidentiality.

Biba   The Biba model was the first model developed to address the concerns of integrity. It does not address availability or confidentiality. It is based on the premise that internal threats are being protected and focuses on external threats.

Clark–Wilson   This integrity-based access control model was developed with the intention to be used for commercial activities. This model dictates that the separation of duties must be enforced, subjects must access data through an application, and auditing is required.

Computer Emergency Response Team (CERT)   An organization developed to provide incident response services to victims of attacks, publish alerts concerning vulnerabilities and threats, and offer other information to help improve the organization's capability to respond to computer and network security issues.

Confidentiality   Data or information is not made available or disclosed to unauthorized persons.

Crossover error rate (CER)   The CER is a comparison measurement for different biometric devices and technologies to measure their accuracy. The CER is the point at which FAR and FRR are equal, or cross over. The lower the CER the more accurate the biometric system.

Data Encryption Standard (DES)   DES is a symmetric encryption standard that is based on a 64-bit block. DES processes 64 bits of plain text at a time to output 64-bit blocks of cipher text. DES uses a 56-bit key and has four modes of operation. Because DES has been broken, 3DES is more commonly used.

Defense in depth   The process of multilayered security. The layers may be administrative, technical, or logical.

Denial-of-service (DoS) attack   A type of attack that denies the organization access to resources. It typically works by flooding the network with useless traffic.

Discretionary Access Control   An access policy that allows the resource owner to determine access.

Encryption   The science of turning plain text into cipher text.

False acceptance rate (FAR)   This measurement evaluates the likelihood that a biometric access control system will wrongly accept an unauthorized user.

False rejection rate (FRR)   This measurement evaluates the likelihood that a biometric access control system will reject a legitimate user.

Hashing algorithm   Hashing is used to verify the integrity of data and messages. A well-designed hashing algorithm examines every bit of the data while it is being condensed, and even a slight change to the data will result in a large change in the message hash. It is considered a one-way process.

Inference attacks   This form of attack relies on the attacker's ability to make logical connections between seemingly unrelated pieces of information.

Integrity   One of the three items considered to be part of the security triad; the others are confidentiality and availability. It is used to verify the accuracy and completeness of an item.

Mandatory access control   A means of restricting access to objects based on the sensitivity (as represented by a label) of the information contained in the objects and the formal authorization (such as clearance) of subjects to access information of such sensitivity.

Redundant array of inexpensive disks (RAID)   A category of `disk drives` that employ two or more disk drives in combination for `fault tolerance` and performance gains.

Role-based access control   A form of access control that assigns users to roles based on their organizational functions and determines authorization based on those unique roles.

Social engineering   A nontechnical type of attack that relies heavily on human interaction and often involves tricking other people to break normal security procedures.

Trusted Computer Security Evaluation Criteria (TCSEC)   A collection of criteria used to grade or rate the security offered by a computer system product. Because each of the books of the series has different color covers, it is also known as the Rainbow Series.

3

Why Risk Assessment

WITH INDUSTRY COMPLIANCY AND INFORMATION SECURITY laws and mandates being introduced in the past four years, the need for conducting a vulnerability and risk assessment is now paramount. These recent laws and mandates include the following:

- The Healthcare Information Privacy and Portability Act (HIPPA) is driving the need for vulnerability and risk assessments to be conducted within any health-care or health-care-related institution.

- The recent Gramm-Leach-Bliley Act (GLBA) is driving the need for vulnerability and risk assessments to be conducted within any banking or financial institution in the United States.

- The recent Federal Information Security Management Act (FISMA) is driving the need for vulnerability and risk assessments to be conducted for all United States federal government agencies.

- The recent Sarbanes-Oxley Act affects all publicly traded companies within the United States that have a market cap greater than $75 million; they are now subject to compliance with the Sarbanes-Oxley Act, Section 404, which also is driving the need for vulnerability and risk assessments to be conducted for publicly traded companies.

- The recent Canadian Management of Information Security Standard (MITS) requires regular security assessments for all Canadian federal government agencies.

The need to conduct vulnerability and risk assessments is being driven by these new laws and mandates. Organizations must now be information security conscious and must develop and implement proper security controls based on the results of their internal risk assessment and vulnerability assessment. By conducting a risk assessment and vulnerability assessment, an organization can uncover known weaknesses and vulnerabilities in its existing IT infrastructure, prioritize the impact of these vulnerabilities based on the value and importance of affected IT and data assets, and then implement the proper security controls and security countermeasures to mitigate those identified weaknesses. This risk mitigation results in increased security and less probability of a threat or vulnerability impacting an organization's production environment.

Risk Terminology

With any new technology topic, terminology, semantics, and the use of terms within the context of the technology topic can be confusing, misused, and misrepresented. Risk itself encompasses the following three major areas: *risks*, *threats*, and *vulnerabilities*.

Risk is the probability or likelihood of the occurrence or realization of a threat. There are three basic elements of risk from an IT infrastructure perspective:

- **Asset**—An IT infrastructure component or an item of value to an organization, such as data assets.

- **Threat**—Any circumstance that could potentially cause loss or damage to an IT infrastructure asset.

- **Vulnerability**—A weakness in the IT infrastructure or IT components that may be exploited in order for a threat to destroy, damage, or compromise an IT asset.

An *IT asset* or *data asset* is an item or collection of items that has a quantitative or qualitative value to an organization. Examples of IT assets that organizations may put a dollar value or criticality value on include the following:

- **Workstations**—Hardware, software, and data assets stored at the end user's workstation location (PCs, PDAs, phones, and so on).

- **Operating systems software**—Operating system software, software updates, software patches, and their configuration and deployment on production services and workstations.

- **Application systems software**—Application software such as databases, client/server applications, software updates, software patches, and their configuration on production servers.

- **Local area network hardware and software**—Local area network infrastructure, TCP/IP, LAN switches, routers, hubs, operating system and application software within the LAN CPE equipment.

- **Wide area network hardware and software**—Wide area network infrastructure, TCP/IP, routers, operating system and application software within the WAN CPE equipment.

- **Network management hardware and software**—SNMP network management infrastructure, operating system and NMS application software, production NMS servers, data collection SNMP polling servers, network-monitoring CPE devices, SNMP MIB I and MIB II data collection and archiving.

- **Telecommunication systems**—Voice communication systems (PBX or IP Telephony), telephone CPE devices on desktops, operating system and application software (IP Telephony), voice-mail systems, automated attendants, and so on.

- **IT security hardware and software**—Operating system and security application software, production servers, DMZs, firewalls, intrusion detection monitoring systems, security monitoring, and alarm notification systems.

- **Systems and application servers, hardware, and software**—Operating systems, application software, client/server application software, production servers, and software code/intellectual property.

- **Intellectual property**—Customer data, customer databases, application data, application databases, information, and data assets. Intellectual property may have an intrinsic value to an organization depending on what the intellectual property is and whether the organization generates revenue from this intellectual property.

- **IT infrastructure documentation, configurations, and backup files and backup data**—Complete and accurate physical, logical, configuration, and setup documentation of the entire IT infrastructure, including backup files, backup data, disk storage units, and data archiving systems.

A *threat* is any agent, condition, or circumstance that could potentially cause harm, loss, damage, or compromise to an IT asset or data asset. From an IT infrastructure perspective, threats may be categorized as circumstances that can affect the confidentiality, integrity, or availability of the IT asset or data asset in terms of destruction, disclosure, modification, corruption of data, or denial of service. Examples of threats in an IT infrastructure environment include the following:

- **Unauthorized access**—The owner of the access rights, user ids, and passwords to the organization's IT systems and confidential information is compromised, and unauthorized access is granted to the unauthorized user who obtained the user ids and passwords.

- **Stolen/lost/damaged/modified data**—Loss or damage of an organization's data can be a critical threat if there are no backups or external archiving of the data as part of the organization's data recovery and business continuity plan. Also, if the data was of a confidential nature and is compromised, this can also be a critical threat to the organization, depending on the potential damage that can arise from this compromise.

- **Disclosure of confidential information**—Disclosure of confidential information can be a critical threat to an organization if that disclosure causes loss of revenue, potential liabilities, or provides a competitive advantage to an adversary.

- **Hacker attacks**—Unauthorized perpetrator who purposely and knowingly attacks an IT infrastructure and/or the components, systems, and data.

- **Cyber terrorism**—Because of the vulnerabilities that are commonplace in operating systems, software, and IT infrastructures, terrorists are now using computers, Internet communications, and tools to perpetrate critical national infrastructures such as water, electric, and gas plants, oil and gasoline refineries, nuclear power plants, waste management plants, and so on.

- **Viruses and malware**—*Malware* is short for malicious software, which is a general term used to categorize software such as a virus, worm, or Trojan horse that is developed to damage or destroy a system or data. *Viruses* are executable programs that replicate and attach to and infect other executable objects. Some viruses also perform destructive or discrete activities (payload) after replication and infection is accomplished.

- **Denial of service or distributed denial of service attacks**—An attack on a TCP/IP-based network that is designed to bring the network and/or access to a particular TCP/IP host/server to its knees by flooding it with useless traffic. Many DoS attacks, such as the *Ping of Death* and *Teardrop* attacks, exploit limitations in the TCP/IP protocols. For all known DoS attacks, system administrators can install software fixes to limit the damage caused by the attacks. But, like viruses, new DoS attacks are constantly being dreamed up by hackers.

- **Acts of God, weather, or catastrophic damage**—Hurricanes, storms, weather outages, fires, floods, earthquakes, and total loss of IT infrastructures, data centers, systems, and data.

A *vulnerability* is a weakness in the system design, a weakness in the implementation of an operational procedure, or a weakness in how the software or code was developed (for example, bugs, back doors, vulnerabilities in code, and so on). Vulnerabilities may be eliminated or reduced by the correct implementation of safeguards and security countermeasures.

Vulnerabilities and weaknesses are common with software mainly because there isn't any software or code in existence that doesn't have bugs, weaknesses, or vulnerabilities. Many vulnerabilities are derived from the various kinds of software that is commonplace within the IT infrastructure. This type of software includes the following:

- **Firmware**—Software that is usually stored in ROM and loaded during system power up.

- **Operating system**—The operating system software that is loaded in workstations and servers.

- **Configuration files**—The configuration file and configuration setup for the device.

- **Application software**—The application or executable file *.exe that is run on a workstation or server.

- **Software Patch**—A small piece of software or code snippet that the vendor or developer of the software typically releases as software updates, software maintenance, and known software vulnerabilities or weaknesses.

Note

Why do software vendors and application software companies have Software Licensing Agreements (SLAs) that protect them from their own software vulnerabilities? Why do software companies have stringent Limited Warranty, Disclaimer of Warranties, Exclusion of Incidental, Consequential, and Certain Other Damages, and Limitations of Liability clauses in all their software products' SLAs?

The answer to these questions can be summarized quite simply: software vendors know they can't create and sell perfect code because of the human element. Software bugs and vulnerabilities are commonplace. Simply put, software vendors cannot guarantee that their software is bug-proof and free of vulnerabilities, so they must protect themselves from potential liability and damages that may be the result of a software vulnerability that is exploited by a hacker or unauthorized user.

Herein lies the fundamental problem—software has vulnerabilities, hackers and perpetrators know there are vulnerabilities, and organizations attempt to put the proper software patches and updates in place to combat this fundamental problem before being attacked. The key word here is *before* being attacked. Many organizations lack sufficient funds for securing their IT infrastructure by mandating a vulnerability window of 0 days or 0 hours, thus eliminating any software vulnerability potential threats. Achieving a vulnerability window of 0 days or 0 hours is virtually impossible given that software vendors cannot provide software patches fast enough to the general public after a vulnerability is exposed. In addition, the time required to deploy and install the software patch on production servers and workstations exposes an organization's IT infrastructure to potential threats from that vulnerability.

This gap in time is reality in IT infrastructures, especially because a majority of IT assets and devices have some kind of software loaded in them. Remember, vulnerabilities in software extend to firmware, operating systems, configuration files, and applications, and must be combated with a software maintenance, update, and patch maintenance plan. This encompasses the entire software, operating, and application software environment exposing potential vulnerabilities in any device that houses and runs this vulnerable software. In large organizations, combating the software vulnerability issue requires an enterprise, automated software patch-management solution.

The Computer Emergency Response Team (CERT) is an organization sponsored by Carnegie-Mellon University's Software Engineering Institute. Until 2003, CERT was the organizational body that was responsible for collecting, tracking, and monitoring vulnerability and incident reporting statistics. CERT can be found at www.cert.org. CERT publishes statistics for the following:

- **Vulnerabilities Reported**—This compilation is for vulnerabilities reported, not those that go unreported.
- **Vulnerability Notes Published**—These notes are published by CERT from data that is compiled from users and the vendor community describing known and documented vulnerabilities.

- **National Cyber Alert System Documents Published**—Information previously published in CERT advisories, incident notes, and summaries are now incorporated into National Cyber Alert System documents.

- **Security Alerts Published**—The total number of validated security alerts published by CERT.

- **Mail Messages Handled**—The total number of email messages handled by CERT.

- **Hotline Calls Received**—The total number of phone calls handled by CERT.

- **Incidents Reported**—Given the widespread use and availability of automated attack tools, attacks against Internet-connected organizations are common given the number of incidents reported.

As of 2004, CERT no longer publishes the number of incidents reported. Instead, CERT is working with others in the community to develop and report on more meaningful metrics for incident reporting, such as the 2004 E-Crime Watch Survey. Figure 3.1 shows the dramatic increase in known and documented vulnerabilities and the number of incidents that have occurred and have been recorded by www.cert.org during the past few years. Note that as the number of vulnerabilities increases, the number of incidents has also increased, but this value is misleading because the number of incidents that go unreported is unknown.

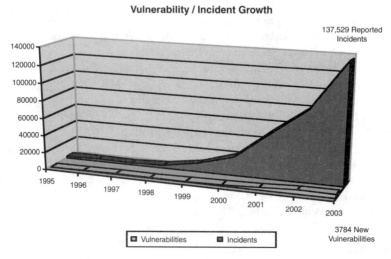

Figure 3.1   Rise in vulnerabilities and incidents.

Many of the security incidents indicated in 2003 on the www.cert.org website were the direct result of software vulnerabilities that were exploited by an attacker. These security incidents can be attributed to the "vulnerability window," which is the amount of time that lapses between when a known vulnerability is identified and documented to when an organization implements the vulnerability fix or deploys the appropriate software patch.

Because of this vulnerability window issue, SQL Slammer, which was a known vulnerability posted by Microsoft in July 2002, affected nearly 90% of the world's SQL databases on Super Bowl Sunday, January 2003, six months after the vulnerability was exposed.

The stages of vulnerability in software are as follows:

1. Vendors release software and code with unknown vulnerabilities to the general public.

2. Vulnerability is discovered, communicated, documented, and published by the vendor. When the vulnerability is identified and communicated to the general public, this defines when the vulnerability window is open. This is referred to as VTopen.

3. A configuration-based software countermeasure (software patch) is created by the vendor and made available to the public.

4. The software patch is released and made available to the public.

5. The software patch is received, deployed, and installed on the affected devices. When the software patch is deployed and installed on the affected device, this defines when the vulnerability window is closed. This is referred to as VTclosed.

In Figure 3.2, the stages in vulnerabilities in software are defined. This gap in time between when a known vulnerability is identified and communicated to when that known vulnerability is mitigated through a software patch is referred to as the vulnerability window.

The Stages of Vulnerability in Software Are:

- Vendors release software and code to the general public (with unknown vulnerabilities)

- Vulnerability is discovered, communicated, and published by the Vendor (Vulnerability window is open, VTopen)

VT
- A configuration-based software countermeasure (patch) is created by the Vendor and made available to the public

- The patch is released and made available to the public

- The patch is received and installed on the affected devices (Vulnerability window is closed, VT closed)

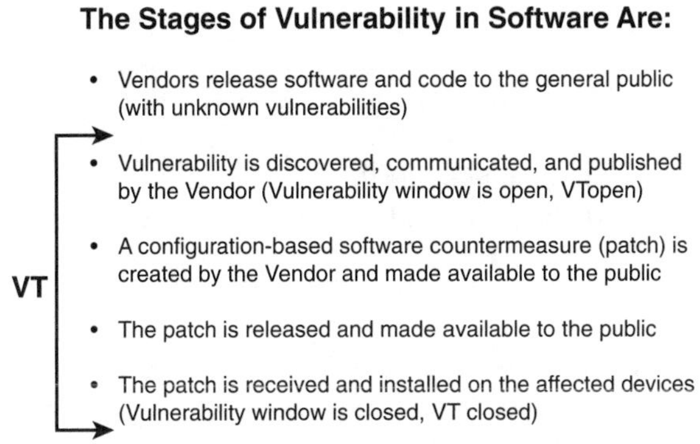

Figure 3.2   The vulnerability window.

From a vulnerability perspective, an IT asset or IT infrastructure is most vulnerable during the vulnerability window exposure time. This exposure time is referred to as vulnerability time:

Vulnerable Time (Vt) = Vt(open) - Vt(closed)

Most organizations, when they first conduct a vulnerability assessment on their IT infra-structure, servers, workstations, and systems, are shocked to realize that they are vulnerable because of software vulnerabilities inherent in the code. Upon realizing this, the ultimate goal for an organization is to prioritize those IT assets and IT infrastructure components to assess which IT assets should have their vulnerability time reduced. Reducing the vulnera-bility time will assist organizations in minimizing the potential risk and threats caused by software vulnerabilities. Many organizations create internal policies that state the maxi-mum vulnerability time exposure for their mission critical IT assets and systems.

Organizations are now realizing that having an IT security architecture and frame-work consisting of policies, standards, procedures, and guidelines for their production IT systems, software, and applications is critical. Many organizations are apt to create a poli-cy that defines the maximum acceptable vulnerability window for its mission-critical and production IT systems. This policy then drives the priorities for how funds are to be invested for risk mitigation via an enterprise patch-management solution.

Tip

When defining a policy for software vulnerability management, identifying and prioritizing mission-critical IT assets to prioritize the confidentiality, availability, and integrity of information assets is paramount.

Software vulnerabilities are documented and tracked by the U.S. Computer Emergency Readiness Team (US-CERT) in a public-accessible list called the Common Vulnerabilities and Exposures (CVEs) list. In 1999, the MITRE organization was con-tracted by the U.S. Computer Emergency Readiness Team to track, monitor, and update the CVE list. Today, the CVE list has grown to more than 7,000 unique documented vulnerability items, and approximately 100 new candidate names are added to the CVE list each month, based on newly discovered vulnerabilities. The CVE list can be found at http://www.cve.mitre.org/.

The CVE is merely a list or dictionary of publicly known information security vul-nerabilities and exposures and is international in scope and free for public use. Each vul-nerability or exposure included on the CVE list has one common, standardized CVE name. The CVE list is a community effort that encourages the support of hardware and software vendors. The CVE list is free and can be downloaded or accessed online at the previously mentioned website.

Tip

Use of the CVE list along with identifying IT and data assets are necessary first steps in conducting an inter-nal risk assessment of an organization. The risk and vulnerability assessor should first identify all known IT assets and build an IT asset inventory using a spreadsheet or similar tool. Then, for each IT asset, the asses-sor should list the firmware, the operating system software, the application software, and the software patches and their version numbers currently loaded in that IT asset. Using the CVE list, a quick global search on known software vulnerabilities to the organization's IT asset list can be conducted, especially if the soft-ware version and software patch numbers from the software vendor can be obtained. This quick examina-tion of known software vulnerabilities will help an organization uncover known software vulnerabilities. This information can be used to assess whether the value of the IT asset or the data asset requires remediation.

Prior to conducting an internal risk assessment, it is important to understand the new laws, mandates, and regulations that are driving organizations to create and implement information systems security plans and conduct vulnerability assessments. These new laws, mandates, and regulations are impacting IT infrastructures and their assets and are driving the need for conducting a thorough risk and vulnerability assessment on an IT infrastructure and its assets.

Laws, Mandates, and Regulations

The U.S. federal government has taken an active role in dealing with computer, Internet, privacy, and corporate threats, vulnerabilities, and exploits during the past five years. This is exemplified by the increase in new laws and mandates that were passed recently. These new laws and mandates encompass the following areas:

- **Cyber Laws and Crimes**—U.S. Code 1029 defines what a criminal activity is in regard to unauthorized access to devices and what the penalties for such crimes will be. U.S. Code 1030 defines what computer fraud is and other related activities in connection with computers.

- **Privacy**—New laws were enacted that protect an individual's confidentiality of personal information, such as social security number, passport number, driver's license number, ID numbers, and so on.

- **Financial Records Confidentiality**—New laws were enacted that protect an individual's confidential financial information, credit report, and any information pertaining to financial records such as user ids, passwords, bank account numbers, and financial data.

- **Corporate Integrity**—New laws were enacted to hold officers of publicly traded companies responsible and accountable for the accuracy and release of financial and annual reports as well as for documenting and ensuring that a proper information security architecture and framework with processes and controls are in place.

When dealing with risk assessment in an organization, there are now many new laws and mandates that impact the requirements and scope of the risk assessment.

Depending on the organization's vertical industry category, different laws and mandates will impact how that organization approaches its internal risk assessment and vulnerability assessment. Many of these new laws and mandates will assist in defining the scope of the risk assessment and vulnerability assessment, given the IT and data assets that must now have the proper security controls, procedures, and guidelines. The following new laws and mandates currently impact information security requirements and are briefly described in this chapter:

- **HIPAA**—Health Insurance Portability and Accountability Act, http://aspe.hhs.gov/admnsimp/pl104191.htm.

- **GLBA**—Gramm-Leach-Bliley Act, http://banking.senate.gov/conf/.

- **FISMA—Federal Information Security Management Act,**
  http://csrc.nist.gov/policies/FISMA-final.pdf.

- **SOX, Section 404**—Sarbanes-Oxley Act, Section 404,
  http://news.findlaw.com/hdocs/docs/gwbush/sarbanesoxley072302.pdf.

Health Insurance Portability and Accountability Act (HIPAA)

The Health Insurance Portability and Accountability Act (HIPAA) was signed into law in 1996 to address the lack of portability that individuals and their families had to deal with when changing jobs. HIPAA provides a way that individuals and their family members can have a continuity of health insurance even through job changes and perhaps even unemployment.

Note

It used to be people stayed in one or two jobs throughout a whole career. In those days people had no need for HIPAA. But today, in a time when jobs and even careers are constantly changing, HIPAA can make a big difference in your personal welfare or the welfare of your family.

Title I of the Health Insurance Portability and Accountability Act of 1996 (HIPAA) protects health insurance coverage for workers and their families when they change or lose their jobs.

Title II requires the Department of Health and Human Services to establish national standards for electronic health care transactions and national identifiers for providers, health plans, and employers.

Under HIPAA law, the U.S. Department of Health and Human Services (DHHS) was required to publish a set of rules regarding privacy. The Privacy Rule was published on August 14, 2002, and the Security Rule was published in the Federal Register on February 20, 2003.

The privacy rule states three major purposes:

- To protect and enhance the rights of consumers by providing them access to their health information and controlling the inappropriate use of that information.

- To improve the quality of health care in the United States by restoring trust in the health care system among consumers, health care professionals, and the multitude of organizations and individuals committed to the delivery of care.

- To improve the efficiency and effectiveness of health care delivery by creating a national framework for health privacy protection that builds on efforts by states, health systems, and individual organizations and individuals.

The security rule states the following:

"In addition to the need to ensure electronic health care information is secure and confidential, there is a potential need to associate signature capability with information being electronically stored or transmitted."

Today, there are numerous forms of electronic signatures, ranging from biometric devices to digital signature. To satisfy the legal and time-tested characteristics of a written signature, however, an electronic signature must do the following:

- Identify the signatory individual;

- Assure the integrity of a document's content; and

- Provide for nonrepudiation; that is, strong and substantial evidence that will make it difficult for the signer to claim that the electronic representation is not valid. Currently, the only technically mature electronic signature meeting the above criteria is the digital signature."

Gramm-Leach-Bliley-Act (GLBA)

The Gramm-Leach-Bliley Act (GLBA) was signed into law in 1999 and resulted in the most sweeping overhaul of financial services regulation in the United States by eliminating the long-standing barriers between banking, investment banking, and insurance. Title V addresses financial institution privacy with two subtitles. Subtitle A addresses this by requiring financial institutions to make certain disclosures about their privacy policies and to give individuals an opt-out capability. Subtitle B criminalizes the practice known as pretexting, where someone will misrepresent themselves to collect information regarding a third party from a financial institution.

Various sections of the GLBA provide support to Title V in a variety of ways. For example:

- **Section 502**—Requires that a financial institution not disclose, directly or indirectly or through any affiliate, any personal information to a third party.

- **Section 503**—Requires the financial institution to disclose its policies annually during the institution's relationship with a given customer.

- **Section 504**—Requires that the Office of the Comptroller of the Currency (OCC), the Board of Governors of the Federal Reserve System (FRB), the Federal Deposit Insurance Corporation (FDIC), the Office of Thrift Supervision (OTS), the Secretary of the Treasury, the National Credit Union Administration (NCUA), the Securities and Exchange Commission (SEC), and the Federal Trade Commission (FTC), after consultation with representatives of state insurance authorities designated by the National Association of Insurance Commissioners, are to prescribe regulations to carry out subtitle A.

Under GLBA law, financial institutions are required to protect the confidentiality of individual privacy information. Under the GLBA definition, financial institutions may include banks, insurance companies, and other third-party organizations that have access to an individual's private and confidential financial, banking, or personal information. As specified in GLBA law, financial institutions are required to develop, implement, and maintain a comprehensive information security program with appropriate administrative, technical, and physical safeguards. This information security program must include the following:

- Assigning a designated program manager for the organization's information security program
- Conducting periodic risk and vulnerability assessments
- Performing regular testing and monitoring
- Defining procedures for making changes in lieu of test results or changes in circumstance

Federal Information Security Management Act (FISMA)

The Federal Information Security Management Act (FISMA) was signed into law in 2002 as part of the E-Government Act of 2002, replacing the Government Information Security Reform Act (GISRA). FISMA was enacted to address the information security requirements for non-national-security government agencies. FISMA provides a statutory framework for securing government-owned and operated IT infrastructures and assets. FISMA requires the CIO to carry out the following responsibilities:

- Develop and maintain an agencywide information assurance (IA) program with an entire IT security architecture and framework.
- Ensure that information security training is conducted annually to keep staff properly trained and certified.
- Implement accountability for personnel with significant responsibilities for information security.
- Provide proper training and awareness to senior management such that proper security awareness programs can be deployed.

The FISMA law also requires the agency head, in this case the secretary of the Navy, to

- Develop and maintain an agencywide information assurance (IA) program with an entire IT security architecture and framework.
- Ensure each agency has a sufficient number of trained information security personnel to ensure agencywide IA.
- Require annual reports from the CIO regarding the effectiveness of the agency's IA programs and progress on any required remedial actions.

The FISMA law also requires each federal agency to develop, document, and implement an agencywide information security program that includes the following elements:

- Periodic risk assessments (at least annually).
- Risk-assessment policies and procedures that cost-effectively reduce the risk to an acceptable level, ensure that information security is addressed throughout the life cycle of each agency information system, and ensure compliance with FISMA.

- Subordinate plans for networks, facilities, and groups of systems as appropriate.

- Security awareness training for agency personnel, including contractors and system users.

- Periodic (at least annually) testing and evaluation of the effectiveness of information security policies, procedures, and practices.

- Processes for planning, implementing, evaluating, and documenting remedial action to address deficiencies in agency information security policies, procedures, and practices.

- Procedures for detecting, reporting, and responding to security incidents.

- Plans and procedures to ensure continuity of operations for information systems that support agency operations and assets.

Finally, FISMA law requires each federal agency to report to Congress annually by March 1. The agency FISMA report must address the adequacy and effectiveness of information security policies, procedures, and practices.

In addition to the annual report, FISMA requires that each agency conduct an annual, independent evaluation of the IA program and practices to determine their effectiveness.

FISMA requirements brought about for the first time in U.S. federal government history a definition for agency information security and human accountability for the protection of federal government IT infrastructure and data assets.

Sarbanes-Oxley Act (SOX)

The Sarbanes-Oxley Act (SOX) was signed into law in 2002 and named after its authors: Senator Paul Sarbanes (D-MD) and Representative Paul Oxley (R-Ohio). This act mandated a number of reforms to enhance corporate responsibility, enhance financial disclosures, and combat corporate and accounting fraud.

Corporate and accounting fraud became commonplace thanks to the Enron and MCI Worldcom fiascos, which were the driving force in the creation and adoption of the SOX law. This was the first law of this kind that requires U.S.-based corporations to abide by new anticrime laws, address a broad range of wrongdoings, and requires a set of comprehensive controls be put in place while holding the CEO and CFO accountable for the accuracy of the information.

SOX law applies to U.S.-based publicly traded companies with market capitalizations of $75 million or more. SOX compliancy commenced in fiscal year 2004, with fiscal year 2005 being the first full year of SOX compliancy. Many organizations are now assessing and eliminating identified gaps in defined control objectives and in particular, information-security-related control objectives.

The SOX structure and charter consists of the following organizational elements:

- **Public Company Accounting Oversight Board (PCAOB)**—The SOX law created and enacted the PCAOB to oversee and guide auditors in maintaining SOX compliancy.

- **PCAOB Was Charted with Creating Proposed Auditing Standards for SOX Compliancy**—PCAOB was tasked with creating consistent auditing standards for SOX compliancy.

- **PCAOB Selected Controls Frameworks from Committee of Sponsoring Organizations (COSO)**—The goal of the COSO was to develop a standardized control framework that provided structured guidelines for implementing internal controls.

To supplement the control framework structure created by the COSO, the PCAOB selected Information Systems Audit and Control Association's (ISACA) control objectives for information and related technology framework (COBIT). Assistance from the IT Governance Institute used COSO and COBIT frameworks to create specific IT control objectives for SOX. The IT Governance Institute Framework includes the following major areas:

- **Security Policies**—Policies are the most important control objectives to define because they encompass the entire organization and act as an element of that organization's overall IT security architecture and framework.

- **Security Standards**—Standards allow the entire organization to follow a consistent definition for how securing the IT infrastructure and assets will be implemented using hardware and software security tools and systems.

- **Access and Authentication**—Requires that the organization have a consistent definition for end user access control and how those users will be authenticated prior to access being granted to the systems and information.

- **User Account Management**—Requires that access control and management of access control be defined consistently across the organization with stringent controls put in place to track, monitor, and ensure system access is not compromised.

- **Network Security**—Requires that the network infrastructure (LAN, WAN, Internetworking, Egress Points, Internet Access, DMZ, and so on) be designed and configured according to the IT security architecture and framework that is defined for the organization.

- **Monitoring**—Requires that the organization have a plan to adequately monitor the security of the IT infrastructure and the various IT systems and assets. This plan undoubtedly requires IT security tools and systems to monitor, audit, and report on network activity and system access.

- **Segregation of Duties**—Requires that the IT organization and, in particular, the roles, responsibilities, and accountabilities for information security be defined and documented in a segregated manner given the layers of responsibilities that are typical in an IT infrastructure.

- **Physical Security**—Requires that physical access and physical security be defined that house and protect the IT infrastructure and assets (for example, data centers, computer rooms, server rooms).

Two sections indirectly and directly impact IT infrastructures and information security: Section 302 and Section 404.

Section 302 impacts information security indirectly in that the CEO and CFO must personally certify that their organization has the proper internal controls. Section 302 mandates that the CEO and CFO must personally certify that financial reports are accurate and complete and that the data they use for financial reporting is accurate and secure. In addition, the CEO and CFO must also report on effectiveness of internal controls around financial reporting.

Section 404 mandates that certain management structures, control objectives, and procedures be put into place. Compliance with Section 404 requires companies to establish an infrastructure that is actually designed to protect and preserve records and data from destruction, loss, unauthorized alteration, or other misuse.

When developing management structures, control objectives, and procedures for SOX Section 404 to protect and preserve records and data from destruction, loss, unauthorized alteration or other misuse, five major areas must be addressed:

- **Control Environment**—The Control Environment defines the scope of the SOX Section 404 responsibility, which includes an organization's IT infrastructure and assets.

- **Risk Assessment**—As per SOX Section 404, a risk assessment for the Control Environment that includes an organization's IT infrastructure and assets is to be conducted.

- **Control Activities**—Specific control activities (for example, asset management, change control board/procedures, configuration management) must be defined and documented for the Control Environment, which usually includes the IT infrastructure and IT and data assets.

- **Information and Communications**—Documentation and communication of the findings and assessment for the Control Environment must be done such that management can take the appropriate steps to mitigate identified risks, threats, and vulnerabilities.

- **Monitoring**—Continuous monitoring, configuration change update tracking, and other internal and external influences to the Control Environment must be done to maintain compliancy with SOX Section 404 on an annual basis.

Organizations today are being forced to create IT security architectures and frameworks to properly address the requirements of these new laws, mandates, and regulations. After an IT security architecture and framework is in place, risk and vulnerability assessments are needed to identify weaknesses and gaps in the deployment of information security architectures and frameworks.

By conducting a risk and vulnerability assessment, an organization will be able to identify and get a baseline for their current level of information security. This baseline will form the foundation for how that organization needs to increase or enhance its current level of security based on the criticality or exposure to risk that is identified during the risk and vulnerability assessment conducted on the IT infrastructure and assets. From here, it is important to understand risk assessment best practices and what the goal of a risk assessment should be for an organization.

Risk Assessment Best Practices

When you're conducting a risk assessment, it is important to define what the goals and objectives are for the risk assessment and what that organization would like to accomplish by conducting one.

Risk and vulnerability assessments provide the necessary information about an organization's IT infrastructure and its asset's current level of security. This level of security allows the assessor to provide recommendations for increasing or enhancing that IT asset's level of security based on the identified and known vulnerabilities that are inherent in the IT infrastructure and its assets.

There are many best practices or approaches to consider when conducting a risk and vulnerability assessment on an IT infrastructure and its assets. These best practices or approaches will vary depending on the scope of the IT infrastructure and its assets. To properly secure and protect an organization's IT infrastructure and assets, a significant amount of design, planning, and implementation expertise is required to ensure that the proper level of security is designed and implemented properly. While preparing and conducting a risk assessment, the following best practices or approaches should be considered:

- **Create a Risk Assessment Policy**—A risk assessment policy will define what the organization must do periodically (annually in many cases), how risk is to be addressed and mitigated (for example, a minimum acceptable vulnerability window), and how that organization must carry out a risk assessment for its IT infrastructure components and its assets. Creation of a risk assessment policy is usually done after the first risk assessment is conducted as a post-assessment activity. In some cases, organizations create a risk assessment policy and then implement the recommendations that the policy defines.

- **Inventory and Maintain a Database of IT Infrastructure Components and IT Assets**—One of the most tedious but important first steps in conducting a risk or vulnerability assessment is to identify and inventory all known IT infrastructure components and assets. Without a complete and accurate inventory of IT infrastructure components and IT assets, an asset valuation, criticality, or importance evaluation cannot be performed.

- **Define Risk Assessment Goals and Objectives in Line with Organizational Business Drivers**—Defining the risk assessment's goals and objectives is the second step in conducting a risk assessment for your IT infrastructure components and IT assets. Aligning these goals and objectives with the organization's business drivers will allow the organization to prioritize and focus on critical systems and assets first given the budget limitations that most organizations face.

- **Identify a Consistent Risk Assessment Methodology and Approach for Your Organization**—Defining and selecting the risk assessment methodology and approach for your organization will be dependent on the organization's ability to identify accurate IT infrastructure components and assets, the ability to identify asset value and/or asset importance/criticality to the organization, and how the organization makes business decisions. This will be further examined in Chapter 4, "Risk Assessment Methodologies."

- **Conduct an Asset Valuation or Asset Criticality Valuation as per a Defined Standard Definition for the Organization**—Depending on the accuracy and availability of inventory documentation and asset valuation data (for example, capital dollars spent on hardware, software, integration, maintenance, staff salaries, G&A overhead), the organization should conduct an asset valuation or asset criticality (importance) assessment to prioritize and determine which IT infrastructure components and assets are most important to the organization (either in monetary value or importance value). This will be further examined in Chapter 4.

- **Define and/or Limit the Scope of the Risk Assessment Accordingly by Identifying and Categorizing IT Infrastructure Components and Assets as Critical, Major, and Minor**—Depending on the scope of the risk assessment, an organization may or may not be faced with a limited budget to conduct a thorough risk and vulnerability assessment. In many cases, organizations have limited budgets to conduct a risk and vulnerability assessment and must limit the scope on the mission-critical IT infrastructure components and assets only. Although this solution exposes the organization to potential risks, threats, and vulnerabilities, a defense-in-depth approach to assessing and mitigating risks, threats, and vulnerabilities can still be pursued.

- **Understand and Evaluate the Risks, Threats, and Vulnerabilities to Those Categorized IT Infrastructure Components and Assets**—After the IT infrastructure components and assets are identified and an asset valuation or asset criticality assessment is conducted, the next step in the risk assessment and vulnerability assessment is to assess the impact that potential risks, threats, and vulnerabilities have on the identified IT infrastructure components and assets. By aligning the potential risks, threats, and vulnerabilities to the prioritized IT infrastructure components and assets, management can make sound business decisions based on the value or criticality of that IT asset and the potential risk, threats, and vulnerabilities that are known.

- **Define a Consistent Standard or Yardstick of Measurement for Securing the Organization's Critical, Major, and Minor IT Infrastructure Components and Assets**—To properly categorize IT infrastructure components and assets, a consistent standard definition or yardstick of measurement needs to be defined. This standard definition refers to how the organization will define and categorize IT infrastructure components and assets to be Critical, Major, or Minor. This definition can be based on monetary value, requirement by law or mandate, or criticality or importance to the organization. The selection criteria or requirements for defining this standard definition should be defined by management and incorporated into the risk assessment policy when it is drafted and implemented.

- **Perform the Risk and Vulnerability Assessment as per the Defined Standard or Yardstick of Measurement for the Organization's IT Infrastructure Assets**—After the standard definition or yardstick of measurement is defined for IT asset categorization, the risk and vulnerability assessment can be aligned to the priorities as defined by the results of the standard definition for categorization of the organization's IT infrastructure components and assets. This is important given that most organizations have a limited budget for implementing information security countermeasures and must prioritize how they spend funds on information security, especially if they are under compliance requirements with new laws, mandates, and regulations that require them to do so or be subject to penalties.

- **Prepare a Risk and Vulnerability Assessment Final Report That Captures the Goals and Objectives Aligned with the Organization's Business Drivers, Provides a Detailed Summary of Findings, Provides an Objective Assessment and Gap Analysis of Those Assessment Findings to the Defined Standard, and Provides Tactical and Strategic Recommendations for Mitigating Identified Weaknesses**—The risk and vulnerability assessment final report is the primary document that presents all the findings, information, assessments, and recommendations for the organization. The final assessment report becomes the instrument for management to make sound business decisions pertaining to the organization's overall risk and vulnerability assessment and how that organization will mitigate the identified risks, threats, and vulnerabilities.

- **Prioritize, Budget, and Implement the Tactical and Strategic Recommendations Identified During the Risk and Vulnerability Assessment Analysis**—After the findings, assessment, and recommendations are presented to management, it is important to prioritize them, create a budget, and have a tactical and strategic plan for implementing the recommendations presented in the final report. These recommendations may impact the entire organization and may take months, if not years, to fully implement. This prioritization of tactical and strategic recommendations will enable the organization to make sound business decisions with the defined goals and objectives of the risk and vulnerability assessment.

- **Implement Organizational Change Through an Ongoing Security Awareness and Security Training Campaign to Maintain a Consistent Message and Standard Definition for Securing the Organization's IT**

Infrastructure and Assets—Implementing organizational change requires an education and security awareness training plan for all employees or authorized users of the organization's IT systems, resources, and data. Mitigating risk requires all employees and users within the organization to abide by security awareness training.

Defining and implementing these risk assessment best practices does not come easily and requires careful analysis and decision making unique to the organization's business drivers and priorities as an organization. For example, a bank or financial institution requires more stringent use of encryption technology to ensure confidentiality of privacy data, whereas an organization that is not subject to stringent confidentiality requirements may put less investment in encryption technology and more investment in other areas.

These risk assessment best practices allow an organization to consider the big picture of why that organization should conduct a risk and vulnerability assessment and how they should methodically approach the assessment. More importantly, these best practices align that organization's business drivers and defined standards to the risk and vulnerability assessment to assist management in making sound business decisions based on available budgets, minimum acceptable vulnerability windows, and importance and criticality of IT infrastructure components and assets.

Understanding the IT Security Process

As defined earlier in Chapter 2, "Foundations and Principles of Security," designing and implementing a sound IT security architecture and framework requires a thorough analysis and examination of how availability, integrity, and availability (A-I-C Triad) is designed and implemented on the IT infrastructure components and assets in the overall information security plan.

Attacks on an IT infrastructure and assets can disrupt availability of service resulting in the following:

- **Loss of Productivity**—Downtime equals lost productivity to organizations. Lost productivity can result in loss in dollars and time.

- **Violation of Service Level Agreements**—Service providers or outsourcing service organizations can be in violation of contractual service level agreements (SLAs) that may result in penalties and financial compensation.

- **Financial Loss**—Lost productivity and violation of SLAs all result in financial loss. Depending on the criticality of the financial loss, this may change the prioritization of how that organization funds and secures its IT infrastructure components and assets.

- **Loss of Life**—System downtime or even loss of data can impact IT infrastructures and systems that are used to maintain, support, and respond to human life issues.

Attacks on an IT infrastructure and assets can disrupt the integrity of information that organizations disseminate:

- **Attack Against the Integrity of a System**—A system's integrity requires sound access control processes and authentication that the user is authorized to access the system. Attacks against the integrity of the system start with access control and include the manipulation of information or data, including destruction of data.

- **Information or Data Can Be Modified, Altered, or Destroyed**—A system's integrity can be compromised if access is granted to a perpetrator and the organization's information or data is modified, altered, or destroyed.

Caution

Attacks on an IT infrastructure and assets can disrupt the confidentiality of information and data assets. Attacks can expose confidential information such as corporate or intellectual property secrets, financial information, and health records, which can result in identity theft. Maintaining the confidentiality of privacy records and financial data pertaining to individuals is now subject to laws, mandates, and regulations dictated by HIPAA and GLBA.

Unfortunately, implementing a robust IT security architecture and framework and conducting a risk and vulnerability assessment is not something that can be taken lightly by an organization. This is true given that many IT systems and applications were not designed with security in mind; many organizations are struggling to deal with the lack of security in their IT infrastructure components and applications that are currently in production. Security was always an afterthought and now for the first time, information security is in the forefront of system requirements definitions and system designs.

Security as a process would define an entire development life cycle that incorporates security requirements into the system or application design from the very beginning. By designing a system (hardware, software, or multiplatforms) or application (software code) from the ground up that includes security requirements for availability, integrity, and confidentiality, minimization of the risks, threats, and vulnerabilities can be designed into the system or application up front. Security as a process would have security requirements incorporated throughout all the steps of the system or application development and design life cycle. These steps include the following:

- **Risk/Threat/Vulnerability Analysis**—Ideally, this is done prior to any system requirements or application requirements being defined and documented. This initial risk, threat, and vulnerability analysis will attempt to identify and mitigate the exposure by incorporating appropriate security countermeasure requirements into the overall system or application design.

- **System Requirements Definition and Design**—After a risk, threat, and vulnerability analysis is conducted, the system's or application's requirements definition can incorporate the technical requirements along with embedded security and security countermeasures requirements to mitigate the identified and known exposures to that system or application.

- **Functional Design**—After the system's technical requirements definition and security requirements definition are complete, a comprehensive system or application functional design can be documented. The functional design will describe the functionality of the system or application and how security is embedded into the functionality of the system or application.

- **Security Design**—After the system requirements definition, technical design, and functional design are completed, the specific security design for the system and application can be conducted based on the security requirements that are identified as being needed. Depending on the criticality and importance of the security design, implementation of security elements into the system or application design will assist the system designers in ensuring the availability, integrity, and confidentiality of the system or application and its data.

- **System/Application Test Plan**—Like any new system or application, a thorough system or application test plan must be developed to ensure that all the technical, functional, and security design elements were developed properly and do not contain identifiable bugs, performance issues, or potential exposure to risks, threats, and vulnerabilities.

- **System Design Verification/Validation**—A thorough system design verification and validation assessment will come from the results of the system or application test plan. The results of the test plan will uncover whether the system design properly incorporated the technical, functional, and security requirements as defined in the system or application development life cycle.

As shown in Figure 3.3, step 4 in the System Development Life Cycle incorporates security design within the design and development phase of the life cycle. This is an important first step to ensure that the proper security controls, security objectives, and security goals are initiated properly.

This IT security process is what is currently missing from many organizations when it comes to designing and implementing new IT systems and applications throughout the organization. As organizations incorporate security requirements and design into the development life cycle, more IT systems and applications will have the inherent security controls to ensure that the availability, integrity, and confidentiality goals and objectives are achieved.

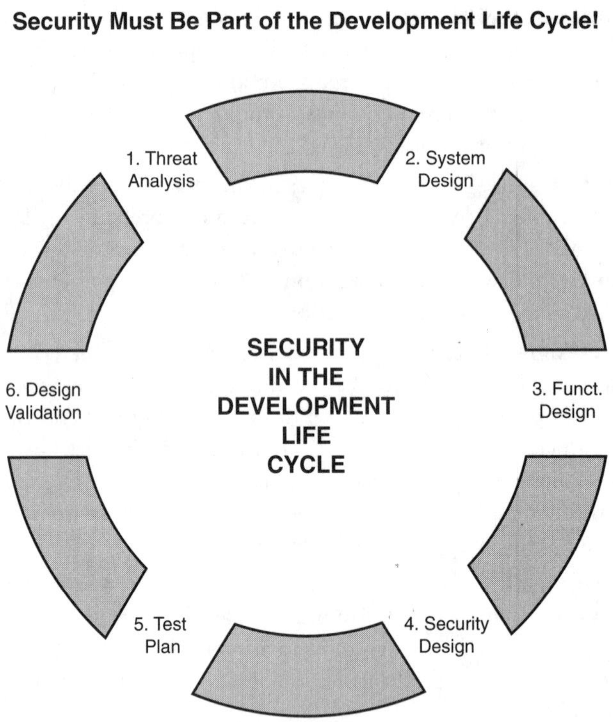

Security Must Be Part of the Development Life Cycle!

Figure 3.3   Security in the development life cycle.

When conducting a risk and vulnerability assessment on IT systems and applications, examination of the defined security goals and objectives can be done. This examination will include a review of the IT system's or applications' security requirements and how they were implemented in production. Understanding this void in the development life cycle will help IT organizations fill the void with proper security requirements and security design steps in the overall development effort. By implementing the proper security controls and requirements into the system and application design up front, minimization of exposure to risks, threats, and vulnerabilities can be achieved, thus eliminating costly security countermeasures and other security controls around the IT system or application that lacks the proper security controls.

The Goals and Objectives of a Risk Assessment

An organization may consider many goals and objectives prior to undergoing a risk and vulnerability assessment. Some of these goals and objectives may be the result of required compliancy to new laws, mandates, and regulations for information security. Security as a process for an IT infrastructure and assets is primarily concerned with prevention, detection, and response. A sound and comprehensive security process coupled with a robust IT security architecture and framework will assist the organization in ensuring the security of the IT infrastructure and assets as per the organization's minimum acceptable risk or exposure level.

Security Process Definition

Security as a process typically includes three key elements: prevention, detection, and response.

Prevention deals with the implementation of security controls and countermeasures or safeguards during the initial security design phase of the development life cycle. By incorporating security requirements into the design phase of the development life cycle, prevention or protection is easier to implement because it is inherent in the system's or application's design up front. Prevention techniques and solutions should be designed and developed into the system or application to ensure that availability, integrity, and confidentiality for the system or application are implemented.

Detection or monitoring deals with monitoring the IT infrastructure and assets. This includes monitoring log files, audit trails, intrusion detection system reporting, and reviewing vulnerability assessments reports and CVE items that are installed within the production IT infrastructure. Continuous monitoring of the IT infrastructure and assets for newly discovered risks, threats, and vulnerabilities is an ongoing process and the responsibility of information security professionals who are responsible and accountable for securing the IT infrastructure and assets.

Response is the reaction that an IT organization takes in response to a security breach or incident from a known or unknown risk, threat, or vulnerability. Response usually encompasses the following four areas:

- **Business Continuity Plan (BCP)**—Organizations that have a significant amount of investment in the IT infrastructure and assets typically create, test, and validate an internal BCP plan to address how to maintain operations and functionality in the event of lost critical assets. A BCP plan typically includes a risk assessment, asset valuation or criticality assessment, and a vulnerability assessment in order for the organization to build the proper BCP plan in the event of risk, threat, or vulnerability incidents affecting the production IT infrastructure and assets.

- **Disaster Recovery Plan (DRP)**—Organizations that have a significant exposure to risks and threats, particularly weather related, act of God related, or war related, must have a plan for dealing with a disaster (for example, hurricane, flood, fire). A DRP plan typically requires an outsourcing solution and/or a hot site that replicates the main IT infrastructure and systems that the organization is fully dependent on to maintain its business operations.

- **Security Incident Response Team (SIRT) and Plan**—Many organizations have their own internal Security Incident Response Team (SIRT) that comprises a cross-section of human resources, legal, IT, and departmental management personnel. The SIRT typically has authority to collect and conduct investigations pertaining to security breaches and/or security incidents. Because of the potential sensitivity and nature of a security breach or incident, confidentiality and maintaining the integrity of data and information used to investigate and collect the data and information must be conducted under certain rules and guidelines. This is critical if forensic data is to be used in a court of law as evidence if a criminal charge is put on the perpetrator or perpetrators for violation of access or unauthorized use of an organization's IT infrastructure and assets.

- **Forensic Analysis Plan**—Depending on the laws, mandates, regulations, and jurisdiction of the security breach and/or incident occurring, a carefully developed forensic analysis plan and computer forensic data and information collection must be followed for the data and information to be admissible in a court of law as evidence for a criminal case in the United States. The CIRT team must be properly trained and the IT security professionals who collect and retrieve data and information must abide by the forensic analysis plan where data and information collected during the security breach or incident investigation is pursued.

Depending on the organization's compliancy requirements to new laws, mandates, and regulations, the priorities, definition of criticality or importance, and the goals and objectives that are identified for conducting a risk and vulnerability assessment will be unique to that organization.

Goals and Objectives of a Risk and Vulnerability Assessment

Some of the more common goals and objectives of conducting a risk and vulnerability assessment are as follows:

- IT organizations can have an accurate inventory of IT assets and data assets.
- IT organizations can have prioritized IT assets and data assets based on different measurements criteria—asset value in dollars, the importance of assets to the organization, or the criticality to the organization.
- Risks, threats, and known vulnerabilities can be identified and documented for the IT organization's production, infrastructure, and assets.
- Risks, threats, and known vulnerabilities can be prioritized based on impact or criticality of the IT asset or data asset that it impacts.
- The vulnerability window can be identified and minimized according to the organization's minimum acceptable tolerance to being vulnerable.
- Remediation or mitigation of the identified risks, threats, and vulnerabilities can be properly budgeted and planned according to the prioritization or criticality of IT assets and data assets.
- Compliancy with new information security laws, mandates, and regulations can be achieved by first conducting a risk and vulnerability assessment.

- Identification of the gaps or voids in the organization's IT security architecture and framework can be found with specific recommendations for closing the gaps and voids.

- A risk and vulnerability assessment identifies the exposures, risks, threats, and vulnerabilities that the organization is subject to and assists the IT organization in justifying the cost of needed security countermeasures and solutions to mitigate the identified risks, threats, and vulnerabilities.

- A risk and vulnerability assessment provides an IT organization with an objective assessment and recommendations to the organization's defined goals and objectives for conducting the risk and vulnerability assessment.

- A risk and vulnerability assessment assists IT organizations with understanding the return on investment if funds are invested in IT security infrastructure.

Summary

Because of the increase in risks, threats, and vulnerabilities and other exploits in IT infrastructures, IT security professionals are not able to address known vulnerabilities in time before the next unknown vulnerability appears. This *catch-22* scenario requires IT security professionals and management to make prioritized decisions pertaining to which IT assets get funding for security controls and security countermeasures first. Many IT budgets are limited, especially for investments in securing the IT infrastructure. This limitation forces organizations to prioritize funding for securing their most critical IT and data assets first. In other organizations, new laws, mandates, and regulations are requiring organizations to invest in information security and IT security infrastructure.

Risk assessments allow the organization to assess from a criticality and importance factor which IT and data assets must be protected and secured more than others. In addition, a risk assessment will allow an organization to make tactical and strategic business decisions pertaining to securing its most valuable IT and data assets. Without a risk assessment, IT management would be guessing as to how best to spend its funds on security for its IT and data assets.

Finally, a risk and vulnerability assessment allows an organization to understand the roles, responsibilities, and accountabilities for the IT professionals and IT security professionals in an organization. Risk and vulnerability assessments typically find gaps and voids in the human responsibility and accountability for dealing with risks, threats, and vulnerabilities. Given the magnitude of the IT security responsibility, segregation of duties and dissemination of these duties to IT and IT security professionals is a critical follow-up step in many IT organizations to properly address the human responsibilities and accountabilities for ensuring that the availability, integrity, and confidentiality of IT infrastructure components and assets are met.

The dissemination of roles, responsibilities, and accountabilities throughout the IT infrastructure or areas of risk management can be clearly defined after the risks, threats, and vulnerabilities are identified within an organization's IT infrastructure.

Key Terms

The following acronyms and terms are used in this chapter. For the explanation and definition purpose of this chapter, these acronyms and terms are defined as follows:

Audit   A term that typically accompanies an accounting or auditing firm that conforms to a specific and formal methodology and definition for how an investigation is to be conducted with specific reporting elements and metrics being examined (such as a financial audit according to Public Accounting and Auditing Guidelines and Procedures).

Assessment   An evaluation and/or valuation of IT assets based on predefined measurement or evaluation criteria. This does not typically require an accounting or auditing firm to conduct an assessment such as a risk or vulnerability assessment.

Disclaimer of Warranties   A legal term that denies or disavows the user's legal claim of warranty of the product, hardware, or software.

Exclusion of Incidental, Consequential, and Certain Other Damages   A legal term that protects and indemnifies the organization from external incidents, consequences, or other certain damages that may arise from the use of the organization's hardware or software.

Hot Site   A remote and secure data center that replicates the production IT infrastructure, systems, applications, and backup data of the production environment.

IT   Information technology.

IT Asset   Information technology asset such as hardware or software or data.

IT Asset Criticality   The act of putting a criticality factor or importance value (Critical, Major, or Minor) in an IT asset.

IT Asset Valuation   The act of putting a monetary value to an IT asset.

IT Infrastructure   A general term to encompass all information technology assets (hardware, software, data), components, systems, applications, and resources.

IT Security Architecture and Framework   A document that defines the policies, standards, procedures, and guidelines for information security.

Law   A rule of conduct or action prescribed or formally recognized as binding or enforced by a controlling authority (U.S. federal government, state government, and so on).

Limitation of Liability and Remedies   A legal term that limits the organization from the amount of financial liability and the limitation of the remedies the organization is legally willing to take on.

Limited Warranty   A legal term that defines but limits the written guarantee of the integrity of a product and of the maker's responsibility for the repair or replacement of defective parts.

Mandate   A formal order from a superior court or official to an inferior one, such as a mandate from the U.S. federal government to state government.

Qualitative Analysis   A weighted factor or nonmonetary evaluation and analysis that is based on a weighting or criticality factor valuation as part of the evaluation or analysis.

Quantitative Analysis   A numerical evaluation and analysis that is based on monetary or dollar valuation as part of the evaluation or analysis.

Regulation   How a law or mandate is implemented.

Risk   The exposure or potential for loss or damage to IT assets within that IT infrastructure.

Risk Assessment   A process for evaluating the exposure or potential loss or damage to the IT and data assets for an organization.

Risk Management   The overall responsibility and management of risk within an organization. Risk management is the responsibility and dissemination of roles, responsibilities, and accountabilities for risk in an organization.

Threat   Any agent, condition, or circumstance that could potentially cause harm, loss, damage, or compromise to an IT asset or data asset.

Vulnerability   A weakness in the IT infrastructure or IT components that may be exploited for a threat to destroy, damage, or compromise an IT asset.

Vulnerability Assessment   A methodical evaluation of an organization's IT weaknesses of infrastructure components and assets and how those weaknesses can be mitigated through proper security controls and recommendations to remediate exposure to risks, threats, and vulnerabilities.

Vulnerability Management   The overall responsibility and management of vulnerabilities within an organization and how that management of vulnerabilities will be achieved through dissemination of duties throughout the IT organization.

4

Risk-Assessment Methodologies

IN THE PREVIOUS CHAPTER, THE GOALS AND OBJECTIVES for conducting a risk assessment were presented. These goals and objectives provide many reasons why an organization should conduct a risk assessment on its IT and network infrastructure. In some cases, new laws, mandates, and regulations such as HIPAA, GLBA, FISMA, and SOX require organizations to conduct periodic risk and vulnerability assessments and implement defined security controls. This, coupled with the creation and implementation of an IT security architecture and framework, provides the necessary foundation for an organization to properly manage and mitigate the risks caused by threats and vulnerabilities to an IT and network infrastructure.

This chapter first presents risk-assessment terminology commonly used when discussing risk management and risk-assessment topics. After these terms and definitions are presented, the chapter will present to the reader the different methodologies and approaches for conducting a risk assessment on an IT infrastructure and its assets. The reader will learn the steps needed to conduct a risk assessment using different methodologies or approaches. However, no matter what methodology or approach is used, it is important that the organization address how asset management and proper inventorying of the organizations IT assets are to be handled. After the IT systems, applications, and data assets are inventoried, the organization must prioritize them based on importance to the organization. This prioritization is critical because many organizations do not have unlimited funds to implement proper security controls and security countermeasures to mitigate the identified risk from threats and vulnerabilities. This prioritization is typically aligned to the organization's business drivers, goals, and objectives. Then, assessing the risk of threats and vulnerabilities on an organization's IT hardware, software, and assets can be done qualitatively, quantitatively, or via a hybrid approach.

Risk-Assessment Terminology

In the previous chapter, the basic elements of risk in an IT infrastructure were identified as assets, threats, and vulnerabilities. Assets typically are items of quantitative or qualitative value to an organization. This can include computers, network equipment, hardware, software, applications, and data assets. One of the most important reasons for conducting a risk assessment on an IT infrastructure and its assets is to assist the organization in adequately managing risk. Risk assessments are a critical component of an overall risk-management strategy for an IT infrastructure and its assets. Developing a risk-management strategy helps organizations manage and mitigate risk to threats and vulnerabilities that are uncovered and identified during the risk and vulnerability assessment. Thus, a risk assessment is a major component of an organization's overall risk-management strategy. Because IT infrastructures grow and evolve, risk management for an organization must include periodic risk assessments. As more and more IT systems, applications, and data assets are implemented, mitigating risk for these production IT assets becomes increasingly important.

Risk-assessment and risk-management terminology include the following terms and definitions:

- **Acceptable risk**— A term used to describe the minimum acceptable risk that an organization is willing to take.
- **Countermeasure or safeguards**—Controls, processes, procedures, or security systems that help to mitigate potential risk.
- **Exposure**—When an asset is vulnerable to damage or losses from a threat.
- **Exposure factor**—A value calculated by determining the percentage of loss to a specific asset because of a specific threat.
- **Residual risk**—The risk that remains after security controls and security countermeasures have been implemented.
- **Risk management**—The process of reducing risk to IT assets by identifying and eliminating threats through the deployment of security controls and security countermeasures.
- **Risk analysis**—The process of identifying the severity of potential risks, identifying vulnerabilities, and assigning a priority to each. This may be done in preparation for the implementation of security countermeasures designed to mitigate high-priority risks.

Risk-Management and Risk-Assessment Requirements

As defined previously, risk management is a process for reducing risk to IT infrastructures and IT assets by identifying and eliminating threats through the deployment of security controls and security countermeasures. Risk management is an ongoing and everyday responsibility for an IT infrastructure and its assets. Because risk assessments are usually done after the fact and on an existing IT infrastructure and its production systems, applications, and data, many organizations attempt to address risk management early in the development life cycle, prior to IT systems, applications, and data being implemented in production. This is the best way to mitigate risk in production IT systems, applications, and data, given the many software vulnerabilities that exist. One approach to risk management is to incorporate it into the system design and system architecture phases of development. By mitigating the bugs and flaws in firmware, operating systems, and applications, exposure to risk from software vulnerabilities can be minimized. Mitigating bugs in software requires incorporating security controls in the software development life cycle (SDLC) as described in the previous chapter.

Ongoing risk management includes conducting periodic risk and vulnerability assessments on an organization's IT infrastructure and assets. Risk and vulnerability assessments can be approached in different ways, depending on the environment and the IT infrastructure. Risk-assessment approaches are best looked at by understanding the landscape first. This landscape is depicted in the seven areas of information security responsibility described in the previous chapter in Figure 3.4. These seven areas require proper security controls and security countermeasures within each area to mitigate risk from threats and vulnerabilities to the overall IT infrastructure. By conducting a periodic risk assessment, the IT organization will know exactly how vulnerable the IT infrastructure and its assets are, and proper remediation can be planned.

Each of the seven areas of information security responsibility has its own risk-mitigation issues that must be analyzed uniquely as well as collectively from an organizational perspective. When identifying and locating an organization's assets, the entire IT infrastructure must be examined, including the end users and IT support staff. By conducting a risk assessment, an organization will be able to align its minimum acceptable level of risk for the IT infrastructure and its mission-critical IT assets with proper risk-mitigation techniques, security controls, and security countermeasures.

Defense-in-Depth Approach for Risk Assessments

Another way of looking at the IT infrastructure and its risk mitigation is to examine the security of an IT infrastructure in a layered fashion. This layered approach to risk mitigation is referred to as *defense-in-depth*. Defense-in-depth is the practice of layering, like an onion, the defenses and security countermeasures into zones, thus distributing the responsibility and accountability for information security over the seven areas of information security responsibility. This multilayered approach to information security provides layers of additional security controls and security countermeasures to slow down as well as mitigate the risk of an internal or external attack. A layered IT security infrastructure plan allows for compartmentalized safeguards and security countermeasures. The overall aggregate security level would be a combination of the defense-in-depth layers, provided they were implemented properly. The security controls and security countermeasures that are implemented throughout the IT infrastructure should be designed so that a failure in one safeguard is covered by another—hence, the layered approach to security. This defense-in-depth approach truly combines the capabilities of people, operations, and security technologies to establish multiple layers of protection, eliminate single lines of defense, and enhance the overall security of the IT infrastructure and its assets.

These layers of protection extend to specific, critical defensive zones commonly found in defense-in-depth risk mitigation approaches:

- **Data defenses**—Security controls and security countermeasures that protect an organization's data assets, such as encryption technology of data within a database.

- **Application defenses**—Security controls and security countermeasures that protect an organization's systems and applications, such as deploying firewalls and IP-based Virtual Private Network (VPN) technology to minimize authorized traffic to specific source IP addresses and authentication capabilities.

- **Operating system defenses**—Security controls with automated software patch management deployments that harden server and workstation operating systems with all security software patches.

- **Network infrastructure defenses**—Perimeter defenses with audit and monitoring at all ingress/egress points in a network infrastructure.

Figure 4.1 shows the defense-in-depth or layered approach to information security controls and security countermeasures.

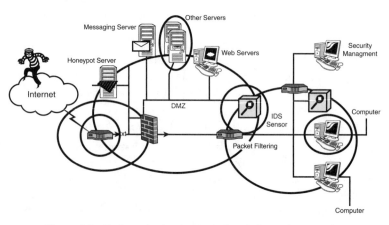

Figure 4.1   Defense-in-depth approach to information security.

The defense-in-depth approach to risk mitigation can best be supported by conducting periodic risk assessments within each layer of the defense-in-depth information security implementation. Conducting a risk assessment on an IT infrastructure that incorporates defense-in-depth strategies allows the IT security professional to focus the assessment on each layer or area within the overall IT infrastructure. Risk assessments are a critical function for the proper implementation and deployment of a defense-in-depth strategy because an organization may knowingly be able to implement security controls and security countermeasures only in specific locations within the IT infrastructure. Conducting a risk assessment will assist the IT organization in addressing the gaps and voids that are uncovered during the assessment, and proper risk-mitigation techniques can be deployed strategically throughout the defense-in-depth layered infrastructure.

Risk Analysis Approach for Risk Assessments

After an IT infrastructure's systems, applications, data, and assets are identified, inventoried, and prioritized by the organization, conducting a risk analysis on those IT assets is required. The process of determining the objective and subjective value of IT assets, the identification of specific threats to them, and the loss or impact to the organization if a threat to the IT asset is realized is part of the risk analysis. This loss or impact to the organization is calculated using either a quantitative or qualitative risk-assessment approach. The results will be a report to management identifying the elements of greatest risk to an IT infrastructure and its assets. This will allow management to make sound business decisions pertaining to the deployment of security controls and security counter-measures to achieve the confidentiality, integrity, and availability goals of the organization.

The following list summarizes the risk-analysis life cycle, which is part of the overall process for conducting a risk assessment on an IT infrastructure and its assets:

- **Asset identification**—An accurate and detailed inventory of IT assets, hardware, software, systems, applications, data, disk storage, and miscellaneous equipment.

- **Asset valuation**—After assets are identified, placing an asset value in dollars or assigning an asset weighted factor value allow an organization's IT assets to be prioritized from highest importance to lowest.

- **Threat identification**—Although there are a multitude of threats to an IT asset, this step in the process requires identifying all possible threats or vulnerabilities for each IT asset identified in the asset inventory. This threat identification or valuation step allows the organization to assess the impact of a threat being realized.

- **Impact or financial loss calculation**—The final step in the risk analysis exercise is to assess the potential impact of a threat to an IT asset and the IT infrastructure and organization and calculate the potential for financial loss.

Asset Valuation Approach for Risk Assessments

Risk analysis requires the identification of an IT infrastructure's assets, including data assets and their valuation. Asset valuation is an important task to conduct as part of an organization's ongoing risk management strategy. Asset valuation is important for the following reasons:

- **Helps prioritize IT asset recovery**—An organization's IT asset valuation provides useful information about an organization's most critical systems, resources, applications, and data, thus providing valuable information for prioritizing investments for security controls and security countermeasures.

- **Assists in the justification for security controls and countermeasures**— Many organizations need to justify the investment needed for proper security controls and security countermeasures. A proper asset valuation will assist an organization's management team in making business decisions regarding deployment of security controls and security countermeasures.

- **Assists in assessing how much insurance to purchase for the IT infrastructure and its assets**—After an asset valuation is completed, an organization will be able to accurately assess its business insurance requirements.

- **Provides financial valuations for the organization to conduct ROI and cost-benefit analyses**—Without an IT asset valuation, it is difficult to conduct a Return On Investment (ROI) or cost-benefit analysis pertaining to the investment in security controls and security countermeasures.

There are two methods for conducting an asset valuation. Deciding which one to use is important because it also represents the foundation for which risk-assessment approach an organization will use. Asset valuation for an IT infrastructure and its assets can be approached either qualitatively or quantitatively.

- A *qualitative valuation* is a subjective determination of an IT asset's value to the organization. This is usually accomplished by creating a valuation model or system that prioritized the criticality or importance of an IT asset to the organization. The qualitative value of an IT asset will include consideration of how critical the IT asset is to the organization, its intellectual property value, or its market value.

- A *quantitative valuation* identifies actual market value for an organization's IT assets. The quantitative value of an asset will include the monetary expenditures required for purchasing and maintenance of the IT asset itself. This may also include such costs as licensing or development and deployments costs, user training, documentation, and upgrades.

At this stage in the risk analysis, identifying all the possible threats to the IT assets can be completed next. It is important that at this stage, all threats are considered and listed. Threats may be categorized in many ways. The best categorization is one that readily fits the needs of the organization. Within these categories will be more specific threats. Information may be available from users, auditors, system administrators with trust relationships, and information sites such as www.cert.org. After the threats have been identified, they must be ranked in order of the magnitude of the impact if they are realized, as well as the likelihood. Because there are so many threats in the IT environment, this ranking may be facilitated by associating the threats that are relevant to vulnerabilities in your particular IT assets. Known vulnerabilities in your software are examples of this.

Quantitative and Qualitative Risk-Assessment Approaches

There are two commonly used risk-assessment approaches that essentially combine elements of risk management and risk analysis with financial impact and financial return on investment calculations. Determining which approach is best depends on the landscape of your IT infrastructure and assets and how your organization makes business decisions. Many organizations lack the adequate asset management, asset valuation, and intrinsic dollar valuation for their IT infrastructure and assets. Without accurate financials and access to financial data, conducting a quantitative risk assessment is difficult, if not impossible. In this case, organizations typically choose to do a *qualitative risk assessment* by assigning mission criticality values and priorities to those IT assets that are critical to the organization. This is a subjective prioritization that typically requires an organization's executive management team to define for the IT organization. This is why it is important to align an organization's business drivers, goals, and objectives with the overall risk assessment. The only tricky part is defining what the yardstick of measurement is for your organization (that is, what is most important to you, what threats you are most concerned with, and so on).

Quantitative Risk-Assessment Approach

Organizations that have accurate asset management, inventory management, annual software and hardware maintenance contracts, and access to accurate financials and depreciation schedules for IT assets typically conduct a *quantitative risk assessment*. A quantitative risk assessment is a methodical, step-by-step calculation of asset valuation, exposure to threats, and the financial impact or loss in the event of the threat being realized. Performing a methodical quantitative risk assessment involves assessing the asset value and threats to those critical IT assets. This is accompanied with several calculations that provide insight into the cost magnitude elements of the security requirement.

Because of the direct relationship between the cost of security and the amount or level of security desired, conducting an asset valuation and a risk and threat analysis is a critical step in conducting a quantitative risk assessment. This critical step will assist organizations in making effective business decisions. By assessing the risks and threats and comparing them to quantitative and measurable financial impacts, an organization's management is better equipped to make sound business decisions pertaining to prioritizing investments for security controls and security countermeasures.

The following steps describe conducting a quantitative risk assessment for an IT asset:

1. Determine the Asset Value (AV) for each IT asset.
2. Identify threats to the asset.
3. Determine the Exposure Factor (EF) for each IT asset in relation to each threat.
4. Calculate the Single Loss Expectancy (SLE).
5. Calculate the Annualized Rate of Occurrence (ARO).
6. Calculate the Annualized Loss Expectancy (ALE).

The first step in conducting a quantitative risk assessment is to identify all the IT assets that will act as the IT infrastructure's asset inventory. These assets should then be prioritized in regard to the systems and applications that support the organization's business processes and functions.

The second step is to identify the likelihood of a threat occurring to those IT assets. These threats include both internal and external threats, natural and man-made threats, accidental or intentional threats, and hardware or software vulnerabilities. For each threat, the risk assessor must calculate the estimated impact of the threat on that IT asset and the likelihood of occurrence or probability that the threat will occur.

The third step is to define the *exposure factor,* which is the subjective, potential percentage of loss to a specific IT asset if a specific threat is realized. The exposure factor (EF) is a subjective value that the risk assessor must define. It is important to identify as many threats or vulnerabilities as possible so that a clear understanding of those risks can be derived when determining the EF value. This is usually in the form of a percentage of the likelihood of it occurring, similar to how weather reports predict the likelihood of rain. For example, a hurricane may be a serious catastrophic threat to an IT asset because it can wipe out an entire data center in an office building, but if that office building is located in New York City, the likelihood of occurrence or exposure factor is negligible. Although there are no scales or predefined percentages or likelihood of occurrence values, the risk assessor must figure out how best to provide the percentage.

The fourth step is to calculate the *single loss expectancy (SLE).* The SLE value is a dollar value figure that represents the organization's loss from a single loss or loss of this particular IT asset. This is a financially calculated value that provides a measurable and comparable value to other IT assets that the organization may have. This allows for a consistent and logical prioritization of all IT assets within an IT infrastructure, which in turn allows an organization to prioritize its security controls and security countermeasures according to the highest SLE calculated for an IT asset. These should be ranked from highest to lowest, providing a prioritization and SLE value that can be compared with all the other critical IT assets of the organization.

Single Loss Expectancy (SLE)

SLE = Asset Value ($)×Exposure Factor (EF)

The single loss expectancy for an IT asset is derived by multiplying the IT asset's value with the exposure factor or probability of occurrence of a specific threat. The SLE value will vary for different threats to the same IT asset, so these must be examined collectively.

Suppose Company ABC has a customer database that is valued at $850,000. This asset value was derived from the IT systems, resources, applications, and hardware, including the profit potential from the customer database for forecasted revenue and profitability.

If the customer database has a potential threat from a critical software bug that the vendor just identified, the potential for a threat being realized is real. Software vendors strive to develop a software patch or software update to address this known critical software bug. Remember, the goal of a software patch is to minimize the software vulnerability window so that users can obtain the software patch, deploy it on production servers systems, and verify that the software vulnerability has been eliminated.

Because of this known vulnerability, the risk assessor assigns an exposure factor of 25%. There is a 25% probability that this known vulnerability can be exploited by an attacker.

The calculated SLE would be as follows:

SLE = $850,000 (Asset Value)×0.25 (Exposure Factor)

SLE = $212,500

If this customer database has a threat from malicious code or malicious software, and the server that the customer database resides in does not have antivirus or personal firewall protection, this could result in a significantly higher exposure factor. The risk assessor may provide a 75% probability that a virus, worm, or Trojan might attack the production server and customer database.

The calculated SLE would be the following:

SLE = $850,000 (Asset Value)×0.75 (Exposure Factor)

SLE = $637,500

When the risk assessor defines an exposure factor or percentage probability of occurrence, many factors should be considered. What is most important is defining a consistent and standard method for probability of occurrence. This will allow for consistent and standard SLE calculations so that a ranking and prioritization of IT assets' SLE values can be accomplished.

The fifth step in a quantitative risk–assessment calculation for an IT asset is to assign a value for the *annualized rate of occurrence (ARO)*. The ARO is a value that represents the estimated frequency at which a given threat is expected to occur. For the preceding customer database example, the two threats that were assessed were a critical software vulnerability and exposure to malicious code or malicious software because of the void in antivirus and personal firewall security countermeasures. Either of these threats being realized could cause a critical or major security incident. In the example of a critical virus infecting the customer database and the server that houses it, the ARO may be once every four years, so the ARO may be 0.25. If the threat was a hurricane and the IT data center was located in a hurricane belt, the ARO may very well be a higher value, such as 0.75 or even 0.80, given the frequency of potential hurricane damage.

The sixth step is to assign a value for the *annualized loss expectancy (ALE)*. The ALE is an annual expected financial loss to an organization's IT asset because of a particular threat being realized within that same calendar year. The ALE is typically the value that executive management needs to assess the priority and threat potential if one were to occur. This is where the ROI or cost-benefit analysis comes into play, especially if you have to justify the cost of security controls and security countermeasures based on the calculated values pertaining to a quantitative risk assessment.

Annualized Loss Expectancy (ALE)

ALE = SLE ($)×Annualized Rate of Occurrence (ARO)

The annualized loss expectancy is derived by multiplying the SLE with the Annualized Rate of Occurrence (ARO).

The ALE is calculated by multiplying the SLE with the defined ARO. For the customer database example with a one-in-four-year threat potential of a critical virus, worm, or Trojan, the ALE would be as follows:

ALE = $637,500×0.25 = $159,375

So what does an SLE value of $159,375 mean? If the ALE for the customer database were $159,375, would the organization invest up to $159,375 in security controls and security countermeasures to ensure that the confidentiality, integrity, and availability goals and objectives of the organization are met? Ideally, yes, the organization would invest this amount of money toward protecting its customer database given the SLE and ALE potential.

> This is where the ROI and cost benefit or cost of no investment warrants a decision from the organization's
> management group. IT security controls and security countermeasures are prioritized by calculating and
> aligning the ALE values for an organization's IT assets.

Qualitative Risk-Assessment Approach

A qualitative risk assessment is scenario based, where one scenario is examined and assessed for each critical or major threat to an IT asset. A qualitative risk assessment examines the asset, the threat, and the exposure or potential for loss that would occur if the threat were realized on the IT asset. A Qualitative Risk Assessment requires the risk assessor to assess and play "What If?" regarding specific threat conditions on IT assets. Qualitatively, the risk assessor must conduct a risk and threat analysis and assess the impact of that threat on the IT asset. This must be done consistently and without bias for all IT assets and their identified threats as part of the scenario-based assessment. For example, a *data classification standard* will dictate the importance of data and the IT systems, resources, and applications that support that data. This data classification standard will dictate the level of security controls and security countermeasures needed for the different types of data—some confidential and some in the public domain.

The purpose of a qualitative risk assessment is to provide a consistent and subjective assessment of the risk to specific IT assets. This typically involves a group or team of members participating in the assessment. All members of the IT organization should participate in risk assessments for various IT assets within the seven areas of information security responsibility; thus, the IT staff and those responsible for maintaining the confidentiality, integrity, and availability of the IT asset all have ownership. Within each of the seven areas of information security responsibility, for example, assets, threats, and their exposure can be assessed. A qualitative risk assessment is scenario based, with an examination of the IT asset, the threat (there can be more than one), and then the exposure of that threat on the IT asset.

Qualitative Risk-Assessment Example

Qualitative risk assessments are based on scenario analyses of threats to specific IT assets and the exposure or criticality of those threats to the IT asset. There can be more than one threat scenario per IT asset that must be considered.

For example, a qualitative risk assessment could consider the customer database example in the following scenarios. This ranking allows the organization to prioritize its investments for security controls and security countermeasures according to the defined exposure or risk factor of the threat occurring.

Asset	Threat	Exposure
Facility Power (A)	Loss of Power	Critical
Customer Database (B)	SW Vulnerability	High
Customer Database (C)	Virus Attack	Medium
Customer Database (D)	Loss of Data	Low

(A) Loss of power as a result of a major weather storm without significant battery backup time or diesel generator for emergency electric power.

(B) The software vulnerability is a critical software defect of which the customer database and the server that it resides in is at risk, especially because the vulnerability window is open for a potential attacker to exploit.

(C) The customer database and server, although unprotected by antivirus and antispyware, has daily automated backups and offsite storage of the customer database. Although a complete system rebuild would take time, the customer database can be recovered minus any lost data that may have occurred from the previous business day. Because viruses can disguise themselves well, it's possible that the backup has been infected as well, increasing the exposure threat to medium.

(D) The customer database, because of daily tape backups and offsite storage of the backup tape, has a low exposure threat given that loss of data would be impacted only by the amount of time from the previous customer database backup to the time that the customer database lost the data.

Best Practices for Quantitative and Qualitative Risk Assessment

Many organizations prefer to do a quantitative risk assessment because it aligns the financial impact of risk so that a return on investment (ROI) or cost-benefit analysis and justification can be presented to management. Many organizations use this quantitative risk assessment to assist in creating budgets for information security controls and security countermeasures. As these controls and countermeasures are implemented, the overall risk is mitigated to the organization's minimum acceptable level of risk. Quantitative risk assessments require accurate IT asset inventories, accurate IT asset valuations, and a consistent method for defining exposure factors for known threats.

For those organizations that do not have accurate IT asset inventory documentation or financial data, conducting a qualitative risk assessment for IT assets is a quick and easy way to prioritize IT assets and their exposure to known threats and vulnerabilities. This still accomplishes the same goal as the quantitative risk assessment—to identify IT assets, prioritize them based on importance to the organization, and assess the risk of known threats and vulnerabilities and their likelihood of occurrence. Either risk-assessment approach will allow an organization to make sound business decisions pertaining to the prioritization and investment of funds towards security controls and security countermeasures.

Quantitative Risk-Assessment Best Practices

When performing a quantitative risk assessment, the following best practices should be followed to maintain accuracy and consistency in the calculations of the AV, EF, SLE, ARO, and ALE:

1. Determine the Asset Value (AV) for each IT asset by identifying the purchase price, incorporating labor, maintenance, and support, and the value of any data assets.

2. Define a consistent scale for the Exposure Factor (EF). Build a table with the threats and vulnerabilities ranked from high to low. This table will act as a consistent EF table for all IT assets. Be sure to define all assumptions and justify your assumptions with supporting historical trends or data.

3. When calculating Single Loss Expectancy (SLE), verify and validate that your business liability and insurance policy can cover a single occurrence of that IT asset being compromised in a calendar year.

4. Define the Annualized Rate of Occurrence (ARO). Depending on what the threat or vulnerability is, use historical data going back in time to get a history or feel for rate of occurrence. For example, how many times has the organization been attacked by a virus, worm, or Trojan in the past five years? This type of data will assist in defining the ARO value for malicious code and malicious software attacks on the organization. Build a table of ARO values for the different threats or vulnerabilities to maintain consistent ARO values. Be sure to define all assumptions and justify your assumptions with supporting historical trends or data.

5. When calculating the Annualized Loss Expectancy (ALE), use this value to justify the cost of investment in security controls and security countermeasures. This ALE investment value is typically used as a cost -benefit justification to invest in proper security controls and security countermeasures to achieve the confidentiality, integrity, and availability goals.

Qualitative Risk-Assessment Best Practices

When you perform a qualitative risk assessment, use the following best practices to maintain accuracy and consistency in assessing the IT assets risk exposure:

1. List all of the organization's critical IT assets in a spreadsheet.

2. Specify the critical threats and vulnerabilities for each IT asset in the spreadsheet. Remember, there may be more than one critical threat or vulnerability for a given IT asset.

3. Develop a consistent exposure severity scale for each asset and its known threats and vulnerabilities. This exposure severity scale should cover critical, high, medium, and low exposure and be assigned accordingly to the IT asset and the specific threat or vulnerability that can be exploited.

4. Organize and prioritize the risk-assessment results from the most critical IT assets and critical exposures first. This will immediately bring to the top those IT assets that have the greatest risk to exploitation from a threat or vulnerability.

5. Prioritize the investment of funds for security controls and security countermeasures for those IT assets that have the greatest importance to the organization with the greatest exposure to risk.

6. Ensure that the organization's critical IT assets achieve the appropriate confidentiality, integrity, and availability goals and objectives.

Choosing the Best Risk-Assessment Approach

Every organization is unique in how it operates and maintains the confidentiality, integrity, and availability of its IT infrastructure and assets. The following are three basic approaches to conducting a risk and vulnerability assessment on an IT infrastructure and its assets:

- **Top-down approach**—A top-down approach requires the existence of the corporate IT policies, standards, procedures, and guidelines. In addition, baseline configurations or minimum acceptable baseline configurations that have incorporated the minimum standard for security are required. With a security framework in place, it is easiest to commence with the vulnerability assessment, starting with these foundational documents. From here, the IT policies, standards, procedures, and guidelines can be reviewed, and then the IT infrastructure and the domains of security responsibility can be assessed according to the defined IT security framework.

Figure 4.2 depicts a top-down risk and vulnerability assessment approach. Top-down refers to an examination of the organization's business drivers and goals and objectives for conducting the risk assessment. This top-down risk and vulnerability assessment approach is dependent on documented organizational business drivers, goals, and objectives for the risk and vulnerability assessment, and an existing IT security architecture and framework or IT security policies, standards, procedures, and guidelines.

Top Down Approach

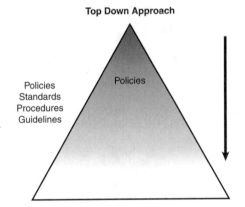

Policies
Standards
Procedures
Guidelines

Policies

Figure 4.2   Top-down risk-assessment approach.

- **Bottom-up approach**—If there are no IT security policies, standards, procedures, and guidelines in place, the risk and vulnerability assessment typically begins in the trenches by examining the IT infrastructure in areas such as the seven areas of information security responsibility. IT assets, configurations, and risk and threat analysis is done on the current production IT infrastructure and its assets. The risk and vulnerability assessment continues upward, meaning that the IT security architecture and framework typically becomes an important next step, deliverable as part of the risk assessment recommendations. A bottom-up risk or vulnerability assessment process can be difficult if it does not gain the support of senior management; without that support, you're attempting to work up from the trenches with little help from above.

Figure 4.3 depicts a bottom-up risk-assessment approach. In many cases, organizations may not have the necessary documentation that the risk and vulnerability assessment can be compared to. In cases like this, conducting a bottom-up risk assessment is common. Prior to beginning the bottom-up risk assessment, the project usually requires the creation of business drivers, goals, and objectives of the risk assessment, and then the creation of an IT security architecture framework. This provides both a baseline definition for the IT infrastructure information security definition as well as the high-level policies, standards, procedures, and guidelines that are needed to implement proper security controls.

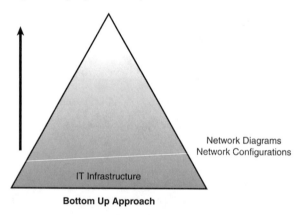

Bottom Up Approach

Figure 4.3   Bottom-up risk-assessment approach.

- **Hybrid approach**—In some cases, organizations have some IT security framework in place, but lack the rock-solid implementation of that framework. The risk and vulnerability assessment can proceed in a hybrid approach. This would be the best solution where an organization has some IT security policies, standards, procedures, guidelines, and baselines in place. The vulnerability assessment would begin by examining whatever IT security framework exists and simultaneously conducting the asset valuation and risk and threat analysis steps.

    Figure 4.4 depicts a hybrid approach to risk management. In this case, both a top-down and bottom-up approach to risk management is conducted in parallel. This will assist in the gap analysis for the provided IT security architecture and framework and an assessment of what is really happening with the security controls and security countermeasures, as defined in the organization's policies, standards, procedures, and guidelines. The hybrid approach to risk management is typical for those organizations that have some IT security policies, standards, procedures, and guidelines, and some network configuration, network documentation, and IT asset inventory data.

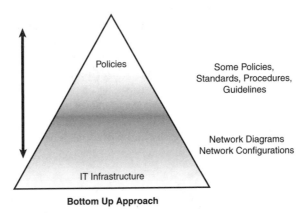

Figure 4.4   Hybrid risk-assessment approach.

Common Risk-Assessment Methodologies and Templates

Many risk-assessment methodologies and templates can be used. Realize that every methodology and approach has it pros and cons. What is most important is learning how to conduct your own risk assessment using elements from each methodology or making the risk-assessment approach fit the organization's environment. This section will present some of the more popular risk-assessment methodologies, such as

- **ISO 17799**—An international standard for conducting a self-assessment and self-certification as per the best practices in information security. ISO17799 evolved from the original BS7799 standard developed out of the United Kingdom.

- **OSSTMM**—The Open Source Security Testing Methodology Manual assists a tester in testing security and conducting a risk and vulnerability assessment in different information security areas.

- **NIST 800-26**—The National Institute of Standards and Technology published the 800-26 publication for U.S. government agencies to conduct their own self-assessment for information security controls.

ISO 17799 is an extremely comprehensive and detailed standard. Compliance, therefore, will require both a methodical and measured approach. It will also require commitment, as well as access to appropriate tools and products. ISO 17799 is a detailed security standard. It is organized into 10 major sections, each covering a different topic or area.

The first step toward ISO 17799 certification is to comply with the standard itself. This is a good security practice in its own right, but it is also the longer term status adopted by a number of organizations that require the assurance of an external measure, yet do not want to proceed with an external or formal process immediately.

In either case, the method and rigor enforced by the standard can be put to good use in terms of better management of risk. It is also being used in some sectors as a market differentiator, as organizations begin to quote their ISO 17799 status within their individual markets and to potential customers, which is another factor to ensure much wider uptake of the standard. Ensuring and managing compliance with ISO 17799 is not an easy task. One tool on the market that was designed to specifically assist with the process of ensuring compliance is the COBRA 17799 consultant. It was designed specifically to make compliance management easier and more straightforward through a series of guided questions. A checklist is another method for managing compliance with ISO 17799.

Note

For more information about the ISO17799 standard go to this URL: http://www.iso17799software.com/.

The OSSTMM assists a tester in dealing with security and risk management. A methodical security testing is different from penetration testing. It relies on a combination of creativeness, expansive knowledge of best practices, legal issues, and the client's industry regulations, as well as known threats and the breadth of the target organization's security presence. This is done by exploiting predictability and best practices to the most thorough extent possible. In other words, we test all extremes of everything considered predictable and fully utilize best practices to test against the worst-case scenarios that may not be as predictable.

In Figure 4.5, the OSSTMM manual defines the different modules that are to be part of the scope of security testing. One of the modules within the OSSTMM is Internet Technology Security. The sub modules are also listed. The OSSTMM guides you through the tests that must be performed to complete a risk assessment. To expand further, the network surveying module is expected to produce the following results: domain names, server names, IP addresses, network map, ISP or ASP information, system and service owners, and possible test limitations.

To produce these results, the OSSTMM guides you through a series of tests and questions to be answered. These tests and questions encompass the following:

- Examine domain registry information for servers.
- Find IP block owned.
- Question the primary, secondary, and ISP name servers for hosts and sub domains.
- Find IPv6 IP blocks in use through DNS queries.
- Use multiple traces to the gateway to define the outer network layer and routers.
- Search web logs and intrusion logs for system trails from the target network.
- Search board and newsgroup postings for server trails back to the target network.

- Logistics and Controls
- Posture Review
- Intrusion Detection Review
- Network Surveying
- System Services Identification
- Competitive Intel Scouting
- Privacy Review
- Document Grinding
- Internet Application Testing
- Exploit Research and Verification

- Routing
- Trusted Systems Testing
- Access Control Testing
- Password Cracking
- Containment Measures Testing
- Survivability Review
- Privileged Service Testing
- Denial of Service Testing
- Security Policy Review
- Alert and Log Review

Figure 4.5 OSSTMM Internet technology security modules.

- Examine target web server source code and scripts for applications servers and internal links.
- Examine email headers, bounced mails, and read receipts for the server trails.

Note

For more information about the OSSTMM testing methodology, go to this URL: http://www.isecom.org/osstmm/.

NIST Special Publication 800-26 builds on the Federal IT Security Assessment Framework developed by NIST for the Federal Chief Information Officer Council. The framework established the groundwork defining five levels of security status and criteria that federal agencies could use as a baseline definition for information security. This document provides guidance on applying the framework by identifying 17 control areas, such as those pertaining to identification, authentication, and contingency planning. In addition, the guide provides control objectives and techniques that can be measured for each area.

Note

For more information about the NIST 800-26 self-assessment methodology for information security, go to this URL:

http://csrc.nist.gov/publications/nistpubs/800-26/sp800-26.pdf

Summary

You learned that assets, threats, and vulnerabilities contribute to the risk factor for IT assets within an IT infrastructure. Determining how an organization approaches its risk and vulnerability assessment is best accomplished by first understanding how the organization makes business decisions. For organizations that require financial impact or return-on-investment calculations to assess the impact of risk on their IT infrastructure and IT assets, conducting a quantitative risk assessment is typical. For those organizations that do not have access to accurate asset management, IT asset inventories, maintenance and warranty contracts, and financial data, conducting a qualitative risk assessment based on different scenarios is typical.

Organizations that have an existing IT security architecture and framework enable the risk and vulnerability assessment to commence in a top-down approach. By examining the organization's policies, standards, procedures, and guidelines, the risk and vulnerability assessment can proceed by comparing what has been implemented with what has been defined. For organizations that do not have an IT security architecture and framework, it is best to approach the risk and vulnerability assessment in a bottom-up or hybrid approach. Creating and investigating the IT infrastructure's threats and vulnerabilities to its IT assets must start at the bottom; however, working in parallel to that effort, it is desirable to create and define the organization's business drivers, goals and objectives for the risk and vulnerability assessment, and baseline definition for information security throughout the organization.

Key Terms

Annualized Loss Expectancy (ALE)—The ALE is an annual expected financial loss to an organization's IT asset because of a particular threat being realized within that same calendar year.

Annualized Rate of Occurrence (ARO)—The ARO is a value that represents the estimated frequency for a given threat.

Asset Value (AV)—The AV is the actual dollar value that is put on the asset itself. Remember that for a data asset, the actual dollar value may be more than the value of the IT hardware, software, maintenance contracts, and so on.

Data classification standard—A standard that defines an organization's classification of its data assets. Typically, a data classification standard will dictate the level of minimum acceptable risk within the seven areas of information security responsibility.

Defense-in-Depth—A term used to describe a layered approach to information security for an IT infrastructure.

End User Licensing Agreement (EULA)—This is the software license that software vendors create to protect and limit their liability as well as hold the purchaser liable for illegal pirating of the software application. The EULA typically has language in it that protects the software manufacturer from software bugs and flaws and limits the liability of the vendor.

Exposure Factor (EF)—This is a subjective value that is defined by determining the percentage of loss to a specific asset due to a specific threat.

Qualitative Risk Assessment—A scenario-based assessment in which one scenario is examined and assessed for each critical or major threat to an IT asset.

Quantitative Risk Assessment—A methodical, step-by-step calculation of asset valuation, exposure to threats, and the financial impact or loss in the event of the threat being realized.

Risk Potential—The potential that a threat or vulnerability will be exploited.

Security Breach or Security Incident—The result of a threat or vulnerability being exploited by an attacker.

Security Controls—Policies, standards, procedures, and guideline definitions for various security control areas or topics.

Security Countermeasure—A security hardware or software technology solution that is deployed to ensure the confidentiality, integrity, and availability of IT assets that need protection.

Single Loss Expectancy (SLE)—A dollar-value figure that represents the organization's loss from a single loss or loss of this particular IT asset.

Software Bugs or Software Flaws—An error in software coding or its design that can result in software vulnerability.

5

Scoping the Project

Scoping the project is the real beginning of the vulnerability assessment. In this phase, a formal document will be developed that will define the activities you and your team will undertake. It will also outline what type of schedule this project will be on and the amount of support that will be needed.

The scoping document will also outline the infrastructure perimeter—that is, what portion of the network will be examined and what portions will be off-limits. This document will act as the road map of planned activities and as such will include evaluation activities, time schedules, and resources available to the team. This document should be approved by a high-level security officer and should contain a nondisclosure clause and a legal clause to protect the team.

Defining the Scope of the Assessment

Defining the scope of the assessment is one of the most important parts of the assessment project. At some point, you are going to be meeting with management to start the discussions of the "how" and "why" of the assessment. Before this meeting ever begins, you're probably going to have some idea as to what is driving this event. Vulnerability assessments usually don't happen in a vacuum, so it's important to understand the business reasons behind it. These can include due diligence, compliance with state or federal laws, a breach in security, or other factors.

Knowing why this assessment is occurring is going to help you get a much better idea of what management is looking for and how much support there is going to be for this project. Much of this can be gauged after you have the initial meeting with management. You'll also have to consider that they may not fully have these answers and to a large part, that's why they are looking to you and your expertise in this matter.

Armed with the proper information, you'll be much better prepared when you initially meet with management to discuss this project. You're going to want to gather up as much documentation as possible about the network, the technologies, and the overall structure of the documents that are presently being used to manage the security process.

During this initial meeting, you are going to want to spend some time ironing out what is critical. The best way to make this determination is by looking at what products your organization offers and how they are delivered to the customer. Then determine the key technologies that support this effort and identify the critical pieces of information that the organization possesses.

With the initial meeting out of the way, you should have some idea of what management is expecting the assessment to accomplish. Now that you have some idea as to the scope and direction of the assessment, you can begin to build your team. After your team is assembled, you will be ready to again meet with management. This formal kickoff meeting is where you will work out the final details of the assessment plan and get the information needed to build an assessment timeline. The important events that occur during the scope include the following:

- Driving events
- Initial meeting
- Becoming the project manager
- Staffing the assessment team
- Kick off meeting
- Building the assessment timeline

Driving Events

The events driving the assessment will affect the scope and the depth of the project. Not all organizations look at security in the same way. Some organizations work in business sectors that deal with a considerable amount of risk, whereas others are situated in lower-risk sectors. The way organizations handle risk is just as varied. As an example, look at how your organization has set up its firewall policies. Many organizations use the "allow all that hasn't been specifically denied" policy. Although this works, it's not the best method. A better approach would be to take the "deny all" route. This method denies everything and explicitly allows only services that have been determined to be a business requirement. This approach is not only much more secure, but also recommended by most security experts and by documents such as NIST Special Publication 800-41 Guidelines on Firewalls and Firewall Policy. Organizations that take the latter approach are going to be much more likely to have a developed policy infrastructure and to take your recommendations much more seriously.

Due Diligence

Due diligence is one of the potential forces that may be driving the assessment. If your organization is serious about security, there will be some assessment work performed during mergers and acquisitions. This can occur before an actual purchase or after the event. These assessments are usually held to a very strict timeline. There is only a limited amount of time before the purchase and if the assessment is performed afterward, the organization will probably be in a hurry to integrate the two networks as soon as possible. In either situation, you have a host of issues to deal with, including the following:

- Technology
- Integration
- Business processes
- Roles and responsibilities
- Training and awareness

Compliance

Compliance with state, provincial, or federal laws is another event that might be driving the assessment. Companies can face huge fines and, potentially, jail time if they fail to comply with state, provincial, and federal laws. The Gramm-Leach-Bliley Act (GLBA), Sarbanes-Oxley (SOX), and the Health Insurance Portability and Accountability Act (HIPAA) are three such laws. HIPAA requires organizations to perform a vulnerability assessment. If this is the type of event driving the assessment, management is going to be concerned that the policies, procedures, guidelines, and training have been put in place. They will be interested to see that a good structure for security has been developed and is being followed.

Caution

Those dealing with compliance issues such as HIPAA and SOX need to have a good understanding of what is required to meet compliance, or have someone on the team who does. Many laws mandate civil and criminal penalties for lack of compliance. For example, Title VII of SOX requires that auditors maintain "all audit or review work papers" for five years.

A Breach in Security

A breach in security will bring about different concerns and driving factors than the ones previously listed for due diligence or compliance with state or local laws. Look for these assessments to be much more technical.

Although you may think that the majority of these events are driven by external factors, that's simply not true. The largest percentage of this type of assessment results from events initiated by insiders. This includes current and former employees. Anytime an employee is unhappy or disgruntled, the organization has a potential problem. This is especially true if this individual has a large amount of knowledge about the internal workings of the network. In these instances, you will be looking at access controls, password policies, system defenses, and system hardening.

If the event is driven by an external attack, management will again want to know if systems have been sufficiently hardened. Are there other holes or technical *vulnerabilities* an attacker can exploit to gain access? These events may not have resulted in a significant loss of revenue. It's possible that only a website was defaced or a brief outage of a service occurred; nevertheless, people will want answers quickly. Management will be looking for technical solutions to secure the infrastructure as soon as possible.

> **Tip**
>
> The best time to deal with incident response is before the event. Your organization should have a well defined incident response plan that details who responds, how they respond, and who will be notified.

Initial Meeting

With some knowledge of what's driving the event, you are now much more prepared for your initial meeting with management. To deal effectively with their questions and start to get a real handle on how much work this is going to be, you are going to want to compile some information to take in the meeting with you. It's best to contact the appropriate personnel before the meeting and let them know what you need to make an appropriate analysis of the situation. By developing a standardized form, you can gather much of the information you'll need to take into the initial meeting.

The information request form will need to provide information that helps define the size and scope of the assessment. If you can't gather all this information before the initial meeting, that's okay, because after management has given the project the green light, you'll quickly get most of the information you need to compile. Following is a list of some of the items you will want to have on your information request form. They can be broadly divided into four categories:

1. Administrative

   - What is the core mission of the organization?
   - How many locations does the organization have?
   - What is the total number of locations?
   - Does the assessment encompass all locations, a limited number of sites, or a sampling across all sites?
   - What event is driving this assessment?
   - Does the organization have existing security policies and procedures?
   - Does the organization have physical controls in place to control the movement of employees and visitors?
   - Do any vendors or corporate partners have access to the network?
   - Are IT services outsourced, and if so, which ones?

2. Technical

   - How many servers are located at each site?
   - What OSs are in place for these servers?
   - How many workstations are located at each site?

- What OSs are in place for these workstations?
- What networking protocols are used?
- Are there any mainframes?
- How many connections are there to the Internet?
- What services are made available externally?
- What services are made available internally?
- Are wireless technologies used?
- Is VoIP used?
- What types of redundant systems are in place?

3. Security

- What type of encryption technologies are used?
- Is there a VPN?
- Is authentication centralized?
- What type of authentication systems are used?
- How is access controlled?
- What type of firewalls are used?
- Is there an IDS in place?

4. Legal

- What state, provincial, and federal laws must the organizations comply with?
- HIPAA
- GLB
- SOX
- Family Education Rights and Privacy Act
- National Institute of Standards and Technologies
- Management of Information Technology Security (MITS)

Becoming the Project Manager

If you are one of the individuals scoping the project, you are most like going to be the team leader or key member of the assessment process. If you are going to be the lead in this assessment, you will need some project management skills. You'll need technical and administrative skills to make this a success. Keep in mind the old saying: "Managing people is like herding cats." By this I mean that a successful team leader is both a manager and a leader. Leaders command respect, are able to inspire and motivate others, and can adapt to different leadership styles as circumstances dictate. As the team leader of the assessment, you are going to be tasked with the following:

- Selecting team members
- Defining the scope of the assessment
- Launching the assessment
- Motivating and focusing the team on its objectives
- Time management
- Organizing the results
- Communicating the findings

You are the one who is ultimately responsible for the assessment. You must make sure that all team members understand their roles and their importance. If schedules cannot be met, it will be up to you to communicate this fact to management and facilitate a resolution.

Staffing the Assessment Team

Depending on the size of the assessment, you will need a capable team to get the job done. You are going to be looking for individuals with a variety of skills. From a technical standpoint, team members will need the following skills:

- Computer expert adept at technical domains
- Knowledge about target platforms (Windows, Unix, Linux)
- Exemplary knowledge in networking and related hardware and software
- Knowledge about security areas and related issues

You will also need team members who can fulfill various roles in the project. If you have spent time managing people, probably you already recognize these traits. These various personalities types can help build a successful assessment team:

- **Inspectors**—Demand high standards
- **Team Builders**—Work toward unity and attempt to pull the team together
- **Idea People**—Encourage diverse thinking
- **Critics**—Analysts, concerned about the team's effectiveness

The specific skills needed, as previously mentioned, depend on what level of assessment is going to be performed. Whereas level I assessments are primarily policy based, level II assessments have much more of a hands-on technical feel. These assessments will require you to add individuals to the team who have sufficient technical skills to set up and run vulnerability scanners, review results from vulnerability scanners, examine firewall rulesets, and perform other hands-on types of activities. If you determine that a level III assessment is going to be performed, you'll need team members with in-depth security skills. You may find that for a penetration test, you are better off contracting out those duties. Be aware that no matter who is on your team, all teams typically go through four stages:

- Form
- Storm
- Norm
- Perform

As you assign duties to each team member, you will want to establish times for each activity. When assigning duties to team members try using the SMART process:

- **Specific**—Goals
- **Measurable**—Outcomes
- **Achievable**—Results
- **Realistic**—Skill set
- **Time limited**—Budget
- **Written**—Project planning

Tip

After you staff the assessment team, a team directory should be assembled. This directory should include

- Assessment team members' names
- Phone numbers
- Email addresses
- Mailing addresses
- Contact information for key stakeholders

Kickoff Meeting

The *kickoff meeting* is the real beginning of the assessment. For the first time, you have a team assembled and you get the opportunity to meet with senior management and the key stakeholders of the assessment. This is the opportunity to develop an overall plan for the assessment. It is also an opportunity for everyone present to ask questions and work out any problems that may come up. For this project to be successful, now is the time to work out the key issues. Therefore, the following items are some of the key issues that should be discussed:

- **Introductions**—You have probably heard this a million times, but introductions serve a useful purpose. They loosen people up, get everyone talking, and help break the ice. Not only do introductions help everyone feel comfortable, but they also ensure that everyone knows everyone else's role.
- **Mission statement**—This is to get everyone on the same page. As project leader, you will want to spend some time talking about what the mission of the business is. If management has input here, listen. Remember that your real role in this assessment is that of a facilitator. Your job is to get the facts from the people who know.

- **Identify critical information and systems**—You may already have this information. If you do not, one quick way to determine critical systems is by using the NSA's information criticality system. More information about the methodology can be found at www.iatrp.com/iam.cfm.

- **Discuss the assessment process**—Now is a good time to review the three levels of assessments and what they entail. *Level I assessments* look at the controls implemented to protect information in storage, transmission, or being processed. It involves no hands-on testing. It is a review of the process and procedures in place and focuses on interviews and demonstrations. *Level II assessments* are more in depth. Level II assessments include vulnerability scans and hands-on testing. *Level III assessments* are adversarial in nature. This form of assessment is also called a *penetration test*, as that is what it is. It is an attempt to find and exploit vulnerabilities. Penetration tests may be performed by *ethical hackers*. The penetration test seeks to determine what a malicious user or outsider could do if determined to damage the organization. It is our belief that organizations performing level II or level III assessments need to have performed a level I assessment because it does little good to find, exploit, and report vulnerabilities that don't have an adequate system in place to manage the remediation.

- **Review the scope**—By this time, you should have a pretty good handle on what the scope of this assessment is going to be. You need to lock in the boundaries of what you are going to do. For example, if this is clearly a level I assessment, you don't need to find out at a later point that management expected you to attempt to hack into the corporate web server. You also want to clarify what type of deliverables that management can expect.

- **Identify candidates and key personnel**—The quality and amount of information you receive from key individuals in the organization will play a large part in the success in the assessment. You probably have a good idea who these individuals are already; if not, you will want to spend some time identifying them. In large corporations or multinationals, these individuals may be scattered across geographically diverse locations. If so, you want to make sure you can schedule time with these individuals by conference call or other means. The risk of not identifying these people or being able to get their input can mean the difference between a successful assessment and a failed one. Schedule time with these individuals as needed.

- **Determine logistics**—If possible, you should seek to arrange a central location for your team to work from. This location will serve as the base location of the operation. Access to phones, computers, and the network are essential. When you're ready to interview employees, having this established location makes life much easier. Otherwise, you will constantly be searching for a conference room to meet in, and these may have booked up well in advance. You don't want to be holding interviews in the lunchroom or other "make do" locations, because it gives an unorganized, haphazard appearance to those you are speaking with and can have a real impact on the type of information gathered.

- **Get written approval**—This is most important. You want to be 100% sure that what has been approved in this meeting is put into writing and signed by management as part of the contract. You don't what to get called on the carpet two weeks later when a team member runs a Nessus scan that brings down a server that was not approved. This is no small point. Not only should you have the scope of the assessment in writing, you should also have the legal department of the company approve its verbiage. If you have brought in external vendors for portions of the assessment, you will want to consider having them sign off on separate legal agreements; don't forget to include the appropriate NDAs.

Building the Assessment Timeline

The timeline establishes guidelines for the completion of the assessment. It also helps establish the scope and duration of the entire project. It will require monitoring on your part to keep the project on schedule. One of the biggest problems you will face is *scope creep*.

Scope creep occurs when you fall under pressure to expand the assessment beyond what it was originally planned to be. It usually results from a failure to define what the assessment will or will not include. The number one way to prevent scope creep is to clearly define the boundaries of the assessment. This should be locked down during the kickoff meeting and defined in the assessment protocol that has been approved by management.

Caution
If you are not alert to scope creep, it can destroy the assessment. Little things add up and before long, the assessment can slip way behind schedule. These are not the events that will make you a management all-star.

As Everett Dirksen said: "A billion here and a billion there and pretty soon, we are talking big money." Organizations do not have unlimited funds; therefore, it's critical that you develop good cost estimates during the preassessment. Time is money and if the schedule begins to slip, costs will increase. As the team leader for the assessment, expect to be held responsible for achieving technical and scheduled goals, but also for the financial costs of the assessment. The cost of the labor will be one of the biggest expenses of a project. As project manager, you must rely on time estimates you develop to predict the cost of the labor to complete the projected assignment on schedule. In addition, the cost of the equipment and materials needed to complete the projected work must be factored into the project's expenses. The relation between the project cost and the project scope is direct: You get what you pay for! Think about it; is it possible to buy a Lexus at a Ford Focus price? That is probably not going to happen. If the project scope expands, expect costs to go up, so plan accordingly.

If you can avoid this and effectively monitor the information as it flows in from the assessment team, you will be on your way toward meeting your projected goals. You will also need an adequate amount of time communicating with the team. They, too, need to know the progress, what tasks have been completed, and what's yet to be done. Just these few simple things can help keep the project on schedule. Overall, there are three clearly defined pieces to the assessment process as seen in Figure 5.1. These include scoping the project, performing the assessment, and post-assessment activities.

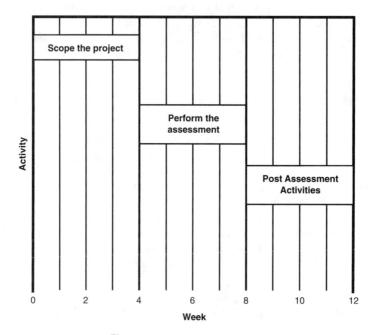

Figure 5.1   Assessment timeline.

The average time for an assessment is 12 weeks. This is only an average, but it should give you some idea of how much time it will take to complete the process. During the scoping process, you'll need to complete seven critical steps before you can actually get started. These are shown in Figure 5.2 and listed next:

1. Determine driving events.
2. Hold the initial meeting.
3. Establish the team.
4. Hold the kickoff meeting.
5. Determine critical items.
6. Create a timeline.
7. Develop a written protocol that details what is going to be done.

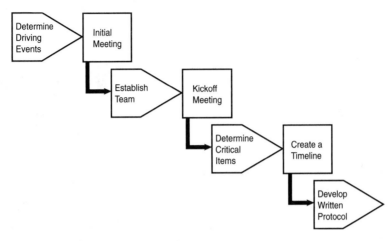

Figure 5.2   Scoping tasks.

Reviewing Critical Systems and Information

If your organization has not sufficiently identified its critical information and systems, this is the point where you're going to want to roll up your sleeves and find out what's most important. Although there are different ways to accomplish this, the best way we have discovered is to follow the methodology laid out by the National Security Agency (NSA) Information Assessment Methodology (IAM). They have developed a quick and easy way to nail down what is critical. It's a *qualitative type assessment* that ranks the system by confidentiality, integrity, and availability. There are two types of criticalities that we will be discussing:

- Organization Information Criticality Matrix (OICM)
- Systems Criticality Matrix (SCM)

Information Criticality Matrix

Criticality is similar to a *business impact analysis* (BIA); you examine the impact on the organization should the information or system be lost. For example, a business would come to a halt if all electrical power was lost but could continue to operate if the cafeteria had to close. These calculations don't replace a BIA, but they do give you and management something to work with if none of this information exists. You are just the facilitator here, so your job is to drive the process while taking input from all those in attendance at the kickoff meeting. There are three broad steps you must go through to make an effective analysis:

1. Identify information types

2. List impact attributes

3. Define impact levels

Let's start off by discussing information and its critical role to the organization. The place to perform this activity is at the kickoff meeting, where representatives from the team and members of management are present. While going through this process, you may want to have someone record notes while you list this information on a flip chart or white board.

Step 1: Identify Information Types

So, what is information? It's basically all the data that your company deals with. It can include customer phone numbers, customer names, customer locations, inventory, purchase orders, finished goods inventory, employee names, HR data, firewall configuration, and so on. If the group you are working with is highly caffeinated, you'll probably come up with a long list of different types of information and data. So, before this thing gets out of hand, you should work through the list and remove any items that have no direct impact on the organization's mission. For example, you may want to remove the data category "cafeteria menu" that the wise guy in the back of the room suggested earlier, because this has no impact on the organization's mission.

Now, you probably still have a pretty long list at this point, so you're still going to need to roll it up some more if it's going to be useful. Therefore, the next step is to roll up the information types. This means that you are going to take all the items that have been presented and roll them up into distinct categories. You'll find that over time, similar industries have very similar information types. Some common information types include the following:

- Human resource data
- Customer data
- Network data
- Management data
- Facilities and physical plant data
- Financial data

One of the biggest pitfalls you will want to avoid is that of allowing individuals to include information systems at this stage. An example of an information system is email. It can carry many types of information in the preceding list. Just remind everyone that systems will come later.

Step 2: List Impact Attributes

After you have compiled this list, you can begin to develop what is going to be used as impact attributes. Impact attributes are items or events that would affect or cause a negative impact on the organization's critical information. This is a qualitative measurement, meaning that it is not something that we place a dollar amount on, but we can rank it. The most common impact attributes are those that you are already probably familiar with:

- Confidentiality
- Integrity
- Availability

Can we add more? Sure, you could add authorizations, accountability, access control, audit, and so on, but the idea is to keep the list fairly short to keep this process manageable. Some security professionals might even make the argument that the big three (CIA) are all that are needed to perform this task.

Step 3: Define Impact Levels

Next up, the impact levels need to be defined. The impact level is the amount of discomfort, damage, or loss that the organization would experience should confidentiality, integrity, or availability of one or more of the information types be lost or degraded. For example, if payroll information is unavailable for a few hours or even a few days, the organization and its employees may not be happy, but the organization could continue to function; however, if the organization was totally based on e-commerce and the web server was down for several days, the company would take a big financial hit and a loss of customer confidence. There are several ways you can define impact levels. You might use ratings of high, medium, or low, 0 to 5, or even a more granular method and rank impact on a scale of 1 to 10. What is going to work for you will depend on the organization, its structure, and its size. To illustrate the process, we will stick with a rating of high, medium, or low. Let's set up some definitions for each so we are in agreement as to what the ranking means.

- **Low**—These are actions that have a low impact on the organization. They can be categorized as items that cause an inconvenience to the company or cause some type of delay.
- **Medium**—These are actions that are going to have a significant impact. This could be a large fine, the loss of customer confidence, or a strategic partner or alliance.
- **High**—These are actions that would have a dramatic impact on the organization. This could be the loss of its most valuable customers, huge legal costs, loss of life, or the exodus of the organization's key employees.

Keep in mind that these rankings are not set in stone. It will be up to your organization to determine how these levels fit. In the end, you can make as many changes as needed to the OICM. But remember, by keeping it as simple as possible, it is much more easily understood and analyzed.

Putting It All Together

Now that you have all the pieces, let's see what the final product will look like. It is shown in Figure 5.3.

	Confidentiality	Integrity	Availability
Information Category 1			
Information Category 2			
Information Category 3			
Information Category 4			

Figure 5.3 Sample blank matrix.

Let's step through an example so that you can get a better feel of how this is actually used. We will use Security Evolutions for the example. Security Evolutions is a security consulting firm that does security training and consulting. Working with management, you have been able to come up with four broad categories of information, which include the following:

- **Training information**—Includes training schedules, classes, course materials, labs, and the like.
- **Client information**—Information about Security Evolutions' clients, such as names, billing addresses, locations, and number of employees.
- **Sales information**—Includes the information the sales group uses to get and maintain clients such as project quotes, profit margin, total sales, and so on.
- **HR Information**—Information relating to employees such as start date, pay scale, dental plan, vacation days, and so on.

These information types are now added down the side of the matrix, as shown in Figure 5.4.

Information Type	Confidentiality	Integrity	Availability
Training Information			
Client Information			
Sales Information			
HR Information			

Figure 5.4   Matrix with information types added.

With the OICM starting to take some shape, you will want to continue your role as facilitator in helping our sample company fill out the matrix. It's up to each company to determine whether an impact level is high, medium, or low. We will start by looking at the loss of confidentiality of training information. It certainly doesn't seem that this kind of loss would cost a loss of life or even critically jeopardize the organization, so this attribute has been rated as low. Losing the integrity of the training information would be an inconvenience, but again, would be only a minor inconvenience. Losing availability of training material would not be fun, but again, not a show stopper. I taught a class once in Canada where customs held up the courseware by four days. Although it wasn't any fun, the class did continue. The results of our initial analysis can be seen in Figure 5.5.

Information Type	Confidentiality	Integrity	Availability
Training Information	Low	Low	Low
Client Information			
Sales Information			
HR Information			

Figure 5.5   Matrix with initial attributes added.

What sometimes happens at this point is that you start to encounter resistance from some individual owners of some information types, because they believe that the items they are in charge of are not being given a high enough level of importance. The truth is that not everything is of critical importance. The objective here is to get a very high-level overview of what types of information the organization most needs to protect. This is not the depth of asset evaluation that was discussed in Chapter 4, "Risk Assessment Methodologies." It is meant to be a high-level evaluation only.

Proceeding with our example, we will continue to fill in the OICM. The final product is shown in Figure 5.6. If you take a minute to look over the results, you can see that the information categories that received the highest ratings were sales confidentiality and integrity. Security Evolutions believes that this is where they should be most concerned and focus their protection mechanisms. If they are bidding on a project and a competitor can access that data or change it, the results could be disastrous for them. You will also notice below the OICM that there is a high-water mark. This is used to roll up the most critical impact attributes. These attributes are calculated by taking the highest impact rating in each category and carrying it down. These should give the organization some idea of what attributes are considered most important.

Information Type	Confidentiality	Integrity	Availability
Training Information	Low	Low	Low
Client Information	Medium	Medium	Low
Sales Information	High	High	Medium
HR Information	Medium	Medium	Low

High Watermark	High	High	Medium

Figure 5.6 The completed informational matrix.

Systems Criticality Matrix

Defining the critical information is only half the work. To finish up this phase of the scope, critical systems will also need to be identified. If these systems have not already been identified, they should be immediately because these are the systems that will need the most thorough investigation. These systems are used to store, process, or transmit the organization's information.

The hardest part of this phase of the assessment is that it is sometimes debatable where one system ends and another begins. So, we will begin our discussion of critical systems by listing some common system types:

- Financial systems
- Research and development systems
- Human resource systems
- Client database systems
- Security monitoring systems
- Sales systems
- Automation control systems
- Order processing systems

The steps to determining critical systems are the same as those used to determine critical information. To keep things simple, we will continue to use the example discussed previously. We can see the final result shown in Figure 5.7. It shows that Security Evolutions has identified four types of systems at its organization. The Internet systems are rated the lowest. No sales are done through these systems and their outage or loss of availability, although inconvenient, wouldn't prevent the organization from continuing business. The sales system, like the sales information previously, is rated as the most critical. Management has determined that the inability to quickly bid on government projects or the loss of integrity to the sales system could seriously damage this growing organization. The high watermark for the company's systems indicates that confidentiality and integrity are the most important attributes.

System Type	Confidentiality	Integrity	Availability
Training Systems	Low	Low	Medium
Internet Systems	Low	Low	Low
Sales Systems	High	High	Medium
HR Systems	High	Medium	Low

High Watermark	High	High	Medium

Figure 5.7 The completed informational matrix.

Compiling the Needed Documentation

With knowledge of the organization's critical systems, you can now turn your attention to directing the team to draw up lists of required documents for review. Several standards clearly define and delineate required security policies. These include ISO 17799, NIST 800-26, and the NSA IAM. Our favorite of the three is the NSA IAM. The NSA revised this list in 2003 to closely match NIST documentation. Unlike the NIST standards, which separate policies into 17 classes of information, the NSA has expanded this to 18. These are divided into the same three categories as used by NIST: management, technical, and operational. All 18 categories are shown in Table 5.1.

Table 5.1 **Documentation Classes and Categories**

Management	**Technical**	**Operational**
INFOSEC documentation	Identification and authentication	Media controls
INFOSEC roles and responsibilities	Account management	Labeling
Contingency planning	Session controls	Physical environment
Configuration management	Auditing	Personal security
	Malicious code protection	Education training and awareness

Table 5.1 **Continued**

Management	Technical	Operational
	Maintenance	
	System assurance	
	Networking connectivity	
	Communications security	

This doesn't mean that all the policies you will want to review will fit into one of these 18 categories, but don't be surprised to find out how well these 18 work in most cases. Although we will spend a considerable amount of time discussing these categories of policies in Chapter 7, "Performing the Assessment," there are a few things worth mentioning here, such as policy documents that can be broadly divided into the following three:

- **Advisory**—The job of an advisory policy is to assure that employees know the consequences of certain behavior and actions. A sample advisory policy follows:

  Illegal copying—Employees should never download or install any commercial software, shareware, or freeware onto any network drives or disks, unless they have written permission from the Network Administrator. BE PREPARED to be held accountable for your actions including: the loss of network privileges, written reprimand, probation, or employment termination if the Rules of Appropriate Use are violated.

- **Informative**—This type of policy isn't designed with enforcement in mind; it is developed for education. Its goal is to inform and enlighten employees. A sample informative policy follows:

  In partnership with the Product Management Team, Instructor Resources job is to serve as advocates for all Security Evolution instructors, providing superior service in recruitment and career development, scheduling services, and fulfillment of administrative needs for our instructors.

- **Regulatory**—These policies are used to make certain the organization complies with local, state, provincial, and federal laws. A sample regulatory policy might state the following:

  Because of recent changes to Virginia state law, the company will now retain records of employee inventions and patents for 10 years; all email messages and any backup of such email associated with patents and inventions will be stored for one year.

Because of potential regulatory requirements, you will also want to review any applicable state, provincial, and federal laws affecting your organization. You will want to make sure that the organization's policies meet these requirements; if not, this will need to be noted.

You will also want to gather all infrastructure documentation. If diagrams don't exist, you have two options: You can ask that they be created or you can provide assistance to get it done. Keep in mind that there are two types of system diagrams needed:

- **Logical diagrams**—From the owners' and users' perspective, these depict the system(s) of information utilization and data flow.

- **Physical diagrams**—Depict the system(s) from the physical component perspective of connectivity and interfaces.

Now you may be wondering how you are going to keep track of all these incoming documents. The best way is to develop a system to track the following:

- Date requested
- Date reviewed
- Date returned/disposed

It is best to appoint one person to collect and distribute all policies and documents requested. A simple form as shown in Table 5.2 can make your life much easier.

Table 5.2 **Document Control Form**

Title	Date Requested	Date Received	Custodian	Date Destroyed, Archived, or Returned
Password Policy	10/20/2005	10/31/2005	David Kim	Returned 11/2/2005
Acceptable Use Policy	10/22/2005	10/25/2005	Guy Bruneau	In use

Making Sure You Are Ready to Begin

You have reached a critical juncture because you are almost to the point to start the real hands-on work. If you have not already done so, you are going to have to choose to what depth to take this assessment. This should be based on what management expects you to accomplish and what your data and analysis shows. The time you spend running this assessment is generally time that you're not spending on other job functions. This can cost your organization money or impact your organization in other ways, so like much of life, this, too, is a balancing act.

With that in mind, it is important to note that most experts agree that good security requires policies, procedures, and guidelines. So, if you haven't much depth and structure there, you should most likely focus on a level I assessment. You will need a good foundation to build effective security. This allows the organization to gain an understanding of critical information, critical systems, and missing and incomplete policies. After these tasks are taken care of, it's much easier to focus on the future of security.

Before the real fun can begin, you need to finish writing the protocol that will outline what's going to be done. Although doing the paperwork is not the most glamorous of tasks, it is required. This not only gives you a map to proceed by, but also clearly serves as the approval for you to move forward. Following are some of the elements you will want to include:

- Approving corporate officer
- Organizational mission
- Organizational Information Criticality Matrix
- Systems Information Criticality Matrix
- Driving factors, concerns, and constraints
- Network configuration and documentation
- Scheduled interviews and demonstrations
- Required documentation
- Assessment team members
- Assessment timeline

Summary

Building a good team will be instrumental in completing a quality assessment. By using individuals from within the organization, you'll have access to the people who best know the network. These individuals can help drill down to get real answers that can help solve problems. You will want to try and build your team from a broad area of the company. This will help give you contacts and inroads into the various departments.

Having a timeline and list of activities that must be completed for the assessment will also help. You will want to use this as a checklist where you can monitor the progress of the team. Remember that this is about more than just checking items off a list. Don't be afraid to ask questions and dig because that's where you will usually uncover the surprising results.

Your success also rests on how well you have worked with management to determine what is most critical. Remember that you cannot protect everything. At some point, the organization is going to have to pick and choose what is most critical and focus its time, effort, and resources on protecting those items.

Attempt to avoid conflicts and heated debates. Although you may be in charge of the assessment, this task is ultimately about the protection and well being of the organization. Concentrate on the findings that will most benefit the organization.

Key Terms

The following acronyms and terms are used in this chapter. For the explanation and definition purpose of this chapter, these acronyms and terms are defined as follows:

Business impact analysis (BIA)   A component of the business continuity plan. The BIA looks at all the components that an organization is reliant upon the continued functionality. It seeks to distinguish which are more crucial than others and require a greater allocation of funds in the wake of a disaster.

Criticality   The quality, state, degree, or measurement of the highest importance.

Ethical hackers   A security professional who legally attempts to break into a computer system or network to find its vulnerabilities.

Kick-off meeting   The initial meeting of the assessment team and management that is used to strategize and plan the assessment activities. It is also an opportunity for everyone present to ask questions and work out any problems that may need to be addressed.

Level I assessments   This type of vulnerability assessment examines the controls implemented to protect information in storage, transmission, or being processed. It involves no hands-on testing. It is a review of the process and procedures in place and focuses on interviews and demonstrations.

Level II assessments   This type of assessment is more in-depth than a level I. Level II assessments include vulnerability scans and hands-on testing.

Level III assessments   This type of assessment is adversarial in nature and is also know as a penetration test. It is an attempt to find and exploit vulnerabilities. It seeks to determine what a malicious user or outsider could do if determined to damage the organization.

NSA IAM   The National Security Agency (NSA) Information Security Assessment Methodology (IAM) is a systematic process used by government agencies and private organizations for the assessment of security vulnerabilities.

Organizational Information Criticality Matrix (OICM)   The OICM is a means of determining critical information types within the organization. IT is based on what the organization determines is most critical. It is a qualitative process.

Penetration test   A method of evaluating the security of a network or computer system by simulating an attack by a malicious hacker but without doing harm and with the owners consent.

Qualitative assessment   An analysis of risk that places the probability results into terms such as none, low, medium, and high.

Scope creep   This is the uncontrolled change in the project's scope. It causes the assessment to drift away form its original scope and results in budget and schedule overruns.

Systems Criticality Matrix (SCM)   Similar to the OICM, the SCM is used to define the organization's critical systems. This allows the organization to identify and focus its security mechanisms on the systems that are most critical to the organization's mission.

Vulnerability   The susceptibility to damage or attack caused by a security exposure in software, application, hardware, or human component.

6

Understanding the Attacker

BY UNDERSTANDING WHO ATTACKS, why they attack, how they attack, and what they do, the IT security professionals conducting the risk and vulnerability assessment can focus on combating threats and vulnerabilities commonly exploited by an attacker. This type of intelligence data can assist in the risk and vulnerability assessment by providing the IT security professional with knowledge about how attacks are conducted. This knowledge can be applied to defense-in-depth security controls and security counter-measures distributed throughout the IT infrastructure and seven areas of information security responsibility. Without this knowledge, the IT security professional cannot con-duct the risk and vulnerability assessment from an attacker's point of view.

This chapter will present an overview of the following characteristics about attackers:

- **Who are the attackers?**—Internal employees, contractors, third-party users, external attackers, hackers, and perpetrators.

- **What do the attackers do?**—Bypass security controls, commit unauthorized access, and exploit software vulnerabilities. Depending on the motivational reasons for the attack, attackers do different things.

- **Why do attackers do it?**—The goals and motivational factors explaining why attackers, hackers, and perpetrators attack an IT infrastructure and its assets will be defined.

- **How do attackers do it?**—The tools, approaches, and methods that attackers, hackers, and perpetrators use to conduct an attack on an IT infrastructure will be described.

With knowledge in these four areas about attackers, conducting a risk and vulnerabil-ity assessment can be done with a specific strategy in mind as well as with knowledge of how attackers attack. This approach to conducting a risk and vulnerability assessment equips the IT security professional with knowledge about how to monitor, prevent, and eliminate various attacks on the IT infrastructure. This knowledge will assist the IT secu-rity professional in developing an appropriate information security strategy for its IT infrastructure that encompasses the seven areas of information security responsibility.

Who Are the Attackers?

Who, from the perspective of an IT infrastructure, are internal attackers and external attackers? Internal attackers are commonly linked to disgruntled employees, contractors, or third-party users who, for whatever reason, have lost respect and integrity for the organization, including its IT infrastructure and its assets. External attackers are commonly linked to one of numerous attacker profiles or types. Figure 6.1 depicts a typical IT infrastructure and the domain between inside and outside threats.

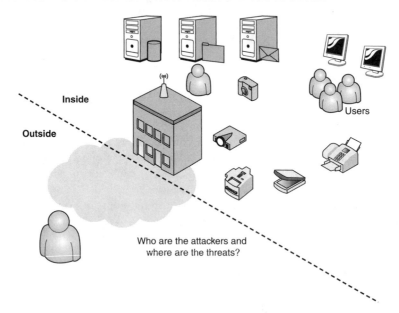

Figure 6.1   Internal vs. external human threats to an IT infrastructure.

Which of the Two Attacker Types Is Potentially More Damaging to the Organization?

It is potentially more damaging to have an attack caused from inside versus outside because that typically means the inside attack was conducted by an employee or individual who has or can obtain access to mission-critical IT systems, resources, and data. More threatening is if the employee was an IT professional with access rights and privileges to the organization's mission critical IT servers, resources, and data. Because of this internal threat caused by IT employees, organizations must have the appropriate Acceptable Use Policies (AUPs) and Confidentiality Agreements in place with key IT personnel who have access to confidential or sensitive IT systems, resources, or data. In addition, human resource procedures and guidelines must be adhered to, especially if an IT employee is to be fired or terminated by the organization. The disgruntled employee situation, along with other human factors and issues, is a serious threat to organizations and IT infrastructures and their assets. This is why conducting thorough background and reference checks for IT employees is a critical and necessary step in the hiring process for many organizations.

Attackers, whether they are internal or external to an organization, are the threat to known or unknown vulnerabilities that can be exploited in an IT infrastructure.

Definition of Threat
by National Information System Security Conference

"A threat is any circumstance or event with the potential to adversely impact a system through"

Unauthorized access—This is when the attacker does not have authorization or permission to access an organization's IT infrastructure and IT assets. Unauthorized access may very well carry a criminal charge, depending on what was compromised and if any monetary damage or loss of productivity was encountered by the targeted victim.

Destruction or damage—After the attacker has completed the initial probing and scanning and has gained access to an IT system or application, the attacker can escalate its user privileges and destroy or damage data assets of the organization after access has been obtained on mission-critical IT systems, resources, and servers.

Disclosure of confidential information—After the attacker has completed the initial probing and scanning and has gained access to an IT system or application, the attacker can access and disclose confidential information to a competitor to damage the organization or collect a payoff if the attacker had monetary motivation.

Modification or alteration of data—After the attacker has completed the initial probing and scanning and has gained access to the IT system, resource, or application, the attacker can escalate its user privileges and modify or alter the data assets of the organization, thus causing monetary damage and loss of data to the organization.

Denial of Service (DoS)—A DoS attack is when the attacker renders production TCP/IP host computers useless or unavailable through the transmission of bogus and invalid packet-sized ICMP echo requests (Ping), SYN flood attacks, or invalid packet transmissions. These invalid or bogus transmissions, in turn, cause a flood of retransmissions between the source and destination IP devices, thus absorbing CPU utilization and resources on the targeted IP device and bandwidth on the network.

By understanding more about the attackers, the risk and vulnerability assessor can "think like an attacker." In the next section, attacker types and their characteristics are presented. This knowledge helps the IT security professional understand who attackers are and how best to combat the kinds of attacks that they commonly engage in.

Attacker Types and Their Characteristics

Many terms and adjectives are used to describe an attacker of an IT infrastructure and its assets. Each type of attacker has a unique profile description along with unique and differentiating characteristics. These profile definitions along with differentiating characteristics are presented next:

- **Black Hat Hacker**—Describes a technically proficient software programmer and information-security knowledgeable individual capable of conducting an attack on an IT infrastructure or its assets merely to prove vulnerabilities or technical prowess and usually without authorization or ethical conduct.

- **Cracker**—Describes an expert software programmer who is capable of programming scripts, solving complex programming problems, and reverse engineering software. Hacker or Cracker are synonyms and used interchangeably, but the Cracker has specific expertise in reverse engineering software and complex programming problems.

- **Cyber-Terrorists/Cyber-Criminals**—Describes an individual or groups of individuals who are funded to conduct clandestine or espionage activities on governments, corporations, and individuals in an unlawful manner. These individuals typically engage in sponsored acts of defacement, DoS/DDoS attacks, identity theft, financial theft, or worse, compromising critical infrastructures in countries, such as nuclear power plants, electric plants, water plants, and so on.

- **Disgruntled Employee**—Describes an employee who has lost respect and integrity for the employer. This is potentially a risk if the employee was fired or terminated without cause, was slighted a deserved promotion or increase in compensation, or was wrongly blamed for a situation. A disgruntled IT employee is potentially a critical threat to an organization, especially if access rights and privileges were provided and managed by the individual.

- **Hacker**—Describes an expert software programmer who is capable of programming scripts, solving complex programming problems, and reverse engineering software. Hacker or Cracker are synonyms and used interchangeably, but the Cracker has specific expertise in reverse engineering software and complex programming problems.

- **Phreakers**—Describes telecommunication and PBX system attackers who break into service provider or corporate telecommunications networks and then exploit and illegally use or provide access to their telecommunication services. This includes physical theft, stolen calling cards, access to telecommunication services, reprogramming of telecommunications equipment, and compromising user ids and passwords to gain unauthorized use of facilities such as voice mail.

- **Program Cracker/Hacker**—Describes a Cracker/Hacker who has specific expertise in reverse engineering software programs and, in particular, software license registration keys used by software vendors when installing software onto workstations or servers.

- **Script/Click Kiddies**—Describes younger attackers who use widely available freeware vulnerability assessment tools and hacking tools that are designed for attacking purposes only. These attackers typically do not have any programming or hacking skills and given the techniques used by most of these tools, can be defended against with the proper security controls and risk mitigation strategies. Script Kiddies and Click Kiddies are synonyms; the term *click* comes from the fact that many tools are automated and have GUI interfaces with buttons to click to launch an attack.

- **System Cracker/Hacker**—Describes a Cracker/Hacker who has specific expertise in attacking vulnerabilities of systems at the operating-system level. These individuals get the most attention and media coverage because of the globally impacting viruses, worms, and Trojans that they create. System Crackers/Hackers perform interactive probing activities to exploit security defects and security flaws in network operating systems and protocols.
- **Whackers**—A whacker was previously a novice or apprentice hacker studying and learning to become a hacker. With the deployment of wireless LAN and WAN technology, hackers who attack wireless LANs and WANs are becoming known as whackers who focus their attacks on wireless networks.
- **White Hat Hacker**—Describes an ethical, information security professional who conducts intrusive penetration tests on IT infrastructures and its assets as part of an overall risk and vulnerability assessment project. A White Hat Hacker is a technically proficient software programmer and information security knowledgeable individual who conducts attacks on an IT infrastructure or its assets with full authorization by the organization.

Who Are the Greatest Threat?

The *greatest threat* to an organization and its IT infrastructure and assets are its internal employees, contractors, and third-party users who have access to the organization's IT infrastructure and its assets. Providing access rights and privileges to internal employees who work with the organization's confidential data and information potentially represents the largest exposure to risk, hence the need for proper human resource procedures when hiring and employing personnel who will be accessing confidential systems and data. Proper background checks, AUPs, and confidentiality agreements must be done for new employees or IT employees who will have access to confidential systems and data. These instruments are the only protection an organization has to prevent an attack made by an internal employee or worse, an internal IT employee. The disgruntled employee represents the single greatest threat to an organization, although the more popular or media-covered security breaches are typically initiated from external attackers.

Insecure Computing Habits Are a Threat

The *second greatest threat* to an organization and its IT infrastructure and assets are its employees' *insecure computing habits*. These insecure computing habits typically include the following:

- **Sharing and exchanging disk media**—Employees and users, whether trusted or not, commonly share data and files on CD-ROMs, USB thumb drives, or floppy disks—all of which are subject to threats from malicious code and malicious software if not properly scanned and quarantined.

- **Installation of unauthorized or pirated software**—Employees and users commonly load unauthorized personal software applications (IM Chat, KAZAA, for example) or pirated software on their company-owned laptops and workstation devices. This can lead to threats from unknown software and data files that are loaded onto the company-owned laptop or workstation as well as software licensing infringements by the employee or user.

- **Downloading and installation of files**—Worse yet is the downloading and installation of freeware or other software applications that may have embedded malicious code or malicious software, such as *spyware* or *adware* that examines the *cookies* and previous Internet destinations of your workstation browser and builds a target profile of the users' habits and likes.

- **Use of email for communications and file transfers**—Employees and users today rely on email communications as the primary business communication tool. Email as a means for file transfer is also another primary application. If the recipient of the email believes it comes from a trusted user, then what is to prevent the user from clicking an email attachment? Hiding a virus, worm, or Trojan in an email attachment that employees and users commonly click is the easiest way to inject a malicious code or malicious software attack into the system.

- **Carelessness with confidential information**—Employees, contractors, and third-party users are often careless with an organization's confidential information and data. This carelessness can be as easy as losing a laptop computer, leaving confidential documents in the back seat of the car, or leaving the computer screen on while the user leaves the work area.

Disgruntled Employees Are a Threat

The *third greatest threat* that an organization may face may be the result of poor firing and termination procedures for employees, and more importantly, IT employees. Many security breaches, both reported and unreported, originate internally to the organization, are perpetrated by current or former employees, and are often undetected because of weak or inefficient human resource procedures and guidelines for the firing and termination of employees. This is particularly important if IT personnel are fired and terminated, with or without cause, or if the employee was slighted a well-deserved promotion, or if other circumstances occur that may lead an employee to lose respect and integrity for the employer. By the time the IT manager or department notifies human resources of the employee termination and human resources notifies the IT manager or department that it was done, the attack could have already happened. In some organizations, it takes days or even weeks before a configuration move, add, or change request is completed, depending on the backlog of trouble tickets and access control procedures; or they get lost and access is never removed until an audit uncovers this loose end.

Organizations must implement proper security controls regarding the deletion of inactive user accounts and access privileges by the appropriate human resources and IT personnel as a final step. Without proper security controls and procedures, such as immediate removal of all access rights and privileges to company-owned IT resources, systems, and applications, an organization may be subject to one of the following threats caused by a *disgruntled IT employee*:

- **Unauthorized access**—This occurs when an attacker accesses an IT infrastructure and its assets without permission or authority to do so. The attacker willingly and knowingly accesses IT systems, resources, and data, and depending upon motives, may do damage or leave unnoticed and undetected.

- **Privilege escalation**—This occurs when an attacker exploits a software vulnerability such as a *buffer overflow error*, and through cracking and hacking steps is able to increase access rights and privileges on the system. This is called privilege escalation and is a critical threat because system administrator rights may be compromised, thus leaving the system and its data unprotected.

- **Disclosure**—This occurs when the attacker willingly and purposely releases confidential information about an individual or organization that is damaging and done with malice.

- **Destruction or defacement of data**—This occurs when the attacker willingly and purposely attacks by destroying data or defacing websites; it is similar to graffiti on city walls and buildings.

- **Use of organization's IT infrastructure and IT assets to initiate an outside attack**—This occurs when the attacker compromises someone else's IT infrastructure and assets and launches an attack from that infrastructure, thus putting an additional layer of protection and anonymity on the attacker.

- **Accidental or intentional release of malicious code or malicious software**—This occurs when the attacker knowingly and purposely launches a virus, worm, or Trojans on the organization's IT assets, thus spreading the mass infection throughout the organization.

What Do Attackers Do?

Attackers can do many things to an unprotected IT infrastructure and its assets, but first must assess who they want to attack in the first place and why. How do attackers select a target and how do attackers carry out an attack? These are questions that only the attacker can answer, but essentially, an attacker must first conduct a risk and vulnerability assessment on the designated target IT infrastructure and IT assets. Depending on the results of the assessment and the degree of the IT infrastructure's security, the attacker may change targets if the target was found to be well protected and secure.

If the motivation is personal and intended to cause embarrassment or financial damage, the target is likely to be highly visible, such as Citibank, eBay, or PayPal. If financial gain is the motivating factor, the highest paying job or opportunity will be given consideration. Choosing the system to attack with the biggest potential payoff is a definite consideration to an attacker; however, the risk versus benefit of the attack must be considered as part of the attacker's internal risk analysis. This is especially true if the security controls and security countermeasures are more stringent on an IT system with thousands of customers' credit card information versus a system with minimal security controls but very few customers' credit card information. In this case, the reward versus the risk may not be high enough to warrant an attack on a specified target that is more secure than others.

Sasser Worm

In the case of the Sasser worm, one of the most globally devastating malicious codes released, it is uncertain if the author of the malicious code went through any kind of risk analysis prior to releasing the worm. The creator of the Sasser Worm was an 18-year-old German student.

The purpose of the worm is uncertain, but it appears the creation of the Sasser worm was ego driven as well as financially motivated because the creator's mother had a PC support and repair business. Unfortunately, the Sasser worm went much further than expected, disabling critical systems for airlines and hospitals. Seeing that the virus was out of control, the creator of the Sasser worm tried to create a version that would instruct users that they needed to patch their machines against the original Sasser. The plan backfired when the newer versions of Sasser also managed to disrupt machines.

This one worm resulted in millions of dollars of losses and damages due to lost productivity, system rebuilds, and loss of revenue experienced by many large organizations. The Sasser worm creator is now facing a mandatory jail sentence for the crime of computer sabotage.

Four Kinds of Attacks

There are four kinds of attacks generally made on an IT infrastructure and its assets. The first three attack types are referred to as structured attacks because they require advance planning; the attacker studies its target and assesses the risk of getting caught prior to launching the attack. An unstructured attack is when an attacker utilizes tools, scanners, and penetration testing tools without any advance planning and specific goal or objective in mind. These four attack types are described next:

- **Coordinated attack**—A coordinated attack involves many people and many systems in a large, well-planned attack. This is typical of the planning done by cyber-terrorists or cyber-criminals. Coordinated attacks are planned well in advance and are usually carried out by numerous remote-controlled agents that have been secretly installed (through other hacking means) on remote high-bandwidth systems. When enough agents have been deployed, the attacker issues a command to the agents to attack en masse. These attacks usually generate enough network traffic to render the target device unavailable, given that its CPU resources are absorbed responding to invalid and bogus transmissions.

- **Direct attack**—A direct attack targets a specific known vulnerability in an IT infrastructure, which is exploited by the attacker. These attacks rely on a known problem existing in a product that has not been protected or patched during deployment and is thus vulnerable to being exploited. The *Ping of Death* attack was targeted to early versions of the Microsoft Windows 95 and Windows NT operating systems; workstations and servers would crash upon receipt of oversize fragmented ICMP echo request packets. Directed attacks are also done on individuals. Modern phishing scams target naïve users by coaxing them to provide confidential information under the pretense of a respected company.

- **Indirect attack**—Indirect attacks are more frequent headline grabbers because of the high visibility that malicious code and malicious software attacks can bring to the world's IT infrastructure and assets. These attacks are a result of prebuilt self-propagating exploits of vulnerabilities in software, operating systems, and applications that are commonly used in IT infrastructures. Common indirect attacks occur in the form of viruses, worms, or Trojans that disguise themselves as trusted applications and email attachments, but that in reality are fronts for sophisticated viruses and worms. These malicious code and malicious software attacks are responsible for millions of dollars annually of lost productivity, downtime, destruction, and damage of IT assets.

- **Unstructured attack**—An unstructured attack is exactly that—an attack usually done by a novice attacker who uses reconnaissance probes and scanners to penetrate an IT infrastructure and collect data on-the-fly in an unstructured manner. Unstructured attacks are common acts of nuisance usually conducted by Script Kiddies or Click Kiddies who initiate vulnerability assessment probing and scanning software on live production IT infrastructures and their assets. Unstructured attacks are not planned and are usually the result of novices using attack tools and password crackers to gain unauthorized access to pay-for websites or engaging in accidental DoS attacks on a targeted device.

Coordinated Attacks

An example of a coordinated attack is a *Distributed Denial of Service* (*DDoS*) attack, which affects the availability of IT systems, resources, and targeted IT assets such as a website or e-commerce website. By transmitting large quantities of bogus network traffic targeted to a specific destination IP address, a DDoS attack relies on the inherent lack of security controls and authentication that the TCP/IP family of protocols uses for communication between TCP/IP devices. This bogus traffic can be in the form of incorrectly formatted packets or part of a *Smurf attack* or *SYN Flood attack*. In a distributed attack, the attacker usually compromises Internet attached workstations to act as agents during the attack. The user is unaware that his or her workstation was compromised via a virus or Trojan program and is now participating in a distributed DDoS attack. When an attacker uses an array of Internet attached workstations to conduct an attack, this is called a *botnet*. Figure 6.2 depicts a DDoS attack using an array of computers, or botnet.

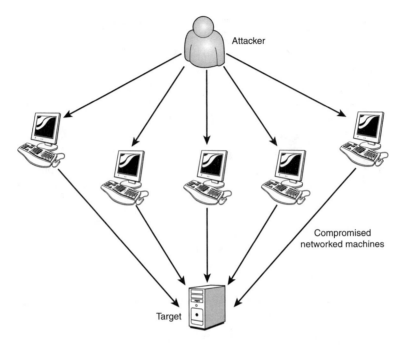

Figure 6.2   Distributed Denial of Service attack.

Coordinated attacks, such as a DDoS attack, utilize specific TCP/IP protocol interactions to exploit the inherent lack of security controls and authentication that the IP network layer protocol has.

Tip

The following presents some security countermeasures that organizations may want to consider as part of their risk mitigation strategy for coordinated attacks:

- **Implement network ingress filtering**—It is a good idea to have your upstream network service provider provide network ingress filtering to stop any downstream networks from injecting spoofed IP packets. Although this does not stop the attack, it makes it easier to identify the source of the attack and terminate it.

- **Rate limit network traffic**—IP routers or Intrusion Prevention Systems (IPS) that can shape traffic or specify the amount of allocated bandwidth so particular kinds of network traffic can be enabled (for example, Committed Access Rate in Cisco IOS software). This will minimize unnecessary ICMP and IP packets, for example, penetrating a server network segment.

- **Implement Intrusion Detection System (IDS) monitoring**—Filters and policies can be set up as IDS alarms to look for specific TCP/IP network traffic patterns and dialogue. IDSs are excellent tools for identifying attackers who utilize compromised workstations from within the IT infrastructure as well as for identifying DDoS network traffic flows. After a DDoS attack is identified, appropriate action can be taken to respond to it. Engaging the organization's *Security Incident Response Team* (*SIRT*) is typically done in the event of a DDoS attack.

Direct Attacks

An example of a direct attack is the *Ping of Death (PoD)* attack, which sends oversized, fragmented ICMP echo request packets in an attempt to crash the targeted IP device. An ICMP echo request packet is generally 64 bytes long, but sending malformed ICMP echo request packets the size of 65,536 bytes causes fragmented IP packet transmissions that often crash the receiving IP device. Other forms of direct attacks occur when the attacker targets a specific and known vulnerability and exploits that vulnerability to gain access. Figure 6.3 depicts a PoD attack in which invalid ICMP echo request packets are transmitted to a targeted IP device in an attempt to crash the IP device.

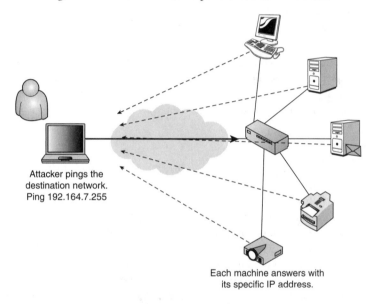

Attacker pings the
destination network.
Ping 192.164.7.255

Each machine answers with
its specific IP address.

Figure 6.3   Ping of Death (PoD) attack with invalid ICMP packet sizes.

Another example of a direct attack is an attack on an individual, or *phishing,* a term used to describe an attacker's attempt at obtaining personal and confidential information. This is a form of *social engineering,* in which the attacker attempts to force the individual into believing that an email message or telephone call from a bogus call center is authentic. Phishing attacks are con artists attempting to obtain personal and confidential information about the individual so that more damaging attacks can then be performed. Attackers often masquerade as banks and other financial institutions in an attempt to obtain personal and confidential information about the targeted user.

Other examples of direct attacks include authentication attacks, database attacks, and application attacks. These are described next:

- **Authentication Attacks**—Direct attacks on systems and authentication techniques where user ids and passwords are compromised. Authentication attacks are easy to deploy but difficult to crack, given stringent access control methods being deployed. Authentication attacks rely on brute-force password attacks, automated password-cracking tools, and even social engineering and phishing tactics to obtain access control information from a user.

- **Database Attacks**—Direct attacks on websites and systems that have a back-end database application that is an attractive target for an attacker because of the wealth of personal, confidential, and financial information that the attack may uncover. In many cases, database attacks can be blamed for recent identify and credit card thefts, causing major banks to terminate all credit card numbers that were compromised and initiate cancellation and reinstatement letters for its customers while issuing them new credit cards.

- **Application Attacks**—Direct attacks on specific applications that have security defects or security limits inherent in them. These attacks are commonly caused by programming errors such as buffer overflows and poor error checking/handling of tainted input in website forms. Buffer overflows will allow malicious code or lines of code to be injected into the application. After this happens, attackers have full control and the capability to do whatever they want with the application and its data.

Indirect Attacks

Examples of indirect attacks are plenty, given that they are usually initiated in the form of malicious code and malicious software, or *malware,* that is developed by software-proficient attackers. Indirect attacks are highly visible because they are directly related to the creation and proliferation of viruses, worms, and Trojans, which are a result of pre-built, preprogrammed, and self-propagating exploits in IT infrastructures and their assets. Creation of indirect attacks requires not only technical knowledge, but a devious mind and intelligence to program and develop a self-propagating indirect attack. Indirect attacks are very costly to clean up and require constant remediation and antivirus, anti-spyware, anti-adware, and anti-pop-up applications. Figure 6.4 depicts an indirect attack where the attack is done on a single targeted IP device. From here, the malware self-propagates and attaches itself to emails and other communications between IP connected workstations and servers, thus spreading the contamination rapidly and throughout the entire IT infrastructure and its assets.

Unstructured Attacks

Examples of unstructured attacks include the entire family of novice attacks that novice attackers like to commit. Most novice attackers initiate unstructured attacks—they are not planned in advance and the attacker is not experienced in conducting an attack. Unstructured attacks are common to websites where the attacker probes, scans, and utilizes tools to conduct an attack such as a password-cracking tool. Password-cracking tools are typically used on e-commerce websites or websites that require user authentication via a login id and password. Unstructured attacks are also usually very targeted and narrow in scope, meaning the attacker does one thing at a time, such as website defacement, attempted password cracking, identifying the server or workstation operating system level, or attaching a virus or work to an email. These attacks are usually sloppy and can easily be identified and prevented with proper monitoring, security controls such as access control lockout when more than three invalid login attempts are tried, and security countermeasures such as an intrusion detection monitoring system, properly configured firewalls, and filtering of specific destination IP addresses.

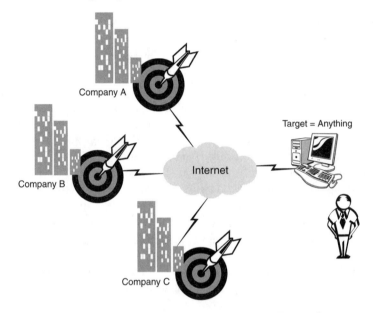

Figure 6.4   Indirect attacks propagate malicious code or malware.

Things That Attackers Attack

Attackers, in general, have the technical prowess to plan, launch, and conduct an attack when they know they can get away with it. Attackers typically attack only when they know there are specific weaknesses or vulnerabilities in the IT infrastructure and its assets. When an attacker launches an attack, they do so by attacking security defects, security limits, and known vulnerabilities in software. In general, anything that an attacker can attack and compromise is considered a *vulnerability*. Vulnerabilities, when identified and compromised, are communicated and shared with other attackers, who then attack the targeted system or IT application. This is known as a security breach or security incident, for which the organization's SIRT team is typically called on to provide a security incident response. Forensic data collection and analysis should be done only by qualified computer and data forensic specialists who can retrieve untainted evidence that may be used in a court of law if charges are filed against the attacker. The following list shows the three main things attackers attack:

- **Security Defects**—An unintended and undocumented deficiency in a product or piece of software that ultimately results in a security vulnerability being identified. A security defect exists when a product or software has a vulnerability that, if properly identified, can be exploited. Security defects are commonplace in software used for firmware, operating systems, software applications, and configuration files, thus presenting a multitude of software defects or vulnerabilities. When a defect is discovered, it must be fixed to minimize the vulnerability window of organization. Vendors and manufacturers typically release *security bulletins* to notify their customers and registered software licensors that there is a known security defect or software vulnerability. Security bulletins usually are accompanied with software patches and instructions for mitigating the risk caused by the security defect.

- **Security Limits**—A known, documented, and well-publicized "deficiency" that might pose a security threat given its vulnerability. No products are 100% secure. By documenting known limits, developers provide customers with the information they need to deploy products in an informed and secure manner. An example of a security limit is the TCP/IP family of protocols such as FTP, SMTP, and POP3 transmissions. These protocols transmit in clear text, allowing confidentiality to be easily compromised with eavesdropping or packet-sniffer devices. This is an example of a security limit inherent in the TCP/IP communication protocols.

- **Software Vulnerabilities**—The result of software bugs and software flaws in the design or coding of the software application itself. These software bugs or software architecture flaws result in software vulnerabilities that, if discovered, can be exploited by an attacker. Bugs in software and lines of code can cause *buffer overflow errors* and leave applications open or vulnerable to injection of malicious code—or worse, access to confidential data can be compromised.

With knowledge of what attackers do and what they look for prior to conducting an attack, the risk and vulnerability assessor can plan risk and vulnerability assessment in accordance with known vulnerabilities in the IT infrastructure and its assets. Software bugs and software flaws result in security defects or security limits, which lead to discovered vulnerabilities in the product or software itself. These vulnerabilities are exploited by attackers and this is what each organization must combat. Remember, all IT components and devices have some kind of software in them and thus have the potential for a vulnerability to be exploited. When an attacker exploits a known vulnerability, this usually triggers a *security breach* or *security incident*. Figure 6.5 shows the relationship between software bugs and flaws, security defects and limits, and vulnerabilities, exploits, and security incidents.

Figure 6.5   Chain of events from software bug to security incident.

Goals and Motivations of the Attacker

Why do attackers attack? What are their goals and objectives for performing an attack? What motivates an attacker to attack? These questions are uniquely answered depending on the situation and the type of attacker. Remember, many attackers and their attacks may not have any particular interest in the target they hit. In other words, the attacker may have not been after anything in particular but simply looking for something to do. An attacker is motivated to conduct an attack for any of the following reasons:

- **Intellectually motivated**—Not all attacks have malicious intent. Intellectually motivated attacks are done to see if the attacker can "beat the system" and gain access to IT systems and resources in an unauthorized manner. Although these attacks may not be intended to be harmful, accidental damage, loss of CPU and processing resources, and other nuisances may occur. In addition, depending on jurisdiction, unauthorized access to IT systems, resources, and data may warrant a criminal charge to the attacker, especially if monetary damage was done.

- **Personally motivated**—This kind of attack motivation is typical of the disgruntled employee when he or she feels jilted that they didn't get a promotion or raise or if they were fired or terminated from employment without cause. Attackers of this type typically like to cause damage or embarrassment to the employer.

- **Politically motivated**—This type of attack occurs when an individual or organization wants to bring their ideals and viewpoints to a larger, mass-media-connected audience. These attacks are meant to showcase an organization's viewpoints using the Internet and the World Wide Web as a sounding board. Website defacements, attacks on critical IT infrastructures and assets, and other cyber-terrorist or cyber-criminal acts are usually politically motivated.

- **Financially motivated**—This type of attack is usually done for financial gain or financial damage. A blackmailer or extortionist paid to do an attack is one example of a financially motivated attack. If an attacker purposely and willingly attacked an organization and destroyed files and/or data used for e-commerce transactions, that organization would lose money and revenue if its system is unavailable during business and peak hours.

- **Ego motivated**—This type of attack and attacker is the one that has no particular motive other than to be a nuisance. Ego can be its own motivation for an attack, especially if that attack is recognized in the various Cracker/Hacker communities and groups that share ideas and stories about their prey. Ego-motivated attacks, although perhaps without malicious intent, carry the same threats as other attacks, such as absorbing CPU resources, accidental damage to data, or embarrassment to an organization.

Note

With Internet access and World Wide Web usage growing, Internet marketers began to deploy aggressive and intrusive tactics to probe and scan individual workstations and their browser settings while examining the *URLs* and *cookies* that the user workstation has archived. Spam, pop-up ads, adware, home page hijacking, and release of spyware applications that monitor and track a workstation's use of the World Wide Web must now be combated, given their nuisance as well as intrusiveness. Although these aren't categorized as attacks, they are definitely a nuisance because they require CPU resources for blocking spam and pop-up ads, and they occupy RAM and require CPU processing power. In addition, an individual's or organization's privacy is violated by having the equivalent of eavesdropping software running in the background of the workstation's primary applications.

Attackers Conduct Their Own Risk Analysis

The goals and objectives of an attacker are varied, as described in this section. How an attacker plans an attack can be attributed to a risk analysis that the attacker may engage in prior to conducting an attack. Attackers are intelligent and they are good at not getting caught. This can be attributed to the fact that they conduct their own internal risk analysis, which typically includes an assessment of the following:

- **Amount of visibility or exposure**—Attackers driven by ego or intellectual reason and motivation are concerned about how visible or how much media exposure the attack will obtain. Some attackers want high visibility and exposure for an attack that they conduct. Other attackers prefer to have their attacks remain in confidence, such as attacks on corporations that do not want to publicly announce they have been attacked or have encountered a security incident.

- **Content or payoff potential**—Attackers who are financially motivated are concerned with how much content or intellectual property can be accessed or how much money they can obtain or steal by compromising an IT system, resource, or application. Financial reward is a great motivator for conducting an attack, especially if that reward is funded by a cyber-terrorist or cyber-criminal organization.

- **Ease of access**—Attackers, after conducting a risk analysis, will attack only if they know what the vulnerabilities are and how to exploit them. An attacker will not attack or will terminate an attack if the target is well protected, secured, has security countermeasures throughout the IT infrastructure, layered protection, or a defense-in-depth strategy for protecting its mission critical IT assets.

After an attacker has decided to conduct an attack, planning and executing the attack must be analyzed, designed, and planned out properly. This planning and execution of an attack requires a thorough knowledge of attack methods, attack tools, and how to use them on an IT infrastructure and its assets. The next section describes how attackers attack, what attackers do, and how they do it.

How Do Attackers Attack?

Attacks on an IT infrastructure and its assets are conducted in a logical, methodical, and sequential manner, where trial-and-error and exploitation techniques are conducted on targeted and known vulnerabilities of IT assets. This section presents the three major stages of a malicious attack on an IT infrastructure and its assets and what tools attackers commonly use when conducting their attack steps. An understanding of how these vulnerability assessment tools work and how best to mitigate the risk caused by them are presented. This same understanding will assist the risk and vulnerability assessment when assessors conduct assessments on their IT infrastructure and its assets. This information will also assist in designing and implementing an appropriate security countermeasure to an identified weakness or vulnerability.

The following list describes the three stages of an attack on an IT infrastructure and its assets:

- **Stage 1: Reconnaissance Probing and Scanning**—Prior to conducting an attack, an attacker must look for and identify a point of entry or vulnerability within the IT infrastructure that can be exploited. This preliminary stage of an attack typically requires the use of vulnerability assessment tools, DNS, SNMP, and IP discovery tools, port scanners, OS fingerprinting scanners, and the dissemination of spyware Trojan applications to collect additional reconnaissance information about workstations and servers.

- **Stage 2: Access and Privilege Escalation**—The second stage of an attack is access, when the attacker uses a system or application exploit to gain privileged access to the IT system or application. The process of increasing a level of authority within a system and gaining system administrator or a higher level of access to a system is known as privilege escalation. An attacker with elevated privileges has access to everything that the access rights or privileges allow. Privilege escalation can occur because of any number of security defects, such as a buffer overflow or a website form reacting in an insecure manner when tainted input or malformed data is injected.

- **Stage 3: Eavesdropping, Data Collection, Damage, or Theft**—The third stage of an attack is the actual clandestine event after access has been obtained. Then the attacker can carry out the final stage of the attack plan by causing damage, eavesdropping for confidential information, collecting information such as usernames and passwords for subsequent attacks, or stealing confidential information or data.

Tools That Attackers Use During the Stages of an Attack

The three stages of an attack typically require the use of vulnerability assessment tools, the use of some of the TCP/IP family of protocols and applications such as DNS, ICMP, and SNMP, and the use of intrusive port scanners and OS fingerprinting scanners. This section presents tools that are commonly used by attackers during the different stages of an attack on an IT infrastructure and its assets. These tools provide the attacker with the necessary information and intelligence data about an IT infrastructure and its assets, such as destination IP addresses, port numbers, applications, operating system version numbers, and application software version numbers. This intelligence data provides the necessary information for an attacker to assess whether to proceed with the next stage of an attack.

Reconnaissance Probing and Scanning Stage

Assuming that an attacker is not intimately aware, as an insider might be, of the IT infrastructure he or she is attacking, the first stage in any attack is for the attacker to conduct a reconnaissance mission to gain an understanding of the IT systems, resources, and applications and identify any potential weaknesses or vulnerabilities for exploitation. This is called the *Reconnaissance Probing and Scanning* stage of an attack, where attackers might employ port scanners to discover IP devices on an active network (for example, IP discovery), the services or applications that they are running, and even OS fingerprinting, which identifies the version of software running on the server or workstation. Port scanner applications such as NMAP can elude intrusion detection systems and even identify version information for remote services; however, the attacker must be careful not to expose the use of NMAP by carefully initiating targeted scans to evade detection. Sophisticated attackers stagger and limit the amount of IP scan packets that are generated (for example, low or slow mode) in an effort to go undetected by intrusion detection monitors. Other popular and frequently used vulnerability assessment and port scanner tools include freeware tools such as Nessus. Nessus even comes with its own vulnerability exploit database, which the risk and vulnerability assessor can use to combat and mitigate the threats caused by use of vulnerability assessment and port scanning tools.

In Figure 6.6, the attacker conducts initial reconnaissance probing steps as part of this initial stage of an attack. This initial reconnaissance probing is typically done externally to the IT infrastructure and its assets and must be conducted in stealth because prior authorization and approval to scan the IT infrastructure was not granted. This type of reconnaissance probing step is intrusive in that TCP/IP packets and network traffic are generated and attempt to connect and pass through the Internet ingress and the organization's egress point in the network infrastructure.

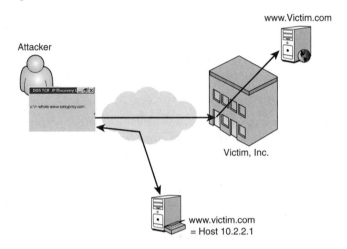

Figure 6.6   Stage 1 of an attack: Reconnaissance probing and scanning.

During the reconnaissance probing and scanning stage that is engaged from an attack workstation, the attacker can use the TCP/IP family of protocols to conduct preliminary reconnaissance probing using *Domain Name System (DNS)* lookups and *WHOIS* to learn valuable information about an organization, its IP addressing information, and DNS names and their IP addresses. DNS is a hierarchy of servers that provide Internet-wide IP-address mapping to hostnames connected to the Internet on the World Wide Web. Publicly available information on registered addresses is obtainable through a number of searchable websites. *Reverse DNS lookup* or *nslookup* are additional commands that will also interrogate DNS information and provide cross-referencing to IP addresses. These services are often provided free on the Internet and can be located by searching on the command name itself. This information becomes the starting point for an attacker, collecting needed IP addressing information and the assigned IP address blocks that were provided to the organization.

TCP/IP Internet Control Message Protocol (ICMP)

Another tool that attackers use is found in the TCP/IP protocol family, the Internet Control Management Protocol (ICMP echo request and ICMP echo reply) or PING command, of which several closely related tools are readily available on most computer operating systems. It can be a key profiling tool to verify that target systems are reachable. The PING command can be used with a number of extension flags to test direct reachability between hosts or as part of the actual attack plan, as in the case of a launched Ping of Death (PoD) attack. After a target network has been located, many attackers perform a Ping Sweep of all or a range of IP addresses within the major network or subnet to identify other potential hosts that may be accessible. This information alone sometimes exposes the likely network size and topology and helps to identify mission-critical IT assets such as routers, switches, and servers that are always on. IP host devices that go on and off are often identified as workstations on an IT infrastructure, given that users typically log off after work hours.

> **Note**
>
> Many IT infrastructures have at the ingress/egress perimeter of the network infrastructure stringent firewall and perimeter security countermeasures that deny ICPM echo request and ICMP echo reply packets and prevent penetration of the perimeter defense. Many attackers know this, so they attempt to penetrate the perimeter defense to initiate PING or PoD attacks on IP devices from within the IT infrastructure using an agent or host device that has been compromised. Many IT infrastructures, including the perimeter of the network infrastructure, deny the transmission and permeation of ICMP echo request and ICMP echo reply packets within a network infrastructure; they only permit network management stations and devices to conduct ICMP echo request and ICMP echo reply packets internally, based on the source IP address of the network management workstations.

PING sweeps are done to identify active IP host devices. Penetrating a perimeter defense and using an agent to conduct a PING sweep is typically done by attackers because many IT infrastructures deny ICMP echo request and ICMP echo reply packets. Figure 6.7 depicts a PING sweep to identify active IP hosts. Denying ICMP echo request packets from outside of the network infrastructure is common.

TCP/IP Simple Network Management Protocol (SNMP)

Another TCP/IP application that is commonly used in TCP/IP-based network infrastructures is the Simple Network Management Protocol (SNMP), which is an application layer protocol that facilitates the exchange of management information between an SNMP manager and SNMP manageable devices. SNMP utilizes the TCP/IP protocol suite and enables network managers to manage network performance, network availability, and configuration management for moves, additions, and changes to the SNMP devices configuration. SNMP enables network administrators to manage network performance, to find and solve network problems, and to plan for network growth. All SNMP manageable devices use the word "Public" as the default password for *SNMP Read-Only (RO) community strings*. The word "Private" is the default password for *SNMP Read-Write (RW) community strings*.

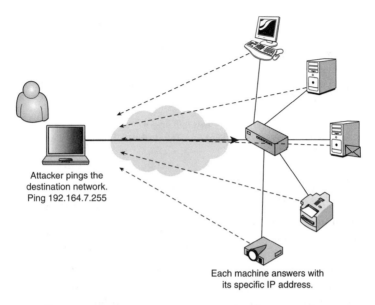

Attacker pings the
destination network.
Ping 192.164.7.255

Each machine answers with
its specific IP address.

Figure 6.7   PING sweeps are done to identify active IP hosts.

> **Tip**
>
> These default SNMP RO and RW community string passwords need to be changed by the SNMP Network
> Administrator in all SNMP manageable devices that are deployed in an IT infrastructure. This must conform
> to the IT organization's policies regarding password creation and password changes. This is a vulnerability
> that is commonly found in SNMP managed IT infrastructures where network administrators and managers
> forget to define security controls when deploying and implementing an enterprisewide SNMP network man-
> agement system.

Reconnaissance Scanning and Probing Tools

Attackers utilize many automated and user-friendly tools during this stage of the attack.
Attackers commonly scan IT infrastructures and IT assets to determine what services and
applications are running on servers, workstations, and other IT devices connected to the
network infrastructure. Scanning is typically done using automated port scanner tools or
OS fingerprinting tools that send reconnaissance packets into and through an IT infrastructure, seeking information about the IT assets that are currently installed.

> **Note**
>
> When a remote machine connects to a server, a banner message often displays with the initial response
> from the server. For example, a Microsoft Exchange 5.5 Server might respond with
>
> 220 ESMTP Server (Microsoft Exchange Internet Mail Service 5.5.2650.21) ready.

> **Tip**
>
> Many IT system administrators create banner messages when a user first accesses an IT system or server. When a user attempts to connect to the IT system or server, there is often a banner message associated with the initial response from the server. Banners can reveal information about the version of the service or application that is running, the features it supports, and even software patches that have been installed. This information can be used to help make an informed decision about whether to attack.
>
> IT system administrators should minimize the amount of data and information contained in the banner message so that an attacker cannot use this data to cross-reference with known software vulnerabilities that can be exploited.

After a target network has been identified, the attacker then commences with a port scanning step to identify the IP host devices, what applications and services are running, and what port numbers are being used by the IP host device. Several popular port scanning applications that an attacker could use are available as freeware applications. One of the most popular is Nmap (available for Unix and Windows). MingSweeper is another network reconnaissance tool for Microsoft Windows NT/2000 workstations and is designed to facilitate large address space and high-speed node discovery and identification. These tools permit an attacker to discover and identify hosts by performing PING sweeps, probing for open TCP and UDP service ports, and identifying operating systems and applications running on IP host devices. This is a wealth of information for an attacker to plan out an attack by finding weaknesses or vulnerabilities in the IT infrastructure and its assets.

Access and Privilege Escalation Stage

The second stage of an attack consists of the *access and privilege escalation* step, in which an attacker attempts to gain access to an IT system, resource, or device within the IT infrastructure based on a known or identifiable vulnerability in the IT device's software. An attacker who knows what IT assets are available within an IT infrastructure and has located potential entry points can proceed with this second stage of the attack. After an attacker gains access to an IT system, resource, or application, the attacker uses a system or application exploitation of a known vulnerability to gain control of the device. The process of increasing or enhancing the attacker's level of authority, administration, and user privileges in an IT system, resource, or application is called *privilege escalation*. An attacker with elevated privileges, such as system administrator, has access to the entire server or workstation, including being able to read and extract data from the server itself. Privilege escalation can occur because of any number of security defects in software, such as a buffer overflow or a website with data fields that react unfavorably to tainted or malformed input data.

After the attacker has obtained unauthorized access, the extent of the damage that unauthorized access can cause depends on the target and the motives for the attack. After gaining access, what can an attacker do? Examples of critical security breaches are listed next:

- **A publicly traded company's financial systems and SEC filings**—This could be a critical security breach or security incident, given that publicly traded companies are under Sarbanes-Oxley compliancy laws, mandates, and regulations and may be subject to penalties and fines if this confidential information is leaked to the public domain.

- **A website with a back-end database of customer credit card information and personal information**—This would be a critical security breach or security incident if the attacker was successful in exploiting a vulnerability on the website and was able to inject lines of malicious code to extract the customer database information, including credit cards and address information of individuals.

- **A hospital's wireless network infrastructure where doctors and nurses access patient record information**—This would be a critical security breach or security incident if the attacker was successful in exploiting a vulnerability on the wireless network and was able to eavesdrop or steal patient privacy information. This would be in violation of the recent HIPAA laws, mandates, and regulations and could potentially subject the hospital to legal ramifications if the individual was damaged or hurt in any way from the hospital's negligence in protecting that patient's information.

- **A bank's online banking system**—This would be a critical security breach or security incident if the attacker was successful in exploiting a vulnerability on the website or back-end database system that is linked to the website. This would be in violation of recent GLBA laws, mandates, and regulations and could potentially subject the bank or financial institution to legal ramifications if the banking customers' privacy data was compromised, financial loss is incurred, or the individual's personal and confidential credit history is altered in the form of *identify theft*.

Access in Compromised and Privilege Escalation Commences

The second stage of an attack, *Access and Privilege Escalation,* is solely dependent on the attacker being able to gain access to an IT device. Access to an IT device usually means compromising user ids and passwords. User ids and passwords can be compromised using various techniques and tools. Some of these are described next:

- **Password guessing**—Password-guessing tools are one of the simplest tools an attacker can deploy. These tools will attack the public authentication interface to a system, such as a web page login prompt, a file server login prompt, an email login, and so on. Password guessing tools rely on the fact that users make bad choices for their passwords. These utilities attempt to use brute force attacks to identify easy-to-exploit accounts. Password-guessing tools are also sophisticated enough to handle simple word reversals and letter and number substitutions as well as conduct dictionary attacks using predefined lists.

- **Password sniffing**—Password-sniffing tools allow an attacker with access to a network to watch that network's traffic for passwords visible within common protocols. Modern password-sniffing utilities incorporate encryption and decryption software. Ettercap, for example, offers support for sniffing SSH1 encrypted traffic. Remember that password sniffing tools cannot remotely sniff network traffic; they must be directly connected to the network segment being monitored.

- **Password cracking**—Password cracking assumes the attacker has gained access to the Unix password/shadow files and/or Windows SAM system files. After these files are retrieved, they can be subject to password dictionary attacks. The password-cracking tool will take this password dictionary and hash each entry and then compare it to the hashed values found within the stolen password file. The strength of the hashing algorithm used by the victim has very little impact on the probability that the attacker will find a correct password. The attacker's success rate diminishes the longer the password is and the more stringent the password change policy is for the organization.

After this access is obtained, the objective of the attack is to increase the level of authority or access right privileges on the IT device. This can be done by exploiting a buffer overflow or some other vulnerability. In Figure 6.8, the attacker accesses the website on www.victim.com by attacking a known vulnerability on the web server itself. After access is obtained, the attacker attempts to increase the level of authority on the web server, thus allowing system administrator or increased levels of authority on the IT device itself. In essence, now the attacker has opened the door to the IT device, and the wealth of information and data on the IT device can be compromised, stolen, or damaged, depending on the motives, goals, and objectives of the attacker.

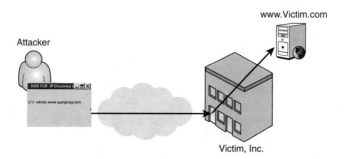

Figure 6.8 Access and privilege escalation on an IT device.

Eavesdropping, Data Collection, Damage, or Theft Stage

After access and privilege escalation has been achieved, the attacker can carry out the final stage of the attack plan by causing one of the following acts:

- **Destruction and damage**—After an attacker has gained access and is successful in escalating privileges on the compromised IT system, destruction of application files, data files, or other damage to the IT system, resource, application, and data can be conducted by the attacker.

- **Eavesdropping and data collection**—Attackers who have gained access to an IT system, resource, or application can eavesdrop or collect user id and password information, can access nonpublic domain information or data that can be used for financial gain or other purposes, and can enable Trojanlike malicious code and malware so that any individual or user who connects and communicates to the IT system, resource, or application will automatically be infected by the malicious code or malware.

- **Theft**—After an attacker has gained access and is successful in escalating privileges on the compromised IT system, the attacker can steal any information or data on the IT system and can delete all reference to this information or data on the production server prior to leaving. This steal-and-delete attack is common in industrial espionage and other acts of a criminal nature.

Gaining unauthorized access to an organization's IT infrastructure and its assets may be a criminal charge in itself, depending on the location of the organization. In addition, after unauthorized access is achieved by an attacker, the preceding list describes common attacks done during the third stage of an attack. This is where the severity of the security breach becomes apparent. Because of the criminal nature of the preceding attacks, attackers seldom conduct direct attacks from their own IT devices, mainly because through proper subpoenas and forensic investigation techniques, the source IP address of the attacker can eventually be found. Remember that attackers are smart enough not to attack from their own IT devices but are capable of using Trojan-like applications and malicious software to gain control of other IT devices that are high speed and connected to the Internet.

An example of the third stage in an attack is a malformed data attack. If an application cannot properly handle inputted data because it was corrupt or it accepted malformed data, applications and systems can behave strangely and possibly be compromised. Malformed data attacks typically inject bad data or malformed data into data fields of the application. Improper error handling or buffer overflow errors are common defects that open an application or system as a result of this type of malformed data attack.

Reducing the Risk of an Attack

Having the knowledge about how attackers attack and what attack tools they use, the risk and vulnerability assessor is better equipped to defend against such attacks. These attacks can be mitigated and prevented from occurring within your IT infrastructure; however, it requires a thorough understanding of how best to implement security controls and security countermeasures to mitigate the risk caused by these attacks.

The following list presents risk mitigation recommendations that an organization can deploy against the attack methods and attack tools commonly used on IT infrastructures and their assets. Note that these recommendations are not a fail-safe solution for preventing an attack, but will certainly deter an attacker because proper security controls and security countermeasures may be enough to discourage the attacker from continuing.

- **PING sweeps**—Risk mitigation for PING sweeps can be accomplished by disabling ICMP echo requests and ICMP echo replies on IP host devices where needed. Also, ICMP echo requests and ICMP echo replies can be blocked at key points throughout the network infrastructure on router and firewall switches. Router Active Control Lists (ACL) can allow ICMP echo request and ICMP echo reply packets only to targeted IP devices and disallow ICMP traffic for all other IP devices.

- **Port scanning**—It is difficult to mitigate the risk caused by port scanners mainly because many port scanners go undetected while performing a port scan on an IT infrastructure and its assets. Use of strategically placed Intrusion Detection Systems (IDS) and IP firewalls will allow the organization to monitor and audit its network traffic so that the IP firewall can be configured to limit the connection attempts between the port scanner and the scanned device. However, by understanding and learning what port numbers, services, and applications are running in production throughout the IT infrastructure, organizations can better plan on how to control network traffic flow, limit access to network segments, and apply appropriate security controls and security countermeasures to protect mission-critical systems, resources, and applications.

- **OS fingerprinting**—Mitigating the risk caused by OS fingerprinting scanners is best supported by an IDS/IPS monitoring system and IP firewalls in strategic locations throughout the network infrastructure. The IDS/IPS will examine the network traffic to look for patterns in responses from targeted machines. Using this information, IP firewalls can be configured to prevent the targeted IP devices from responding to the OS fingerprinting requests for information.

- **Password sniffing**—Mitigating the risk caused by password sniffing requires understanding that a local network connection is required to exploit password sniffing. This can be mitigated by using switched ethernet ports for LAN connectivity, rather than shared media ethernet LAN segments. Use of encrypted passwords so that they are not visible as clear text in the payload of an IP packet is also recommended.

- **Password cracking**—Mitigating the risk caused by password-cracking attack tools is best handled with an access control and password changing policy and standard. The longer the password and the more alphanumeric and nonalphanumeric characters, the more difficult it is to crack that password. With proper security controls for periodic password changes and standards for how to create a password, users and their login IDs and passwords can mitigate the risk caused by password-cracking attack tools.

- **Malformed data attack**—Mitigating the risk of malformed data attacks requires a more stringent software development life cycle process that incorporates security into the actual design of the application. Because many applications were developed without security in mind, the bugs, flaws, and vulnerabilities in software are commonplace. With proper security design requirements and testing and quality assurance, data fields can be more stringently designed to accept only certain data inputs and no others. This will eliminate the malformed data input vulnerability that can cause a buffer overflow error or other exploit.

- **Banner grabber**—Developers and applications programmers should not put in plain English or other language any information that could potentially be used in an attack. By eliminating confidential information pertaining to the IT asset on banner messages, the attacker will not have anything to grab or review, thus eliminating the ease of identifying potential vulnerabilities in known IT assets.

- **Password guessing**—Mitigating the risk from password-guessing attacks and tools is best supported with an access control and password changing policy and standard. The longer the password, the more alphanumeric and nonalphanumeric characters, the more difficult it is to crack that password. With proper security controls for periodic password changes and standards for how to create a password, users and their login IDs and passwords can mitigate the risk caused by password-guessing attack tools.

Reducing the risk caused by these attack methods and attack tools requires an understanding of how these attacks are conducted at the TCP/IP protocol level as well as at the services and applications level. This understanding allows the risk and vulnerability assessor to focus the assessment project on these known attack methods and attack tools and how they would attack the IT infrastructure and the assets that are being assessed. This puts the assessor in the shoes of the attacker when the assessment project is under way. By understanding the attacker, the risk and vulnerability assessor will be able to focus on the defense and security countermeasures on these known attack methods. Specific recommendations will be presented that address risk mitigation of the threats and vulnerabilities that the IT organization must face, including risk mitigation from attacks and attack tools commonly used on IT infrastructures and their assets.

How to Respond to an Attack

Response to an attack is typically initiated by a user, employee, contractor, or third-party user calling the IT help desk, network operations center, or security operations center. After an attacker exploits a vulnerability in an IT infrastructure or its assets, a security incident is created. This security incident may manifest itself into an immediate confidentiality, integrity, or availability issue that must be called in to the IT help desk. Upon receipt of the security incident call, the IT help desk must initially assess the criticality factor of the security incident. The criticality factor for the security incident will dictate the level of response that is needed to respond to this attack or security incident. Critical, Major, and Minor classifications will typically define the level of response that must be provided given the severity of the security incident.

Many organizations create and deploy a Computer or Security Incident Response Team (CIRT) or (SIRT). These teams are usually composed of a cross-section of human resources, legal, IT, and IT security personnel and are led by a team leader who has full authority and power to resolve the security incident quickly and without damage or altering of any forensic data or physical evidence that may be collected as part of the security incident investigation. SIRT teams are dispatched when security breaches or incidents occur in real-time, and live monitoring and auditing of the affected IT assets and devices is conducted. Depending on whether the attack and the attacker are internal or external to the organization, the SIRT team reacts and responds uniquely to the situation. This is especially important if it is suspected that the attacker is an internal employee and proper human resource procedures and guidelines must be followed, especially if the employee is to be fired on the spot.

In Chapter 10, "Post-Assessment Activities," SIRT team goals and objectives, SIRT team functions, security workflow definitions, and security incident severity classifications are discussed in greater detail. Chapter 10 also discusses what an organization should do to put the proper response team in place to handle information security breaches and security incidents. Security incidents are the by-product of exploitations of vulnerabilities in software that are inherent in most IT infrastructures and their IT assets.

Summary

This chapter presented an overview of who attackers are, what motivates them to attack, what they do when they attack, and how they attack. By understanding how attacks are conducted and with what tools, the IT security professional stands a better chance of building the proper information security controls and security countermeasures to combat known vulnerabilities and exploits. Prior to conducting a risk and vulnerability assessment, the assessor can gain a better understanding of potential weaknesses and vulnerabilities in the IT organization by understanding how an attacker thinks.

If the risk and vulnerability assessment project incorporates how to mitigate risk from attacks and known attack methods and tools, the organization will be able to implement the recommendations that are presented in the final report. These recommendations typically address the risk mitigation of known vulnerabilities as well as attacker methods and attacker tools. Many of the vulnerabilities are related to the use of the TCP/IP family or protocols. This puts the burden of security on other elements within the IT infrastructure. IT infrastructures are populated with many security defects, security limits, and software vulnerabilities.

Because of this, organizations must conduct a periodic risk and vulnerability assessment in an attempt to close the vulnerability window on the organization's IT infrastructure and its assets. The gap in time from when an organization realizes it has a threat from a known vulnerability to when the organization actually implements the proper security controls and security countermeasures is known as the vulnerability window. Closing this vulnerability window is what organizations must define as part of their minimum acceptable level of risk in the seven areas of information security responsibility.

Key Terms

Acceptable Use Policy (AUP)   A policy that defines what employees, contractors, and third parties are authorized to do on the organization's IT infrastructure and its assets. AUPs are common for access to IT resources, systems, applications, Internet access, email access, and so on.

Adware   A software program that automatically forces pop-up windows of Internet marketing messages to users' browsers on their workstation devices. Adware is different from spyware in that adware does not examine a user's individual browser usage and does not examine this information on a user's browser.

Botnet   A term used to describe robot-controlled workstations that are part of a collection of other robot-controlled workstations.

Buffer overflow   In computer programming, this occurs when a software application somehow writes data beyond the allocated end of a buffer in memory. Buffer overflow is usually caused by software bugs and improper syntax and programming, thus opening or exposing the application to malicious code injections or other targeted attack commands.

Confidentiality Agreement   An agreement that employees, contractors, or third-party users must read and sign prior to being granted access rights and privileges to the organization's IT infrastructure and its assets.

Cookies   A message from a website given to an individual's web browser on the workstation device. The workstation browser stores this text message in a text file. The message is sent back to the web server each time that the browser goes to that website.

Defense-in-Depth   A term used to describe a layered approach to information security for an IT infrastructure.

Denial of Service (DoS)   A type of attack on a network or an IT device where unnecessary or bogus network traffic renders the network or a targeted IT device inoperable. This attack negatively impacts availability of an IT system, resource, or application.

Distributed Denial of Service (DDoS)   Similar to DoS, except the attack is launched from multiple, distributed agent IP devices.

Domain Name System (DNS)   A hierarchy of Internet servers that translate alphanumeric domain names into IP addresses and vice versa. Because domain names are alphanumeric, it's easier to remember these names than IP addresses.

Enterprise vulnerability management   The overall responsibility and management of vulnerabilities within an organization and how that management of vulnerabilities will be achieved through dissemination of duties throughout the IT organization.

Finger   On some Unix systems, finger identifies who is logged on and active and sometimes provides personal information about that individual.

Hash   A mathematical algorithm that is used to ensure that a transmitted message has not been tampered with. The sender generates a hash of the message, encrypts it, and sends it with the message itself. The recipient then decrypts both the message and the hash, produces another hash from the received message, and compares the two hashes. If they're the same, there is a very high probability that the message was transmitted intact.

Honeypots   An Internet-attached server that acts as a decoy, luring in potential hackers in order to study their activities and monitor how they are able to break in to a system.

Identify theft   An attack where an individual's personal, confidential, banking, and financial identify is stolen and compromised by another individual or individuals. Use of your social security number without your consent or permission may result in identify theft.

Insecure computing habits   The bad habits that employees, contractors, and third-party users have accumulated over the years can be attributed to the organization's lack of security-awareness training, lack of security controls, and lack of any security policies or Acceptable Use Policies (AUPs).

Intrusion Detection System (IDS)   A network-monitoring device typically installed at Internet ingress/egress points used to inspect inbound and outbound network activity and identify suspicious patterns that may indicate a network or system attack from someone attempting to break into or compromise a system.

IT security architecture and framework   A term used to describe a hierarchical definition for information security policies, standards, procedures, and guidelines.

Minimum acceptable level of risk   The stake in the ground that an organization defines for the seven areas of information security responsibility. Depending on the goals and objectives for maintaining confidentiality, integrity, and availability of the IT infrastructure and its assets, the minimum level of acceptable risk will dictate the amount of information security.

Phishing   The act of misleading or conning an individual into releasing or providing personal and confidential information to an attacker masquerading as a legitimate individual or business.

Security bulletins   A memorandum or message from a software vendor or manufacturer documenting a known security defect in the software or application itself. Security bulletins are typically accompanied with instructions for loading a software patch to mitigate the security defect or software vulnerability.

Security defect   A security defect is usually an unidentified and undocumented deficiency in a product or piece of software that ultimately results in a security vulnerability being identified.

Security Incident Response Team (SIRT)   A team of professionals that usually encompasses human resources, legal, IT, and IT security to appropriately respond to critical, major, and minor security breaches and security incidents that the organization encounters.

Smurf attack   A DDoS attack where the attacker transmits large amounts of ICMP echo request (PING) packets to a targeted IP destination device using the targeted destination's IP source address. This is called spoofing the IP source address. IP routers and other IP devices that respond to broadcasts will respond back to the targeted IP device with ICMP echo replies, thus multiplying the amount of bogus traffic.

SNMP community strings   An assigned authentication keyword or password that allows a remote application to access specific SNMP objects in the Management

Information Base (MIB) tree. Standard SNMP installations support Read-Only (RO) SNMP community strings and Read-Write (RW) community strings.

SNMP community strings "Public" and "Private"   This is an inherent vulnerability in SNMP management and SNMP manageable devices because "Public" is the default password used for Read-Only (RO) SNMP community strings. "Private" is the default password used for Read-Write (RW) SNMP community strings. These default passwords must be changed in all SNMP manageable devices appropriately according to the password creation and changing policies of the IT organization.

Social engineering   The act of obtaining or attempting to obtain otherwise secure data by coaxing an individual into revealing private or confidential information.

Software bug   An error in software programming. A software bug that typically requires an immediate fix (such as a software patch) to minimize the vulnerability window and potential for exploitation by an attacker.

Software flaw   An error in how the software or application was architected. Typically a software flaw cannot be fixed with a software patch because a flaw requires a reengineered solution to fix.

Spyware   Any software application that covertly gathers information about a user's Internet usage and activity and then exploits this information by sending adware and pop-up ads similar in nature to the user's Internet usage history.

SYN flood attack   A DDoS attack where the attacker sends a succession of SYN packets with a spoof address to a targeted destination IP device but does not send the last ACK packet to acknowledge and confirm receipt. This leaves half-open connections between the client and the server until all resources are absorbed, rendering the server or targeted IP destination device as unavailable because of resource allocation to this attack.

URLs   A Uniform Resource Locator is the global address on the Internet and World Wide Web where domain names are used to resolve IP addresses.

WHOIS   An Internet utility that returns information about the domain name and IP address.

7

Performing the Assessment

The NEXT PHASE OF BUILDING A SECURE INFRASTRUCTURE is the actual assessment. This is one of the most critical steps of the project. Presented in this chapter is an overall process, a proven method for finding problems and securing the organization's infrastructure. If you keep to the methodology and practice due diligence, you can complete this portion of the assessment successfully.

Introducing the Assessment Process

The assessment process can be carried out in one of three ways: level I, level II, or level III types. A level I assessment is focused on information. Level I assessments require you to request and review all the security policies and procedures the organization has. This job has been simplified because the documentation has been broken into 18 distinct classes, which are shown in Table 7.1. Each of the classes of policies will be discussed in this chapter. After these documents are reviewed, you can progress to employee interviews. The interviews are with the people who carry out the day-to-day tasks outlined in the various policies that were reviewed. They will be able to provide you with valuable information about how things are actually done versus how procedure describes that they should be done. They can also offer insight into ways to improve security. It's important to note that interviews are not interrogations. Employees should be able to speak freely with you and not worry that their comments will be attributed to them or used against them.

Table 7.1 **Categories and Classes of Policy Control**

Management	Technical	Operational
INFOSEC documentation	Identification and authentication	Media controls
INFOSEC roles and responsibilities	Account management	Labeling
Contingency planning	Session controls	Physical environment

Table 7.1 **Continued**

Management	Technical	Operational
Configuration management	Auditing	Personal security
	Malicious code protection	Education training and awareness
	Maintenance	
	System assurance	
	Networking connectivity	
	Communications security	

The next item to be tackled in a level I assessment is system demonstrations. System demonstrations give you the opportunity to match up what is stated in policy versus what is actually done. System demonstrations are just as the name implies—demonstrations. You will let employees who normally perform a task go through the process while you observe.

With the completion of system demonstrations, you will have completed a level I assessment. Will you need to go further? Well, it depends. Level II and III assessments focus on technology. Items such as vulnerability scanning, password cracking, and exploiting vulnerabilities are all part of level II and III assessments. Performing a level III assessment or *ethical hack* just to show that someone can break in is important only to demonstrate that it endangers the organization or its key business processes. By itself, a level III assessment provides only an adversarial view, is usually external in nature, and does not examine policies, procedures, or the underlying security structure and may provide only a short-term fix. Figure 7.1 outlines the assessment process and details the flow of level I, II, and III assessment activities.

Figure 7.1 Assessment process.

Let's start by taking a look in more detail at what needs to be accomplished during a level I assessment.

> **Note**
>
> An assessment is not an *audit*. Whereas audits are focused on ensuring compliance with established policies and operational procedures, assessments are more concerned with the big picture. Some of the questions an assessment seeks to answer are the following: Are procedures in place? Do you adequately protect the organization's core business? Do employees have suggestions on how to improve security or make changes to current procedures? Assessments, unlike audits, are based on a policy of nonattribution. If the janitor reports that he has seen confidential information in the trash, there's no need to attribute that statement directly to him; simply state that media control policies are not being followed.

Level I Assessments

The heart of a level I assessment includes the policy review, interviews, and system demonstrations. The policy review should have been started during the scoping phase as that was the time at which you should have requested all of the various policies that control the security mechanisms developed by the organization. Before we move on to discussing interviews and system demonstrations we should first turn our attention to what reviewing the documentation should entail.

Reviewing the Documentation

As discussed at various points throughout this book, policies are of vital importance to an organization. It's important that the organization's existing policies be reviewed. This is one of the most important activities of a level I assessment. First, we will look at how NIST and the IAM break up the categories and classes of information. We will then take a look at some of the other standards that can be useful during an assessment.

NIST 800-26 Security Self-Assessment Guide for Information Technology Systems divides policies into three categories:

- Management
- Technical
- Operational

Within these three categories are a total of 17 classes. This is close to the NSA IAM, except that the IAM has 18; so it's a little more granular. By adding an additional category the IAM has provided use with a more specific list to work from. This list of the categories and classes was shown in Table 7.1.

Management

NIST 800-26 defines management controls as "controls that focus on the management of the IT security system and the management of risk for a system. They are techniques and concerns that are normally addressed by management."

INFOSEC Documentation

For security to be effective, it must start at the top of an organization. Decisions have to be made on what should be protected, how it should be protected, and to what extent it should be protected. These decisions should be crafted into written documents. These INFOSEC documents should clearly state what is expected from each employee and what the result of noncompliance will be. These documents can be divided into the following hierarchical levels and types:

- **Policies**—*Policies* are the top tier of formalized security documents. These high-level documents offer a general statement about the organization's assets and what level of protection they should have. Well-written policies should spell out who is responsible for security, what needs to be protected, and what is an acceptable level of risk. They are much like a strategic plan in that they outline what should be done but don't specifically dictate how to accomplish the stated goals. Those decisions are left for guidelines and procedures. Security policies can be written to meet advisory, informative, and regulatory needs. Each has a unique role or function.

- **Guidelines**—A *guideline* points to a statement in a policy or procedure by which to determine a course of action. It's a recommendation or suggestion of how things should be done. It is meant to be flexible so it can be customized for individual situations. Sometimes guidelines are referred to as best practices.

- **Procedures**—This is the most specific of security documents. A *procedure* is a detailed, in-depth, step-by-step document that lays out exactly what is to be done. Because procedures are detailed documents, they are tied to specific technologies and devices. You should expect to see procedures change as equipment changes. For example, suppose your company has replaced its Cisco PIX with a Checkpoint firewall. Although the policies and standards dictating the firewall's role in your organization probably would not change, the procedure for configuration of the firewall would.

INFOSEC Roles and Responsibilities

It important to provide a clear division of roles and responsibilities. This will be a tremendous help when dealing with any security issues. Everyone should be subject to this policy, including employees, consultants, and vendors. Common roles include the data owner, data custodian, user, and security auditor.

- **Data owner**—Usually a member of senior management, such as chief executive officer, chief information officer, chief security officer, or information owners. After all, senior management is responsible for the asset and if it is compromised, can be held responsible. The *data owner* can delegate some day-to-day duties, but cannot delegate total responsibility. Senior management is ultimately responsible. They are responsible for leading the security effort and for providing support and guidance to other levels to ensure that policies can be implemented.

- **Data custodian**—This is usually someone in the IT department, such as systems administrators, security administrators, network security administrators, and the like. Although the *data custodian* does not decide what controls are needed, he does implement controls on behalf of the data owner. Other responsibilities include the day-to-day management of the asset, controlling access, adding and removing privileges for individual users, and ensuring that the proper controls have been implemented.

- **User**—This is a role that most of us are familiar with because this is the end user in an organization. Users do have responsibilities; they must comply with the requirements laid out in policies and procedures. They must also practice due care.

- **Security auditor**—This is the person who examines an organization's security procedures and mechanisms. How often this process is performed depends on the industry and its related regulations. For example, the health-care industry is governed by the Health Insurance Portability and Accountability Act (HIPAA) regulations, which state that audits must be performed yearly. Regardless of the industry, the audit process should be documented and approved by senior management.

Contingency Planning

Contingency planning is about preparing to deal with disasters before they occur. The two types of contingency planning include business continuity planning (BCP) and disaster recovery management (DRM). *Business continuity planning* is about planning ways to keep key organizational units operational while minimizing the impact of natural or manmade disruptions. The impact a disruption has on a business is usually measured in downtime. Critical systems are those that the organization cannot survive without for more than a short period of time. Downtime examples are shown in Table 7.2.

Table 7.2 **Maximum Tolerable Downtime**

Item	Required Recovery Time
Critical	Minutes to a few hours
Urgent	1 day
Important	3 days
Normal	1 week
Nonessential	One month

Disaster recovery management is focused on the steps that must be taken to restore business operations if a disaster occurs. Contingency planning documentation should include the following information:

- Identifies who is responsible for executing BCP or DRM plans.
- Identifies critical functions and priorities for restoration.
- Specifies the location of recovery facilities.
- Notes who will manage the restoration and testing process.
- Details how the organization will interface with external groups, such as customers, shareholders, the media, the community, and regional, provincial, and state emergency services groups.
- Communicates how the plan has been tested. Common methods include the following: checklist, table-top, walk through, functional, or full interruption.

Configuration Management

Configuration management is the process of controlling and documenting any changes made to networks, systems, or software. In 1962, the American Air Force responded to the control and communication problems in the design of its jet aircraft by authoring and publishing a standard for configuration management, AFSCM 375-1. This was the first standard on configuration management. Configuration management should be a documented, formalized process having the purpose to control modifications. Although it can be implemented many ways, it's generally a six-step process:

1. Define change management process and practices.

2. Receive change requests.

3. Plan and document the implementation of changes.

4. Implement and monitor the changes. Develop a means of backing out of proposed changes if necessary.

5. Evaluate and report on implemented changes.

6. Modify change management plan if necessary.

Many organizations have a change control board set up to handle this activity. A good reference document is NIST 800-14, "Generally Accepted Principles and Practices for Securing Information Technology Systems." You can find this document at http://csrc.nist.gov/publications/nistpubs. Configuration management is a big concern when moving from one version of software to another or moving from beta development to the final release of a product.

Beta Development

The term *beta testing* is thought to have originated at IBM during the 1960s. *Alpha tests* are the first round of tests performed by the programmers and quality engineers to look at how applications will function. Beta testing comes next. Beta testing is widely used throughout the software industry. This second round of product development has evolved to include testing that is performed internally and externally by prospective users.

Although the software is potentially unstable, it is much more user friendly than in its alpha stage and gives the programmers, quality engineers, and users a good look at how the end product will act and perform. After collecting feedback from these initial users, the application is typically run through another round of improvements before it is released in its final form.

Technical Controls

What are technical controls and how are they categorized as policy? NIST 800-26 defines technical controls as "controls that focus on security controls that the computer system executes. The controls can provide automated protection for unauthorized access or misuse, facilitate detection of security violations, and support security requirements for applications and data." There are nine primary technical controls discussed in the following sections.

Identification and Authentication

Identification and authentication are two big security controls. Identification is the process of identifying users. Authentication is the process verifying their identification. Together these two mechanisms are what are primarily used to control physical and logical access to an organization's assets. The following list describes three ways in which users are authenticated:

- **Something you know**—Passwords, pin numbers, secret handshakes, the combination to a door lock.
- **Something you have**—This could be your bank ATM card, your set of keys, or a token.
- **Something you are**—Usually a personal characteristic such as a fingerprint, voice pattern, retina scan, and so on.

Passwords are the most widely used form of authentication. If passwords are used, password policy should dictate the complexity and frequency in which passwords should be changed. The frequency with which passwords should be changed will depend on the sensitivity of the data. Password change times must be balanced because periodically changing passwords will reduce the damage done by stolen passwords, but too frequent changes will sometimes frustrate the users and can lead to security breaches such as users writing down passwords or using obvious ones in an attempt to keep track.

Account Management

Some surveys have found that as many as 60% of the access accounts in some organizations are no longer valid. If you find this to be true, you need to look closely at policy. Either the policy is not effective or it is not being followed. Account management is the process of handling access to the organization's logical assets. Account management policies should address the following:

- Account initialization
- Account change control
- Privilege access control
- Account termination
- Account lockout
- Password change policies

Account management systems must also address the following issues, which are closely related to session controls:

- **Password request**—Allow users to register for access.
- **Password synchronization**—Policies specifying how passwords are synchronized between multiple systems.
- **Lost passwords**—Policies that specify how users who have forgotten passwords authenticate with some other means and reset them.
- **Help desk**—Allow IT support staff to authenticate callers for password management.

Session Controls

Session controls are automatic features used to limit the amount of time a user's logon is held open; they are used to discourage attackers and misuse. Session controls can be used to prevent someone from attempting to log in at 3 a.m. and can set a limit on the number of attempted logins.

- **Account lockouts**—Limits the number of failed attempts a user can make before an account is temporarily or permanently disabled.

- **Screensaver locks**—Useful when people get up or move away from their terminal without logging out. Can be preconfigured to activate after a predetermined period of time.

- **System timeouts**—An automated control that logs out individuals automatically after a preconfigured period of inactivity. Useful for people who forget to log out at lunch or before going home.

- **Warning banners**—Used for legal notification. They identify acceptable and unacceptable use. Warning banners are useful in establishing legal precedence and informing would-be intruders or attempted security policy violators that their intended activities are restricted and additional activities will be audited and monitored. According to CERT.org, "failure to include a logon banner regarding acceptable use of a computer system can make it difficult to prosecute violations when they occur. Indeed, legal cases exist in which defendants have been acquitted of charges for tampering with computer systems because no explicit notice was given prohibiting unauthorized use of the computer systems involved." A real-life example of a warning banner can be seen in Figure 7.2.

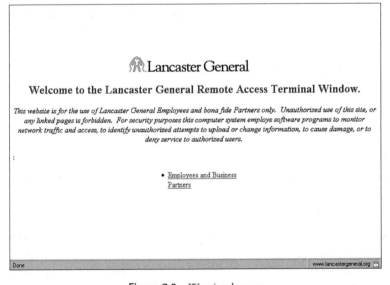

Figure 7.2 Warning banner.

Auditing

Auditing is the measurement of how well the other controls we are discussing actually work. Auditing is by nature a detective control. It's usually not looked at closely until something goes wrong. Many audit trails have alarm thresholds called *clipping levels*. A clipping level is the point at which an alarm threshold or trigger occurs. For example, setting an account lockout after three failed login attempts is an established clipping level. You can mistype your password once or twice, but on the third try, a mistyped attempt will trigger an alert and lock out your account. Well-written audit policies will specify the following details:

- **Log review policy**—Detailed information about how the audit logs are reviewed.

- **Process automation**—Transmit audit logs to a remote system and utilize tools that parse the data, which will free the operator from having to review hundreds of entries manually. By doing so, it will encourage administrators to use the logs in a preventive function rather than in a detective one, and they will be more likely to follow policy.

- **Centralize logging**—Again, this eases and simplifies the burdens of the administrators by having all the information in one location.

- **Exporting audit logs**—This makes it more difficult for individuals to tamper with the logs or cover their activities.

- **Maintain manageable audit log size**—Limit auditing to useful information. Almost always, the tendency is to either not log anything or to log everything.

Malicious Code Protection

Hopefully, this will be one area of policy that has been responsibly addressed. Malicious code includes all types of malware, including *viruses*, *worms*, *spyware*, and *Trojans*. Protection mechanisms need to be in place for workstations and servers. Not only are software mechanisms important, but user training as well, because many types of viruses, phishing schemes, and other forms of malicious code initially function by tricking the end user into some type of interaction or response. All malware threatens either availability, integrity, or confidentiality.

Maintenance

Maintenance is another important security concern. Many times, you'll find inadequate policies for verifying maintenance personnel before allowing them into sensitive areas. Stories abound on the Internet about fake maintenance workers stealing company equipment.

System Assurance

System assurance addresses the need to validate systems and equipment. This formal process is used to validate the system. The two terms you'll hear most commonly used during this process are certification and accreditation. *Certification* is the process of validating that the systems that are implemented are configured and operating as expected. It also validates that the systems are connected to and communicate with other systems in a secure and controlled manner and that they handle data in a secure and approved manner. The certification process is a technical evaluation of the system that can be carried out by independent security teams or by the existing staff.

On completion of the certification process, the results are reported to the organization's management for mediation and approval. If management agrees with the findings of the certification, the report is formally approved. The formal approval of the certification is the *accreditation process*. This is typically accomplished by issuing a formal, written approval that the certified system is approved for use and specified in the certification documentation. If changes are made to the system, it is reconfigured; if there are other changes in the environment, a recertification and accreditation process must be repeated. Some examples of documents designed for system assurance follow:

- **The Rainbow Series**—An aptly named series of books because each book in the series has a different colored label. This six-foot-tall stack of books was developed by the National Computer Security Center (NCSC). These guidelines were developed for the Trusted Product Evaluation Program (TPEP), which tests commercial products against a comprehensive set of security-related criteria.

- **ITSEC**—A European standard that was developed in the 1980s to evaluate confidentiality, integrity, and availability of an entire system. ITSEC designates the target system as the Target of Evaluation (TOE). The evaluation is divided into two parts: One part evaluates functionality and the other evaluates assurance.

- **Common Criteria (ISO 15408)**—An amalgamated version of TCSEC, ITSEC, and the CTCPEC. Common Criteria is designed around TCB entities. These entities include physical and logical controls, startup and recovery, reference mediation, and privileged states.

- **ISO 17799**—A comprehensive standard in its coverage of security issues that is divided into 10 sections, including security policy, security organization, asset control and classification, environmental and physical security, employee security, computer and network management, access controls, system development and maintenance, business continuity planning, and compliance.

Networking Connectivity

Policies addressing network connectivity must address all the ways in which users can connect to the network:

- Wireless
- LAN
- WAN
- VPN

- Internet
- Modem
- Third-party connectivity

> **Note**
> Protection mechanisms that can be used include ACLs, firewalls, mandatory access control techniques, VLANs, and by implementing "deny all" policies.

Communication Security

Communication security addresses the need to protect data while it is in transit. Before you think strictly about data communication, voice and fax communications should also be examined. Encryption is the most direct way to provide additional protection. IPSec, PGP, WPA, and VPNs are a few examples of how this can be accomplished.

Operational Control

NIST 800-26 defines operational controls as follows: "controls address security methods focusing on mechanisms primarily implemented and executed by people (as opposed to systems). These controls are put in place to improve the security of a particular system (or group of systems). They often require technical or specialized expertise and often rely upon management activities as well as technical controls." As you can see, operational controls deal with items such as media controls, document labeling, training, personal security, and physical security. This is of vital importance when you think of the number of people who carry cell phones with built in cameras, which could be used to move confidential information discreetly out of an organization. Other items such as USB thumb drives can hold 1 to 2 gigabytes of data or more and fit easily in a pocket or purse.

Media Controls

Media controls examine the ways in which paper documents, floppy disks, CDs, DVDs, hard drives, USB drivers, and other forms of media are handled throughout their life cycle. Sensitive media must be handled and destroyed in an approved manner.

Sensitive media should be handled with the same care that sensitive documents receive.

> **Caution**
> Anyone looking for a good example of how not to handle sensitive media needs to look no further than the June 2000 incident at Los Alamos in which hard drives containing nuclear secrets were discovered missing. Later, they were discovered behind a copier, but no one knew how they got there.

Media can be disposed of in many acceptable ways. Paper documents can be shredded, CDs can be destroyed, and magnetic media can be degaussed. Hard drives can be wiped. Wiping is the process of overwriting all addressable locations on the disk. The DOD (Department of Defense) drive wiping standard #5220-22M states: "all addressable locations must be overwritten with a character, its complement, then a random character and verify." By making several passes over the media, an organization can further decrease the possibility of data recovery. For organizations worried about proper disposal of used media, this provides clean, unrecoverable media.

Labeling

As discussed in Chapter 2, "Foundations and Principles of Security," labeling addresses the need to have a formal document classification system. The two most widely used are government classification and commercial.

Physical Environment

Physical security is another import control that should be documented in policy. Logical security does little good if someone can just walk in and remove a server's hard drive and leave. Physical security includes items such as

- Locks
- Guards
- CCTV
- Fences

Personal Security

Personal security addresses the administrative process of ensuring that personnel are not a risk to an organization. For governmental positions, this is usually accomplished by requiring a security clearance. A security clearance is a determination that an individual is able and willing to safeguard classified national security information. Typically, the first step in obtaining U.S. government security clearance is to complete a Standard Form 86, Questionnaire for National Security Positions. In private industry, personal security is usually accomplished by the following:

- **Hiring practices**—Employees should have their personal backgrounds thoroughly checked. Organizations should comply with all federal, state, provincial, and local laws in regard to personal information.
- **Preemployment**—Reference check, criminal check, educational history, and background investigation.
- **Nondisclosure Agreements (NDAs)**—These should be provided to new employees and reviewed during the exit interview. The purpose of a nondisclosure agreement is to provide a limited amount of protection against nondisclosure, proprietary information to your competitors. This does not guarantee that an employee will not reveal proprietary information; however, it does assure you the right to sue and seek monetary damages.

- **Termination**—Exit interview, reminder of NDA, account lockout, and password change.

Education Training and Awareness

Employees need to be trained in proper security. Awareness programs are effective in increasing employee understanding of security. Security awareness training policies should take into account the different groups that make up an organization. Training will be focused differently for each group. Not only will the training vary, but the topics and types of questions you'll receive from the participants will also vary. Well-written security awareness programs tailor the message to fit the audience. Following are three of the primary groups that security awareness training should be targeted to:

- **Data owners**—Senior management is not going to want to hear an in-depth technical analysis from this group. Because they are mainly concerned with costs, benefits, and ramifications of good security practices, they should also be informed about how they can support the organization and promote good security practices.
- **Data custodians**—This group of midmanagement requires a more structured presentation on how good security practices should be implemented, who is responsible, and what the individual and departmental costs are for noncompliance.
- **Users**—End-user training should align with an employee's daily tasks and map to the user's specific job functions.

Besides security awareness training, you will also want to see what policies are in place to make sure employees are properly trained on specific security tasks. That new Checkpoint firewall is of little use to the organization if no one has been properly trained as to how to set it up and configure it. This might consist of in-house training programs that teach new employees needed security skills or the decision to send the security staff offsite for a more in-depth educational program. The most common types of training programs are

- Degreed programs
- Continuing education programs
- In-house training
- Web-based training
- Classroom training
- Vendor training
- On-the-job training

Common Policy Problems

While reviewing documentation, you need to be on the lookout for things such as missing policies, outdated policies, or poorly written ones. You may find a policy that goes into detail about how employees are not allowed to connect to unauthorized modems, but find nothing that mentions wireless devices.

Regardless of what you find, you're going to want to record the results and make some recommendations on how any problems can be fixed. Policy problems are usually indicative of underlying problems. You need to make sure that the organization has the necessary items in place to support your recommendations. A well-designed documentation system should have the following components:

- **Policy development**—The development of good policy should take into consideration the organizational needs, requirements, and environment. Senior management must set the tone of what's required and work to motivate and educate the employees as to why these policies are required and their end result.

- **Change management**—Change happens, and when it does, how will the organization deal with it? Maybe a major flaw in the security policy exposed a vulnerability that a hacker was able to exploit. How will this be dealt with? Controls should be in place to indicate how policy changes can be approved, how they are documented, and who is allowed to make changes.

- **Acceptance**—All policies must have acceptance. If policies are routinely bypassed or ignored, they will be deemed ineffective; therefore, employee buy-in is important.

- **Testing**—An important part of any policy is testing. There is no way to gauge effectiveness without testing policies to see if they are effective. For example, you may have a procedure that dictates what can and cannot pass through the firewall. A series of penetration tests would help confirm that the procedure works and allows only acceptable traffic.

- **Implementing**—Policies must have a scheduled implementation. Once I heard, "Yeah, we have a strong password policy but it wasn't implemented because of hardware/software issues."

- **Reviewing**—Have you ever gone to your boss's office and asked about a questionable policy only to have a dusty book pulled from the shelf in an attempt to research the answer? Static policies are bad policies! Policies are living documents. Times change, technologies change, laws change, and so should policies. They should change with the times and adapt to meet the organization's needs. Assessments and audits are useful at analyzing policies as well as the effectiveness of the policies.

> **Tip**
>
> If you end up being responsible for the development of policies, remember that their real purpose is to clear up confusion, not generate new problems. When creating policy, write the document for the specific audience to which it is targeted. It's not likely that you will be able to sit down with each reader and explain what each item means or how it benefits the organization. Individuals who have become proficient at writing policy usually remember the "Five Ws of Journalism 101":

- What—What is to be protected (the topic)?
- Who—Who is responsible (responsibilities)?
- Where—Where within the organization does the policy reach (scope)?
- How—How will compliance be monitored (compliance)?
- When—When does the policy take effect (timing)?
- Why—Why was the policy developed (reason)?

Assessing the organization's documentation requires not only reading it, but also asking employees what it means to them. During the upcoming interview process, ask the interviewees how they interpret the policy.

Additional Organizational Guidelines and Controls

Depending on the nature and scope of the security assessment, different standards might be appropriate. Some of the most well known are described next.

ISO 17799

ISO 17799 is a good benchmark to reference during a vulnerability assessment because it represents industry-recognized best practices.

- **Security Policy**—Discusses what policies should look like as well as how the policies should be reviewed.
- **Organizational Security**—Addresses roles and responsibilities for all aspects of information security.
- **Asset Classification and Control**—Deals with the ownership of assets and asset classification.
- **Personnel Security**—Maps closely to NIST and IAM as it discusses all aspects of someone's employment with the organization.
- **Physical and Environmental Security**—Specifies physical and environmental security controls that should be taken to prevent unauthorized physical access or damage to facilities.
- **Communications and Operations Management**—These controls address secure communications and items such as change management and media handling.
- **Access Control**—These controls are focused on the principle of least privilege.
- **Systems Development and Maintenance**—Requirements in this section are to ensure that security is built in to information systems.
- **Business Continuity Management**—Controls in this section deal with business continuity.
- **Compliance**—This section defines certain legal and operational compliance. This includes regulatory, legislative, and contractual security-related requirements that are applicable to the organization.

RFC 2196

RFC 2196 is another good standard to reference during the vulnerability assessment. The basic approach it outlines is shown next:

1. Identify what you are trying to protect.

2. Determine what you are trying to protect it from.

3. Determine how likely threats are.

4. Implement control measures that will protect your assets in a manner that is cost effective.

5. Periodically review the process and make improvements each time a weakness is found.

Control Objectives for Information and Technology (COBIT)

Control Objectives for Information and Technology (COBIT) consists of 34 high-level IT control practices. Corresponding to each is an Audit Guideline to enable the review of IT processes against COBIT'S 318 recommended, detailed control objectives to provide management assurance and advice for improvement. COBIT helps its users develop good control policies and good practices for IT control. COBIT is a tool that allows users to bridge the gap between control requirements, technical issues, and business risks and communicate that level of control to stakeholders.

Interviewing Process Owners and Employees

At this step in the assessment, you'll want to get an idea about how day-to-day processes are carried out. You have data that was provided from the initial information request, and you have done a review of the organization's documentation. Armed with this data, you will want to learn more about how operations are actually carried out. The interview process will provide that information.

Interviews should be handled by individuals who have good people skills. You need people who can interact well with others and know when to probe for more in-depth answers. You don't want this to come off like a poorly written episode of *Dragnet*. Your goal here is to see how well policy actually matches up to reality. For example, you may find that a certain security policy states that the IT manager must personally clear all individuals who enter the server room. Because this is somewhat of an inconvenience, you may find that the IT manager just leaves the access key for the second- and third-shift managers in case they need access. Interviews help identify where policy and practice deviate. The other purpose of the interview is to hear from other employees how they feel about the security of the organization. Employees truly are an organization's greatest asset and will bring many good ideas to the table if asked. Interviews are the place to solicit this information.

Interview Candidates

You will want to interview a cross section of employees from your organization. The idea is to get a feel for what the individuals at the top all the way down to the end user feel about security. What are their attitudes and perceptions? Table 7.3 shows some potential interview candidates. This should give you some idea of the range of employees you'll want to talk to.

Table 7.3   **Potential Interview Candidates**

Data Owners	Data Custodians	End Users
Chief security officer	Network manager	Users
Chief executive officer	Security administrator	Privileged users
Chief technology officer	Department heads	Database admin
Executive staff	Facilities manager	Janitorial staff

Interview Techniques and Schedule

Unfortunately, Security Assessment Interviewing 101 is not a course offered in most colleges. As mentioned previously, you're going to need to use care in choosing the interviewer. The individual who conducts the interview needs to have good interpersonal skills. Individuals don't like feeling that they are being interrogated. Also, that is not the purpose of the interview. The goal here is to have a dialog with the employees as to what their thoughts and concerns are and how they carry out day-to-day activities. Three items must be considered when planning and performing the interviews:

During the interview, you want to make the person being interviewed is as comfortable as possible. Position yourself where there is no table or obstruction between you and the interviewee, move from behind your desk, and take a chair next to the candidate. Interviews should be held in a private location. You will want to keep supervisors and others out of the room at the time of the interview. The objective is to have an open, honest dialog. Schedule individuals from the same groups at different times to try and keep the atmosphere from becoming stilted, self-serving, and defensive. The presence of a microphone inhibits some employees, so it's best not to record interviews. Have a second person in the room take notes. It's important to remind the interviewee that this is not an audit, and nonattribution is the policy.

Nonattribution means that whatever is said in the interview will not be attributed to a specific person outside of the meeting. You will not report the results of the interview in such a way that would identify or expose the participant's identity. This is an issue because some participants will be concerned about what they say or how their participation in the assessment interview process may be viewed by colleagues and department heads. If individuals lie or attempt to misrepresent the truth during an interview, you can usually tell by their body language, tone of voice, or the words they use. Classic body language giveaways include individuals scratching their nose and not looking directly at the interviewer when they are speaking. Guaranteeing confidentiality is an important part of establishing trust and helps to remove the feeling that the interviewee should hide the facts from you. You're not doing this to find a guilty party or accuse someone of doing anything wrong; the purpose here is to learn what's right and wrong with the organization's security posture.

> **Tip**
>
> Another important consideration is the interview schedule. You will want to allow adequate time for each person you are going to talk to. You will also want to leave some time between interviews to gather your notes, record any findings, and keep the interviewees from stacking up in a queue while waiting for you. A general rule is to allow the following:
>
> - Thirty minutes or so for each end user
> - One hour for data custodians and data owners
> - One and a half hours for technical interviews

Interview Topics

Topics discussed during the interview will vary based on which group of individuals you are interviewing. NIST 800-26 has a good list of potential questions tied to the specific categories, but there will also be some general questions you will want to ask most interview candidates. These may include

- Who is the employee and what is his or her relationship to the organization?
- How long has the employee worked for the organization?
- What data can the employee access, how is this accomplished, and what applications are made available to the employee?
- What does the employee perceive to be critical or sensitive data and resources?
- What knowledge does the employee have of where security policy and security practice deviate?
- What changes would the employee recommend to improve corporate security practices?
- What security vulnerabilities does the employee believe the organization is not addressing?

System Demonstrations

When you have an in-depth knowledge of the organization's policies and have completed a thorough set of interviews, it will be time to observe some system demonstrations. The purpose of system demonstrations is to clarify any disagreements between stated policy and interviews. For example, during an interview, you may have been told that there is no lockout policy in place. That is, users can enter one, two, three, four, or more incorrect passwords and still not have their account locked out or disabled. Because you know that policy dictates a lockout after three tries, a simple system demonstration can prove or disprove this problem. If a system demonstration shows that a lockout policy has not been implemented, you can then get more information from the individuals in charge and try to find out why. Is it a technical limitation, a failure to adhere to policy, or what?

Another example could be that the cleaning crew stated that they have seen restricted documents thrown in the trash and not disposed of by shredding as policy dictates. This can be verified by taking a walk around some of the work areas late at night or doing a little dumpster diving.

The importance of demonstrations is that they are used to prove facts that have thus far been uncovered and that when possible, you are having the employee perform the action or procedure stated in the policy. Remember, your goal is to determine where policy and actual practice deviate.

Although system demonstrations go a long way in demonstrating that policy and action agree, they are not perfect, nor can they solve or answer all problems. Suppose that you review the ACL policy and even observe the organization's firewall administrator enter it in. Does this demonstrate that the ACL works as policy dictates? Maybe, maybe not. Items of this nature are best verified by performing a level II assessment.

Level II Assessments

Congratulations, you've done most of the work needed for a level I assessment. Level II assessments rely heavily on vulnerability scans and more intrusive forms of technical testing. Although many organizations are quick to want to jump directly to level II assessments, to do so overlooks the entire administrative and operational side of security. Vulnerability scans are important, but they deal mainly with the technical side of the organization. Up to this point of the assessment, what you should really have been trying to do is to figure out the core mission of the organization, what processes it takes to accomplish the core mission, and how well policies map up to real life activities. If you've done a thorough job, you will already be able to see if the policy structure is sufficient or whether changes need to be made to better protect key assets. With this done, you can focus your activities on technology.

> **Tip**
>
> Chapter 8, "Tools Used for Assessments and Evaluations," will go into detail on the various technical assessment tools and the guidelines and standards that are available. ISO 17799 and *The Open Source Security Testing Methodology Manual* (OSSTMM) are two examples. The OSSTMM focuses on the technical details of what should be tested, what to do before, during, and after a security test, and how to measure technical test results. The OSSTMM is divided into sections that collectively test the following:
>
> - Information and data controls
> - Personnel security-awareness levels
> - Fraud and social-engineering control levels
> - Computer and telecommunications networks, wireless devices, and mobile devices
> - Physical security access controls, security processes, and physical locations

Vulnerability Scans

Vulnerability scanners are one of the primary tools used for a level II technical assessment. Vulnerability scanners can probe the network, evaluating firewall rule sets, network configurations, vulnerable systems, unpatched services, and more. If you discover critical vulnerabilities, you should inform others immediately; otherwise, general findings should be noted for the final report. Some common vulnerability scanners and assessment tools are

- Nessus
- SAINT
- ISS Internet Scanner
- NetRecon
- Retina
- SARA

It is important to stay focused on key systems and information types you identified while scoping what are most critical. Performing a level II assessment has much more value after you have verified that the needed policies and procedures are in place and that overall compliance with these documents is acceptable.

Level II Assessment Caveats

A major caveat of level II assessments is that individuals sometime think that you can just stroll in, run a vulnerability assessment tool, and then you have secured the network against all possible threats. First, these results need to be correlated against the administrative and operational findings discussed earlier. Second, vulnerability scanners typically produce tons of paperwork. Most networks are quite large, and a blind scan against all possible devices will produce a lot of data that will need to be processed and analyzed. It may be necessary to have the supporting infrastructure groups assist in running these tests and analyzing the results. Vulnerability scanners are good at identifying foundational security issues but require substantial input to analyze how the results map to bigger organizational issues. In the end, some organizations are so large that it may not be possible to audit all network devices. You may be able only to do a sampling in various sections of the network and indicate that in the report.

Level III Assessments

Having completed a level I and level II assessment, you may have determined it is necessary to continue your technical analysis. Some of the tools you will need for this level of the technical assessment include the following:

- Information-gathering tools and techniques
- Scanning tools
- Enumeration tools

- Wireless tools
- Password auditing tools
- Vulnerability scanning tools
- Automated exploit tools

NIST 800-42 is a good foundational document to review to help guide you through this portion of your testing. Level III assessments can be performed for several reasons:

- To see what attackers can access and infiltrate if they so desire
- To determine what types of information leakage is occurring
- To demonstrate the end result of some of the uncovered vulnerabilities.

Simply stated, if discovered vulnerabilities are not addressed, this may be the result. You may perform these activities yourself or hire outside consultants for this task. If you outsource any aspect of the assessment, check the vendor's references and prior experience to see if this third party is reliable. It is also advisable to run background checks to see whether outside consultants have been involved in any criminal activities.

Vulnerability Exploitation

Vulnerability exploitation is an attractive option because you can tell some people about vulnerabilities, but showing them their passwords, talking about the secret plans for next year's product launch, or producing a file stored only on the CEO's laptop can have a very dramatic effect. Although exploiting vulnerabilities won't always be necessary, when they are used, they can produce some dramatic results. A big drawback to level III assessments and the never ending hunt for potential weaknesses to exploit is that there will always be weaknesses or potential vulnerabilities; you will want to identify which risks concern your organization most and then concentrate on them while ensuring that the policy structure is in place so that long-term security can be maintained. Tools used for vulnerability exploitation include

- Metasploit
- CANVAS
- Core IMPACT

If you believe this level of assessment is necessary, planning becomes an important issue. These activities most likely will not run from 8 a.m. to 5 p.m. Therefore, it is important that team members are not scheduled for long periods of continuous work, even if they are being fueled by Snickers and Mountain Dew! These activities can take substantial amounts of time, so make sure to

- Plan the best time to perform these activities, possibly late night and weekends. Think about what result a network outage would have during peak business hours.

- Maintain phone numbers and contact information of key network professionals. If something does go wrong, you will need the appropriate contact numbers.
- Plan your activities to have the least level of impact on the organization.

> **Tip**
>
> Throughout this assessment process, you should be in close contact with management to keep them abreast of your findings. There shouldn't be any big surprises at the conclusion of the process. Management should be kept informed of your findings as the project progresses. At the conclusion of these assessment activities, you will want to report on your initial findings even before you have developed a report. You shouldn't be focused on recommendations here, but on what you found and its potential impact. Some key decisions will start being made at this meeting, so it is essential to prepare in advance.

Summary

To be successful, you will need to focus on what issues are of most importance to the organization. Which of the potential threats and risks can do the organization the most harm? This can be a big undertaking, so you will need managerial, technical, and project management skills to be successful. But also remember, it's not your project; it is the organization's project. Listen to those around you, solicit input from key business unit managers, and pay attention during the interviews. The end users can provide you with a wealth of information.

Key Terms

The following acronyms and terms are used in this chapter. For the explanation and definition purpose of this chapter, these acronyms and terms are defined as follows:

Audit   An independent examination of records, actions, and activities to assess the adequacy of security controls and to ensure compliance with established policies and operational procedures.

Business continuity planning (BCP)   A system or methodology to create a plan for how an organization will resume partially or completely interrupted critical functions within a predetermined time after a disaster or disruption occurs. The goal is to keep critical functions operational.

Clipping level   The point at which an alarm threshold or trigger occurs.

Configuration management   The process of controlling and documenting any changes made to networks, systems, or software.

Contingency planning   The process of preparing to deal with calamities and non-calamitous situations before they occur so that the effects are minimized.

Control Objectives for Information and Related Technology (COBIT)   A third-generation document that has 34 high-level objectives that cover 318 control objectives categorized in four domains. Its purpose is to provide organizations with a set of generally accepted information technology control objectives to help them fully benefit from their IT infrastructure and develop good IT governance and control procedures.

Data owner   The individual responsible for the policy and practice decisions of data.

Data custodian   The individual responsible for implementing controls on behalf of the data owner.

Ethical hack   A term used to describe a type of hack that is done to help a company or individual identify potential threats on the organizations IT infrastructure/or network. Ethical hackers must obey rules of engagement, do no harm, and stay within legal boundaries.

Guidelines   Points to a statement in a policy or procedure by which to determine a course of action.

NIST 800-42   The purpose of this document is to provide guidance on network security testing. It deals mainly with techniques and tools used to secure systems connected to the Internet.

Nonattribution   The act of not providing a reference to a source of information.

Policies   High-level or the top tier of formalized security documents.

Procedure   A detailed, in-depth, step-by-step document that lays out exactly what is to be done and how it is to be accomplished.

RFC-2196   The purpose of RFC 2196 is to provide practical guidance to organizations trying to secure their information and related services.

Spyware   A general term for a program that surreptitiously monitors your actions. These programs can sometime be acquired by simply browsing the Web.

Trojan   A program that does something undocumented that the programmer or designer intended, but that the end user would not approve of if they knew about it.

Virus   A computer program with the capability to generate copies of itself and thereby spread. Viruses usually require the interaction of an individual and can have rather benign results, such as flash a message to the screen, or it can have malicious results that destroy data, systems, integrity, or availability.

Worms   A self-replicating program that spreads by inserting copies of itself into other executable code, programs, or documents. Worms typically flood a network with traffic and result in a denial of service.

8

Tools Used for Assessments and Evaluations

Assessments are not all about paperwork, policy, and documentation. Numerous tools can be used to help analyze, assess, and test the network's security infrastructure. Good security will require that funds be spent, but a multitude of excellent open source software products are available and some of them may just suit your needs. Therefore, the goal here is to introduce you to a variety of commercial and open source tools and offer you a high-level overview. These tools have also been divided into categories, because after all, nothing is used in a vacuum.

> **Note**
>
> If you want to know more, the vendor's website is always a good place to start. If you are looking for a real in-depth examination, there are books that have been written about many of these tools. Two good choices are
>
> *Hacking Exposed* (ISBN: 0072260815)
>
> Anti-Hacker Tool Kit (ISBN: 0072230207)

A Brief History of Security Tools

The tools described in this chapter are designed to search for vulnerabilities. They can be used by security administrators to find and fix problems or by hackers to exploit system and network weaknesses. Vulnerability assessment tools have been around for a while. Dan Farmer and Wietse Venema helped start this genre of software in 1995 when they created one of the first vulnerability assessment programs called Security Administrator Tool for Analyzing Networks (SATAN). This program set the standard for many tools to follow; it made it possible to scan for vulnerable computers through the Internet and provided a variety of functions in one package. Although SATAN was a great tool for security administrators, it was also useful to hackers.

Today, there is an untold number of tools that can be used to scan for vulnerabilities and probe for "open doors." Some of these are legitimate security tools and others have been written by hackers or those without the best of intentions. As a security professional, you will probably want a keep a variety of these tools handy. Just make sure you have written authorization before using them on a network.

Putting Together a Toolkit

The tools we are about to discuss have been arranged into a logical order. Assessments usually follow a well-defined methodology. That is the focus here—to step you through the process and briefly discuss some of the tools that can be used at each particular step. The tools are divided into the following categories:

- Information-gathering tools and techniques
- Scanning tools
- Enumeration tools
- Wireless tools
- Password auditing tools
- Vulnerability scanning tools
- Automated exploit tools

Note

Remember that tools come and go, but the methodology of an assessment stays the same. Some of these tools are free, such as Nmap and SuperScan, whereas others, such as L0phtcrack and LANguard, must be purchased.

Information-Gathering Tools and Techniques

This first step of the assessment is about discovery: How much information is exposed to outsiders and what is its potential damage? One of the best tools you can use at this step of the engagement is your brain. This step is all about old-fashioned detective work. Before you fire off a single port scanner or ping sweep, you'll want to start here and see what the rest of the world may already know.

Begin with the organization's website. It's surprising what type of information can be found there. Email addresses, employee names, organization locations, and technologies are just a few of the items you may dig up. Spend a little time and use a site ripper like Blackwidow Pro or Wget to pull down the contents of the site. Again, you may be surprised at what you find. While you quest for information, also check out SiteDigger. Foundstone developed this tool to automatically scan websites and report security vulnerabilities available via public search engines. It's possible to uncover additional amounts of sensitive information that should not be publicly available with this tool. The biggest drawback is that it's structured around Google's API; you'll be limited to 1,000 searches per day.

On the subject of manipulating Google searches, you should also check out the *Google Hacking Guide* by Johnny Long; his website is at http://johnny.ihackstuff.com. It offers insight into some of the ways you can easily find exploitable targets and sensitive data by using Google's built-in functionality. Google commands such as *intitle* instruct Google to search for a term within the title of a document; others, like *filetype,* allow individuals to search only within the text of a particular type of file.

Next, take a look at the *IANA/ARIN/RIPE* databases. You can manually step through this process or use one of the many websites set up for this purpose, including dnsstuff.com, centralops.net, all-nettools.com, and geektools.com. Many organizations have removed names and other information from these databases. but sometimes you still get lucky.

It's sad but true that not everyone in an organization may be happy about his or her current status. Offshoring, outsourcing, and reductions in force can add to individuals' frustrations. These unhappy individuals are also potential sources of information leakage. This information may be posted on a blog, some type of "sucks" domain, or other site. Shown in Figure 8.1 is the stinky gateway domain that was up for a while before Gateway computer corporation found out and requested that the former employee remove it.

Figure 8.1 Stinky Gateway site.

Frustrated employees will always find some way to vent their thoughts, even if not from a "sucks" domain. One such site that may offer other insider information is internalmemos.com. This site lists information that is usually sensitive and probably shouldn't be released to the world. Although some of the content is free, other content is considered premium and must be purchased to be viewed. A sample shot of the site is shown in Figure 8.2. Don't be surprised if you find some of your company's memos there!

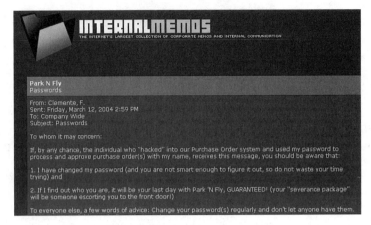

Figure 8.2   Internalmemos.com.

Other Footprinting Tools and Techniques

A host of other tools and techniques can be used for basic information gathering. The following list describes some of them:

- **Job searches**—Monster.com, Careerbuilder.com, and other job site boards are prime targets for infor-mation. If your organization uses online job sites, you'll want to pay close attention to what type of information is being given away about the company's technology.

- **Financial records**—Publicly traded companies are the focus of much more scrutiny than private firms. 10-Qs and 10-Ks are two items that outsiders can access to find names, addresses, financial data, and information about acquired or divested industries. The Edgar database at the ftc.gov site is a good place to start.

- **Banner information**—No one has said anything about scanning a site yet, but you'll probably want to take a look at www.netcraft.com. Netcraft has a handy little feature that lets you see what a website is running.

- **Old website content**—The Wayback Machine keeps about 40 billion web pages all the way back from 1996. It can be seen at www.archive.org.

More information can be found at

Blackwidow Pro—www.soft32.com

Wget—www.gnu.org/software/wget/wget.html

SiteDigger—www.foundstone.com

Google Hackers Guide—http://johnny.ihackstuff.com

With some basic information gathering completed, we can move on to more in-depth techniques. In the following sections we will discuss scanning tools, enumeration tools, wireless tools, password auditing tools, vulnerability scanning tools, and automated exploit tools. Combined, these will provide you with most of what is needed for a level II or level III assessment.

Scanning Tools

With the basic information gathering out of the way, it's time to start getting interactive. At this phase of an assessment, you are looking for active machines and networks. No matter which tools you use, activity here can be boiled down to three steps:

- The first step is network discovery. Network discovery tools use ICMP ECHO_REQUEST/REPLY packets to see if a target is live. If ping hasn't been blocked, it can reveal which machines are active on the network.

- The second step is port scanning. *Ports* are tied to services and as such, provide a list of what potential applications are active. Ports are placed into *TCP* and *UDP* packets so the correct application can be passed to the required protocols. Although applications can be made to operate on nonstandard ports, the established port numbers serve as the de facto standard. Although there are approximately 65,000 ports, they are divided into well-known ports (0-1024), registered ports (1024-49151), and dynamic ports (49152-65535).

  Just finding an open port in no way means that vulnerability has been found. Further analysis must be performed to pry additional information from the server. Port-scanning programs typically manipulate the *TCP handshake* process to find out what's really running on that open port. These techniques can include the following:

  - **TCP SYN scan**—This half-open scan was developed to evade IDS systems, although most now detect it. Open ports reply with a SYN/ACK, whereas closed ports respond with a RST/ACK.

  - **TCP FIN scan**—Forget trying to set up a connection; this technique jumps straight to the shutdown. This type of scan sends a FIN packet to the target port. Closed ports should send back a RST. This technique is effective on Unix devices.

  - **TCP NULL scan**—Sure, there should be some type of flag in the packet but a NULL scan sends a packet with no flags set. Closed ports should return a RST.

  - **TCP ACK scan**—This scan attempts to determine rulesets or identify whether stateless inspection is being used. If an ICMP destination unreachable message is returned, the port is considered to be filtered.

  - **TCP XMAS scan**—Sorry, no Christmas presents here, just a port scan that has toggled on the FIN, URG, and PSH flags. Closed ports should return a RST.

- The third step is *OS identification*. Tools that fingerprint the OS can be passive or active. Passive tools sniff network traffic and make a determination of what type of

OS is generating the traffic. Passive identification requires a large amount of traffic but offers a level of stealth that is lacking in active tools. Active fingerprinting tools can be very accurate but can easily be detected by IDS systems. Active fingerprinting tools can craft packets and probe for responses by using the following:

- The FIN bit
- Various TTL options
- The TCP Win Size
- The Don't Fragment (DF) setting in the IP header
- Manipulating TOS settings

Each of the scanning tools is covered in detail next.

Nmap

Nmap (as shown in Figure 8.3) was developed by a hacker named Fyodor Yarochkin. This popular application is available for Windows and Linux as a GUI and command-line program. It is probably the most widely used port scanner ever developed. It can do many type of scans and OS identification. It also has the capability to do blind scanning, zombie scanning, and allows you to control the speed of the scan from slow to insane. Its popularity can be seen by the fact that it's incorporated into other products and was even used in the movie *Matrix*.

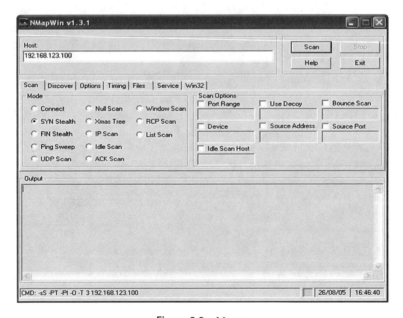

Figure 8.3   Nmap.

SuperScan

SuperScan is a Windows GUI-based scanner developed by Foundstone. It will scan TCP and UDP ports and perform ping scans. It will allow you to scan all ports, use a built-in list of defined ports, or specify the port range. As far as the price, it's free and offers great features if you are looking for a Windows GUI scanner. It's shown in Figure 8.4.

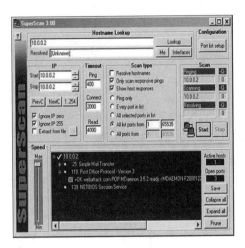

Figure 8.4 SuperScan.

Scanrand

Scanrand is part of a suit of tools known as Paketto Keiretsu developed by Dan Kaminsky. Scanrand is a fast scanning tool. What makes this tool so fast is that it uses a unique method of scanning TCP ports. Most TCP scanners take the approach of scanning one port at a time. After all, TCP is a stateful protocol, so traditional scanners must probe each port, wait for the response, store the connection in memory, then move on. Traditional scanning is a serial process.

Scanrand implements *stateless* scanning. This parallel approach to scanning breaks the process into two distinct processes. One process sends out the requests at a high rate of speed while the other independent process is left to sort out all the incoming responses and figure out how it all matches up. The secret to the program's speed is in its use of something called *inverse SYN cookies*. Basically, Scanrand builds a hashed sequence number that is placed in the outgoing packet that can be identified upon return. This value contains information that identifies source IP, source port, destination IP, and destination port. If you're tasked with scanning a large number of IP addresses quickly, this is something you'll want to check out.

Xprobe2

Xprobe 2 is an active operating system fingerprinting tool with a different approach to operating system fingerprinting. Xprobe2 relies on fuzzy signature matching. In layman's terms, this means that targets are run through a variety of tests. These results are totaled and the user is presented with a score that tells the probability of the targeted machine's OS—for example, 75% Windows XP and 60% Windows 2000. Xprobe is also unique in that it uses a mixture of TCP, UDP, and *ICMP* to slip past firewalls and avoid *IDS* systems.

THC-Amap

THC-Amap is another example of scanning and banner grabbing. One problem that traditional scanning programs have is that not all services are ready and eager to give up the appropriate banner. For example, some services, such as SSL, expect a handshake. Amap handles this by storing a collection of responses that it can fire off at the port to interactively elicit it to respond. Another is that scanning programs sometimes make basic assumptions that might be flawed. Many port scanners assume that if a particular port is open, the default application for that port must be present. Amap probes these ports to find out what is really running there. Therefore, this tool excels at allowing a security professional to find services that may have been redirected from their standard ports. One of the ways to use this program is by taking the greppable format of nmap as an input to scan for those open services. Defeating or blocking Amap is not easy, although one technique would be to use a *port knocking* technique.

Port Knocking—A Defensive Technique Against Scanning

Port knocking is a defensive technique that requires users of a particular service to access a sequence of ports in a given order before the service will accept their connection. Initially, the server presents no open ports to the network, but it does monitor all connection attempts. The service is triggered only after the client initiates connection attempts to the ports specified in the knock. During this knocking phase, the server detects the appropriate sequence and opens a connection when the knocking sequence is correct.

Although this technique may not be suitable for publicly accessible services, it could be used for applications that are available to only a limited number of users. It's also important to note that anyone who has the capability to sniff the network traffic will be in possession of the appropriate knock sequence. Finally, this technique does not harden the underlining application. If accessible, it may still be vulnerable to attack.

Want to Know More?

If, after this brief introduction to these tools, you would like to learn more, the best place to start is the vendors' websites. These URLs are provided next, as are several URLs that discuss port knocking and passive fingerprinting in-depth.

Port scanning basics—www.garykessler.net/library/is_tools_scan.html

Passive fingerprinting—http://project.honeynet.org/papers/finger/

Nmap—www.insecure.org

SuperScan—www.foundstone.com/resources/freetools.htm

Scanrand—www.lurhq.com/scanrand_dissected.pdf

Xprobe—www.net-security.org/article.php?id=540

TCH-Amap—http://thc.org/thc-amap/

Port Knocking—www.portknocking.org

Enumeration Tools

Enumeration is the process of gathering information from a system without logging on. It can be seen as an extension of the scanning process. Information that can be obtained from enumeration includes the following:

- Usernames
- Open shares
- Active Directory information
- Router information
- Device information

Although not all the tools and techniques are guaranteed to produce results, it is worth the time to investigate each of them. Services that can be used to target and enumerate Linux include finger, SNMP, SMTP, RPC, and TFTP. Many of the techniques used to target Windows rely on the weaknesses of the *null session*. The null session is the result of the Windows IPC$ (InterProcess Communications) share. This default share can be found on Windows NT, 2000, and XP. The purpose of the IPC$ share is to handle communication between applications located on one machine or distributed between two or more systems. There is quite a bit of information that can be leaked by probing this process. This can be done with an array of tools or manually by executing the following command:

C:\>net use \\IP_address\ipc$ "" /u:""

You'll be happy to know that there are ways to lock down the IPC$ share, which is what Microsoft attempted to do in Windows 2003 when it changed the default restrict anonymous setting. Linux can also be subjected to this type of enumeration if Samba is being used. Table 8.1 will give you some idea of what type of information can be extracted from the system running the default settings.

Table 8.1 **Enumeration**

Operating System	Enumerate Shares	Enumerate Usernames	Enumerate SIDs	Enumerate Running Services
Windows 2003 and XP	Yes	Yes	Yes	No
Windows 2000	Yes	Yes	Yes	No
Windows NT	Yes	Yes	Yes	Yes

SolarWinds IP Network Browser

Following is a technique that you would expect to fail, but we have been amazed at the number of times we have seen this tool enumerate information that shouldn't be available. SolarWinds IP Network Browser is a tool that probes Simple Network Management Protocol (SNMP) communication. SNMP version 3 offers data encryption and authentication, although version one, which is a clear text protocol, is still widely used. The key to SNMP is the community strings. SNMP uses both public and private community strings. Therefore, if they have not been changed or if they have and someone can sniff the traffic, they can then launch this tool effectively. Although the tool is not free, you can download a demo from the solarwinds.net website. A screen shot is shown in Figure 8.5.

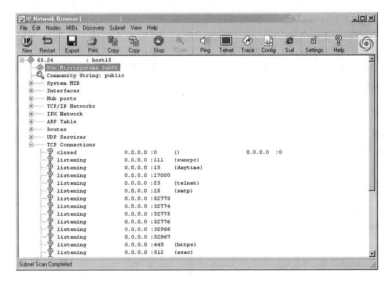

Figure 8.5 SolarWinds SNMP enumeration.

DumpSec

DumpSec is a Windows-based tool from SomarSoft. It allows you to remotely connect to Windows machines and dump account details, share permissions, and user information. It is shown in Figure 8.6. Its GUI-based format makes it easy to take the results and port them into a spreadsheet so that holes in system security are readily apparent and easily tracked.

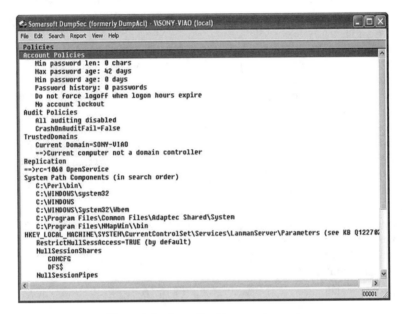

Figure 8.6   DumpSec Enumeration tool.

USE42

USE42 is a combination of three existing tools combined into a Windows GUI program. USE42 includes NBTscan, IPEye, and Enum. This combination of tools enables you to obtain a list of NETBIOS names, portscan a range of devices, pull down password policies, user account information, group information, and share details on Windows computers.

Want to Know More?

If, after this brief introduction to these tools, you would like to learn more, the best place to start is the vendors' websites. You can download the tools there as well as gather more information. Their URLs follow:

Windows Enumeration—http://www.sans.org/rr/whitepapers/windows/286.php

SolarWinds—www.solarwinds.com

DumpSec—www.somarsoft.com

USE42—www.inetcat.org/software

Wireless Tools

802.11 wireless connectivity is probably something you are going to want to look at during the assessment. Even if your organization is not officially using wireless, you will want to make sure that there are not any rouge wireless access points. Wireless networks have become popular because of their low cost and convenience. It's so much easier to plug in a wireless access point (WAP) than to run 1,000 feet of cable. Unfortunately, many end users who are moving to wireless still don't have any appreciation of the security measures they should employ.

Originally, 802.11 wireless was protected with Wired Equivalent Privacy (WEP). WEP encrypts data with the RC4 encryption algorithm. The key was limited to 40 bits. This provides a very limited level of encryption that is relatively easy to compromise. This weakness led to several changes in the industry. First, many WAPs began incorporating 802.1x into many wireless devices. 802.1x provides port-based access control. Second, the industry released WiFi Protected Access (WPA). WPA is much more secure because it uses Temporal Key Integrity Protocol (TKIP). In 2004, the IEEE approved the next upgrade to wireless security, which was WPA2. It is officially known as 802.11.i. This wireless security standard makes use of the Advanced Encryption Standard (AES). WAPs can now be found with key sizes of up to 256 bits, which is a vast improvement from the original 40-bit encryption WEP used. Now that you are primed to perform a wireless assessment, you'll need a few items for the task:

- **Software**—Discussed in the sections that follow. A nice collection is available on the Linux Auditor distribution.

- **Wireless card**—Prism and Orinoco chipsets offer the most compatibility with existing software.

- **External antenna**—You don't really want to go around holding that laptop over your head, do you? One popular choice is the cantenna from cantenna.com.

NetStumbler

NetStumbler is a Windows-based GUI tool that acts as a wireless scanner. It operates by sending out a steady stream of broadcast packets on all channels. It's useful for checking the coverage of an organization's wireless LAN. A screenshot is shown in Figure 8.7. It displays signal strength, MAC addresses, SSID, and integrates with GPS systems to facilitate mapping. MiniStumbler is a version of the software that is available for handhelds.

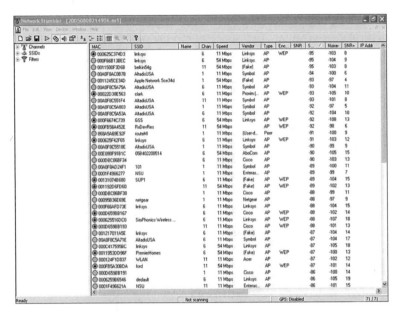

Figure 8.7   NetStumbler wireless capture.

Kismet

Kismet is a Linux-based 802.11 wireless sniffer that can monitor and sniff raw packets from wireless networks. Kismet can detect standard and hidden network names and doesn't analyze beaconing hidden networks. Kismet is useful for detecting rogue access points and can be used for site surveys.

LinkFerret

If you're looking for a Windows tool to handle a similar task, you'll want to consider LinkFerret. This commercial 802.11 network monitor and packet sniffer can also detect rogue assess points, provide signal monitoring for site surveys, and can perform WEP decryption. LinkFerret is an easy-to-use tool that will pay for itself very quickly.

WEP Cracking

If you are interested in cracking *WEP* and would like to see how strong the keys are, you'll want to consider the following tools. If the access point is vulnerable to this type of attack, you may be able to crack the WEP keys in a very short period of time. The tools are shown in their order of use:

1. **Airodump**—This program scans a *wireless network* for packets and captures these packets into files.

2. **Void11**—This program will deauthenticate wireless clients from the *wireless access point* and force them to reassociate to the AP, creating many ARP requests.

3. **Aireplay**—This program takes *ARP* requests generated by VOID11 and resends it to the AP, spoofing the ARP request from the valid wireless client.

4. **Aircrack**—Takes the captured files generated by airodump and extracts the WEP key.

Want to Know More?

If, after this brief introduction to these tools, you would like to learn more, the best place to start is the vendors' websites. You can download the tools there as well as gather more information. Their URLs are provided next. The first link in the list provides some useful information about cracking WEP.

Cracking WEP—www.tomsnetworking.com/Sections-article120-page1.php

Auditor—http://new.remote-exploit.org/index.php/Auditor_tools

NetStumbler—www.netstumbler.org

Kismet—www.kismetwireless.net

LinkFerret—www.linkferret.ws

Aircrack—www.cr0.net:8040/code/network/

Password Auditing Tools

Password auditing tools can test the strength of your passwords in one of three ways: dictionary, hybrid, and brute force attacks.

- Dictionary password cracking pulls words from a dictionary or word list to attempt to discover a user's password. A *dictionary attack* uses a predefined dictionary to look for a match between the encrypted password and the encrypted dictionary word. Many times, dictionary password audits will recover a user's password in a very short period of time. If passwords are well-known, dictionary-based words, dictionary tools will crack them quickly.

- A *hybrid attack* uses a dictionary or word list, then prepends and appends characters and numbers to dictionary words in an attempt to crack the user's password. These programs are comparatively smart because they can manipulate a word and use its variations. For example, take the word "*password*." A hybrid password audit would attempt variations such as 123password, abcpassword, drowssap, p@ssword, pa44w0rd, and so on. These various approaches increase the odds of successfully cracking an ordinary word that has had a little variation added in.

- *Brute force attacks* use random numbers and characters to crack a user's password. A brute-force audit on an encrypted password may take hours, days, months, or years, depending on the complexity and length of the password. The speed of success here will be dependent on the speed of the CPU's power. Brute force audits attempt every combination of letters, numbers, and characters.

Historically, the preceding three approaches were the primary methods that someone would use to test the strength of a password or attempt to crack it. Some passwords were considered secure because of the time it would take to crack them. The time factor was what made these passwords seem secure. Sure, it could be cracked, but who is going to spend a month trying. This theory no longer holds completely true. A relative new approach is to use a rainbow table. The RainbowCrack technique is the implementation of Philippe Oechslin's faster time-memory trade-off technique. It works by precomputing all possible passwords in advance. Once this time-consuming process is complete, the passwords and their corresponding encrypted values are stored in a file called the rainbow table. An encrypted password can be quickly compared to the values stored in the table and cracked within a few seconds. This should drive home the point that you should:

- Select and configure strong network authentication protocols.
- Protect password databases.
- Have a strong password policy, enforce it, and schedule awareness training and password audits.

Ophcrack

Ophcrack is a password cracking tool that implements the rainbow table techniques previously discussed. It has several tables that can be downloaded, or you can search the Web for others. What's most important to note here is that if a password is in the table, it will be cracked quickly. Their website also lets you enter a hash and reveal the password in just a few seconds. An example of this is shown in Figure 8.8.

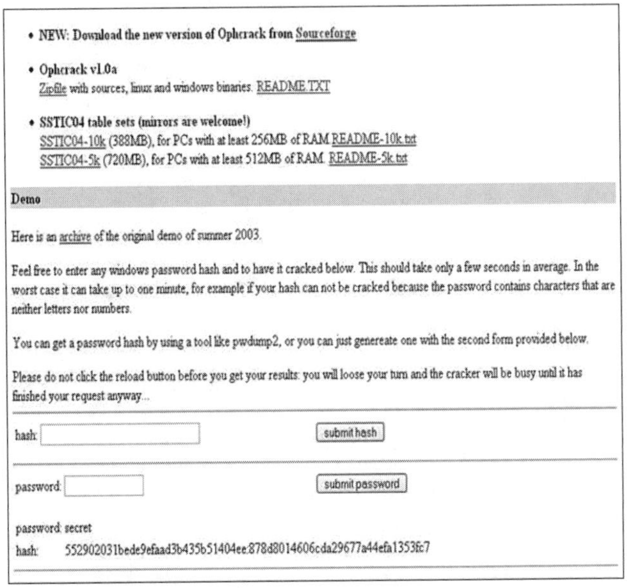

Figure 8.8   Ophcrack online password cracking.

John the Ripper

John the Ripper is a great password auditing tool. It is available for 11 types of Unix systems plus Windows. It can crack most common passwords, including Kerberos AFS and Windows NT/2000/XP/2003 LM hashes. There is also a large amount of add-on modules available for John that can allow it to crack OpenVMS passwords, Windows credentials cache, and MySQL passwords.

L0phtCrack

L0phtcrack was released way back in 1997 and became famous as the premiere Windows password cracking tool. Symantec now owns the rights to this tool, but it continues to be improved. LC5 is the current version. It can extract hashes from the local machine, a remote machine, and can sniff passwords from the local network.

Cain

Cain is a multipurpose tool that has the capability to perform a variety of tasks, including Windows enumeration, sniffing, and password cracking. Cain is shown in Figure 8.9. The password-cracking portion of the program can perform dictionary and brute force attacks and can use precomputer hash tables.

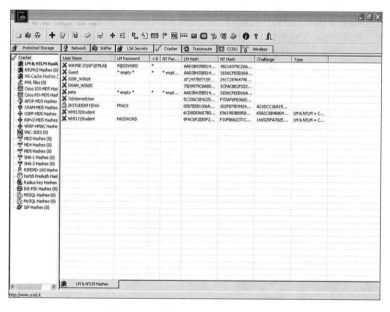

Figure 8.9 Cain password cracking.

Want to Know More?

If, after this brief introduction to these tools, you would like to learn more, the best place to start is the vendors' websites. You can download the tools there as well as gather more information at

Rainbow tables—www.antsight.com/zsl/rainbowcrack

Ophcrack—http://lasecwww.epfl.ch/~oechslin/projects/ophcrack/

John the Ripper—www.openwall.com/john

Cain and Abel—www.oxid.it

Vulnerability Scanning Tools

You'll find that there is no shortage of vulnerability assessment tools on the market. These tools can be used to scan internal or external computers for vulnerabilities. Some of these tools are commercial and may require an annual subscription, whereas others are open source and won't cost you anything to initially acquire. All of these tools can be broken into three basic categories:

- Source code scanners examine the source code of an application.
- Application scanners examine a specific application or type of application.
- System scanners examine entire systems or networks for configuration or application-level problems.

Source Code Scanners

Source code scanners can be used to assist in auditing security problems in source code. Many of these tools are available for free; Rough Auditing Tool for Security (RATS) and FlawFinder are two such tools. Source code scanners can detect problems such as buffer overflows, race conditions, privilege escalation, and tainted input. Buffer overflows allow data to be written over portions of your executable, which can allow a malicious user to do just about anything. Race conditions can prevent protective systems from functioning properly or deny the availability of resources to their rightful users. Privilege escalation occurs when code runs with higher privileges than that of the user who executed it. Tainting of input allows potentially unchecked data through your defenses, possibly qualified as already-error-checked information.

Application-Level Scanners

Application-level scanners are the next type of vulnerability scanner we will examine. Application scanners provide testing against completed applications or components rather than the source code. They scan applications for vulnerabilities that occur at runtime and they test such issues as user input and bounds testing. Application-level scanners aren't just useful for security testing either; the amount of time that you can save by using automated bounds-testing software and the like can be amazing. AppDetective is an example of one of these programs. AppDetective scans, locates, examines, reports, and fixes security holes and misconfigurations in database applications.

System-Level Scanners

The final category of scanners is system-level scanners, which are intended for probing systems and their components rather than individual applications. The scanners can be run against a single address or a range of addresses and can also test the effectiveness of layered security measures, such as a system running behind a firewall. Nessus is an example of a well-known system-level scanner.

The primary advantage of system-level scanners is that they can probe entire local or remote systems or networks for a variety of vulnerabilities. If you need to test a large number of installations, remote system-level scanners can be far more efficient than auditing the configuration of each machine individually. System scanners do have their disadvantages as well. For example, it is not possible to audit the source of the processes that are providing services. Additionally, scanning results have to rely on the responses of a service to a finite number of probes, meaning that all possible inputs cannot be reasonably tested. If the production environment of your organization is experiencing services unexpectedly coming online or going offline, you might run a system scanner to see if the cause of the problem can be detected. In another example, if the target system has been patched or experienced other recent upgrades, you might run a system scanner to double-check everything.

Probably most important, system scanners do not substitute for more thorough measures in that they are a part of the vulnerability assessment process, but not the sole component. They are intended to supplement other measures, such as secure architecture and design practices and decisions. Source code and application scanning should also be done where applicable. An in-depth vulnerability assessment consists of all the components we have discussed: information gathering, wireless surveys, password audits, source code scanners, application-level scanners, and system-level scanners. None can be substituted for another component.

Nessus

Nessus is an open source, comprehensive cross-platform vulnerability scanner with CLI and GUI interfaces. Nessus has a client/server architecture, with clients available for Unix, Linux, and Windows and servers available for Unix, Linux, and Windows (commercial). Nessus is a powerful, flexible security scanning and auditing tool. It takes a basic "nothing for granted" approach. For example, an open port does not necessarily mean that a service is active. Nessus tells you what is wrong and provides suggestions for fixing a given problem. It also supports many types of plug-ins, which range from harmless to those that can bring down a server. The plug-in menu is shown in Figure 8.10.

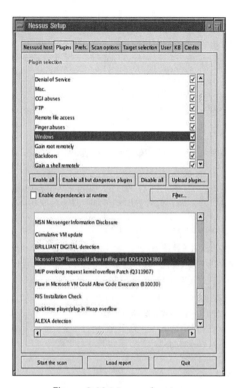

Figure 8.10 Nessus plug-ins.

SAINT

SAINT is a commercial application from Saint Corporation, providing industry respected vulnerability scanning and identification. It has a web-based interface and the deployment platforms for this product are Linux and Unix. It is certified CVE-compliant and allows you to prioritize and rank vulnerabilities to determine which critical security issues you should tackle first.

ISS Internet Scanner

ISS Internet Scanner is one of the products available from Internet Security Systems. Its deployment platform is Windows NT/2000/XP/2003. The package provides extensive vulnerability scanning and identification across network platforms and devices via CLI and GUI interfaces. It can identify more than 1,300 types of networked devices. After these devices have been scanned and identified, Internet Scanner can analyze their configuration, patch levels, operating systems, and installed applications. Then it can generate a report identifying vulnerabilities.

NetRecon

NetRecon is a commercial scanner produced by Symantec. It provides vulnerability scanning and identification with a unique, "cooperative" approach. NetRecon actually learns about the network as it scans it. If it finds and cracks a password on one machine, that password will be tried on others. The application has a GUI interface and its deployment platform is Windows NT/2000.

Retina

Retina is a commercial product from eEye Digital Security. It provides "gentle" vulnerability scanning across systems and network devices. Not only can it scan a class C network in about 20 minutes, it also discovers devices through wired and wireless connections. Retina has a GUI interface and its deployment platform is Windows NT/2000/XP/2003.

Security Auditor's Research Assistant (SARA)

SARA is a CLI and web-based GUI freeware application. Instead of inventing a new module for every conceivable action, SARA is adapted to interface to other open source products. For example, SARA works with NMAP and SAMBA to perform OS fingerprinting and SMB security analysis. It's considered a gentle scanner. The term *gentle* means that the scan does not present a risk to the operating network infrastructure. It's compliant with SANS Top 20, supports CVE references for identified vulnerabilities, and can be deployed on Unix, Linux, and Mac OS X.

Other Choices

A host of other scanners are available. Several are mentioned next:

- **VLAD**—An open source vulnerability scanner. Written in Perl, VLAD is designed to identify vulnerabilities in the SANS Top 10 list.
- **N-Stealth**—Another vulnerability assessment product that specifically scans web servers to identify security problems and weaknesses that might allow an attacker to gain privileged access.
- **LANguard**—A full service scanner that reports information such as the service pack level of each machine, missing security patches, open shares, open ports, services/application active on the computer, key Registry entries, weak passwords, users and groups, and more.

Want to Know More?

If, after this brief introduction to these tools, you would like to learn more, the best place to start is the vendors' websites. You can download the tools there as well as gather more information. Their URLs follow:

Nessus—www.nessus.org

SAINT—www.saintcorporation.com

ISS—Internet Scanner www.iss.net

NetRecon—www.symantec.com

Retina—www.eeye.com

SARA—www.arc.com

VLAD—www.bindview.com

Automated Exploit and Assessment Tools

If the tools you've seen so far have piqued your interest, you're bound to find the next three tools very interesting. These tools represent where vulnerability assessment tools are headed. Tools such as Nessus and others have had the capability to integrate scanning, assessing, and reporting functions. The tools described in the following sections take this functionality to the next step by tightly integrating the capability to exploit a suspected vulnerability.

Metasploit

Metasploit is an all-in-one exploit testing and development tool. Metasploit allows you to enter an IP address and port number of a targeted machine and run the chosen exploit against the targeted machine quite easily. This is an open source tool that can be compared to CANVAS and Core IMPACT. Metasploit was developed using Perl, C, and Python. It is available for Linux and Windows and is shown in Figure 8.11. It can have the victim connect back to you, open a command shell on the victim, or allow you to execute code on the victim.

Figure 8.11   Metasploit demo.

CANVAS

CANVAS is a tool developed by Dave Aitel of Immunity.com. It was written in Python so it is portable to Windows and Linux. It's a commercial tool that can provide the security professional with attack and penetration capabilities. Like Metasploit, it is not a complete all-in-one tool. It does not do an initial discovery, so you must add your targets manually. It's cleaner and more advanced than Metasploit but requires you to purchase a license. This does, however, provide you with updates and support. Overall, this is a first-rate tool for someone with penetration and assessment experience.

Core IMPACT

This is by far the most advanced of the three tools discussed here. Core IMPACT is a mature point-and-click automated exploit and assessment tool. It's a complete package that steps the user through the process starting at scanning and continuing through the exploit and control phase. One of its unique features is that it supports a feature known as pivoting. Basically, *pivoting* allows a compromised machine to be used to compromise another. This tool is useful for everyone from the novice to the seasoned security professional. Take a look at the interface shown in Figure 8.12.

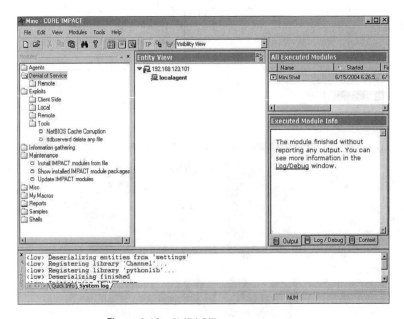

Figure 8.12 IMPACT target assessment.

Want to Know More?

If after this brief introduction to these tools you would like to learn more the best place to start is the vendors website. You can download the tool there as well as gather more information at:

Metasploit—www.metasploit.com

CANVAS—www.immunitysec.com/products-canvas.shtml

Core IMPACT—www.coresecurity.com

Determining What Tools to Use

Now that you've seen a few of the tools that can be used, it's time to start thinking about which ones you're going to use. A large part of this will be determined by what type of assessment you'll be performing. You will probably find that system-level scanners will be one of the most useful tools to use regularly. You'll also want to consider the disruption factor. For example, the analyst must determine what processes, both human and computer, must be put on hold during a VA scan. Certain scanning tools run intrusive scans that can disrupt network or computer systems as part of their operation. Many tools, however, can be automated. They can scan machines and networks and report their progress or generate a report when done, or both. With these tools, it is possible to perform scans in off hours, reducing or eliminating downtime. What degree of disruption, if any, the user can tolerate, is a big factor to be considered.

What's the Best Platform to Install Your Tools On

Not all the tools you'll collect will run on Linux and Windows. This raises the issue as to what the perfect test platform is. Setting up a laptop to use for assessment activities is a really good idea. It's portable and gives you the capability to take it where you need it. No matter if you're running a port scanner or *wardriving* for *rouge access points*, you'll be ready for action. There are several ways you can go about setting up the laptop to get maximum mileage.

- Set the machine up as dual boot. Load Windows and your favorite flavor of Linux on the machine; you can switch between OSs as needed.
- Use a virtual machine. VMWare and VirtualPC both offer you the capability to run both OSs at the same time. This is the preferred method of choice because you can quickly move between each OS.

Additional Items for the Toolkit

After reviewing this chapter, you should have some idea of what's needed to put together your own toolkit; however, there will be a few other items you'll want to add to round out your toolkit. Items such as Excel spreadsheets, documentation forms, and so on will also help you not only collect, verify, and validate your findings, but also ease the burden of implementing change. Having implemented some type of patch management system will also help. Clearly, if you're conducting a vulnerability assessment, the capability to capture, organize, review, and assess data and information in a tabular, checklist manner is critical. This allows you to examine your data and information and make recommendations based on your IT security goals and objectives.

Summary

Tools don't fix problems. They can only identify problems—and then, only the ones that are known. Security tools are important and help to address security issues in your networks and the environment, but you can't stop there. Any given tool can produce false positives, false negatives, or simply wreak havoc on your network. You need to plan to use these tools at the appropriate time, and you will also need a remediation plan to address how discovered problems will be addressed.

The vulnerability assessor must be trained in the use of the tools, use them carefully, and then interpret any information that has been produced by that tool. Finally, you should never use these tools on a network unless you have been given explicit permission in writing to do so. You run the risk of being considered a Black Hat, you may face legal penalties, and anyway, it is simply polite to ask.

Key Terms

Active fingerprint   An active method of identifying the OS of a targeted computer or device.

File type   Search for non-HTML file formats including .pdf, .doc, .ppt, and others.

Gentle scan   A type of vulnerability scan that does not present a risk to the operating network infrastructure.

IANA   A primary governing body for Internet networking. IANA oversees three key aspects of the Internet: top-level domains (TLDs), IP address allocation, and port number assignments. IANA is responsible for preserving the central coordinating functions of the Internet for the public.

Internet Control Message Protocol (ICMP)   Part of TCP/IP that supports diagnostics and error control. Ping is a type of ICMP message.

Intitle   If you include [intitle:] in your query, search engines such as Google will restrict the search to documents containing the specified word or phrase in the title.

Intrusion Detection System (IDS)   IDS systems inspect all inbound and outbound network activity and identify suspicious patterns or unusual types of traffic that may indicate a network or system is under attack or being probed.

Inverse SYN Cookies   A method for tracking the state of a connection that takes the source address and port, along with the destination address and port, and puts them through a SHA-1 hashing algorithm. This value becomes the initial sequence number for the outgoing packet.

Matrix   A movie about a computer hacker who learns from mysterious rebels about the true nature of his reality and his role in the Matrix machine. A favorite movie of hackers.

Null session   A Windows feature where anonymous logon users can list domain user-names, account information, and enumerate share names.

OS identification   The practice of identifying the operating system of a networked device through either passive or active techniques.

Passive fingerprint   A passive method of identifying the OS of a targeted computer or device.

Port knocking   Port knocking is a defensive technique that requires users of a particular service to access a sequence of ports in a given order before the service will accept their connection.

Ports   Ports are used by protocols and applications. Port numbers are divided into three ranges: Well Known Ports, Registered Ports, and the Dynamic and/or Private Ports. Well Known Ports are those from 0 through 1023. Registered Ports are those from 1024 through 49151, and Dynamic and/or Private Ports are those from 49152 through 65535.

Rogue access point   An 802.11 access point that has been set up by an attacker for the purpose of diverting legitimate users so that their traffic can be sniffed or manipulated.

Sniffer   A hardware or software device that can be used to intercept and decode network traffic.

SNMP   An application layer protocol that facilitates the exchange of management information between network devices. Version one uses well-known public and private community strings.

TCP handshake   A three-step process computers go through when negotiating a connection with one another. The process is a target of attackers and others with malicious intent.

Transmission Control Protocol (TCP)   One of the main protocols of IP. It is used for reliability and guaranteed delivery of data.

User Datagram Protocol (UDP)   A connectionless protocol that provides very few error-recovery services, but offers a quick and direct way to send and receive datagrams.

Wardriving   The act of driving around in a vehicle with a laptop computer, an antenna, and an 802.11 wireless LAN adapter to find and possibly exploit existing wireless networks.

Wi-Fi Protected Access (WPA)   A security standard for wireless networks designed to be more secure than WEP. Developed from the draft 802.11i standard.

Wired Equivalent Privacy (WEP)   Based on the RC4 encryption scheme. It was designed to provide the same level of security as that of a wired LAN. Because of 40-bit encryption and problems with the initialization vector, it was found to be insecure.

9

Preparing the Final Report

ALTHOUGH THE HANDS-ON PORTION of the assessment is complete, you still have a report to write. You also have data to analyze. This chapter discusses one method you can use to accomplish this. This step of the assessment is just as important as the scoping and the hands-on activities. Before you start thinking that you're going to take on this work by yourself, remember that your team can be as big an asset here as they were during the previous assessment activities.

Maybe you're thinking, "Hey, people aren't fired for being poor report writers." Maybe not, but don't expect to be promoted or praised for your technical findings if the report doesn't communicate your findings clearly. The post-assessment report should present the results of the assessment in an easily understandable and fully traceable way. The report should be comprehensive and self-contained. Because this is such an important topic, we'll spend time in this chapter discussing what should be in the final report and how you can format this document. Let's get started!

Preparing for Analysis

Now that you are ready to dig into the data, use the skills and abilities of your team to help formulate solutions. Get the team involved. As project manager, you will be responsible for the report and its overall look and feel. Individual team members can be given responsibility for portions of the report. Assign them to the areas that they worked in or to a task that fits with their strengths. Working as a group, they can also help you analyze the findings and develop risk-ranking scores. When meeting with the team, the project manager should set the agenda. Encourage all team members to take an active role and offer input. Remind the team to stay focused on what is best for the organization. When it is time to write the report, you should also set deadlines for each team member's individual assignments, follow-ups, or additional information that you've requested. One way to work through the bulk of the findings as a team is by using a three-tiered approach:

1. Multimodal (Brainstorm)—As you review your findings and discuss specific problems, let the group come up with possible solutions. Much of the analysis is qualitative, so it is open to discussion. During this free flow of information, don't

discount any ideas or opinions. One approach is to list each possibility on a white-board.

2. Bimodal (Evaluate)—Now that the team has provided you with many possible solutions, go through the list and narrow it down to the few that really seem possible.

3. Unimodal (Decide)—Maybe more than one solution will work, but you'll need primary solutions and recommendations. You might consider dividing the solutions into three categories: good solutions, cheap solutions, and quick fixes. This helps the organization to maintain some flexibility when trying to budget the needed improvements.

The organization may not be able to implement all the items you recommend, so target the ones with the highest risk/highest probability. To help stay focused on what's important, keep in mind the organization's OICM and SCM. These matrixes identified what was critical for the organization's mission.

Ranking Your Findings

During the assessment, you may have discovered potential problems that will need to be presented to management in a structured order. This can be done by calculating a *risk score*. A risk score gives us a way to quantify our findings and determine a prioritized list of what is most important. The risk score takes into account two key items: *raw risk* and *policy control*.

> **Tip**
>
> Raw risk has two basic components, which are *probability* and *impact*. What's probability? It is the likelihood of an event happening. Impact can be best defined as an attempt to identify the extent of the consequences should a given event occur. If you multiply the probability by the impact, you can get a raw risk score that is easy to chart.
>
> *Probability * Impact = Raw Risk*

Policy control is an analysis of the current state of the organization's policies. This has been discussed throughout the book—good policies are a real requirement. Policies that are deficient or nonexistent will factor heavily into our final calculations. The real objective here is to use raw risk and policy control to develop a risk ranking. This risk ranking can be used to group potential risk. It gives us a way to identify high-impact, high-probability risks, as seen in Figure 9.1. This is the area where management should concentrate on improving policy control.

This methodology assigns a numerical value to both the raw risk and policy control. This is not an exact science and is quite subjective. Let's continue this discussion by reviewing the first variable in the raw risk formula: impact.

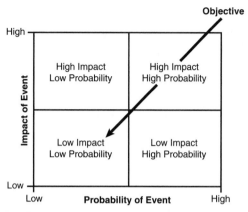

Figure 9.1   Impact and probability matrix.

Caution

Calculating impact and probability is highly subjective, so it's important to work with your team as you work through your analysis. Their input and judgment can be of help here. Make sure to clearly document your thought process so those reviewing the final report can see how you arrived at specific findings.

Impact Rating

As previously stated, impact ratings are highly subjective. The following scale is based on a numeric scale of one to three. For your analysis, you may decide that a scale of one to five should be used. In the end, this is just a method of gauging potential damage. The larger the scale, the more granular the results. We like a one-to-three scale because it is easy to work with and users relate well to a high, medium, and low scale. When discussing impact, you are basically asking what the potential damage is if a particular risk becomes a problem. Our three-tiered scale defines damage as follows:

- High (3)—Significant loss of revenue, core business process significantly affected, permanent loss of customers

- Medium (2)—Some loss of revenue, core business processes somewhat affected, customers upset with loss of service or outage

- Low (1)—No loss of revenue, but inconvenient; work around if possible so that core business process continues, customers unaware or unaffected by loss of service or change in service

Other criteria can be used or added to the preceding descriptions as needed. Overall, what's important is to classify your findings in a consistent manner.

Probability Scale

Although we have no way of being able to actually predict what potential risks may become a problem, the capability to determine the probability can help us quantify the risk. Probability is seeking to answer what the likelihood is of a particular risk becoming a problem. For our calculations, we will again use a scale of one to three to measure probability.

- High (3)—Significant probability of occurrence
- Medium (2)—Some possibility of occurrence
- Low (1)—Low probability of occurrence

Note

Does the scale have to be one to three? Of course not, you could just as easily use a probability scale of one to five. If this is what you decide to do, be sure to clearly quantify each level and be consistent with its use.

Determining Raw Risk

We have now discussed impact and probability. They are the two components of raw risk. With these values established, we can now calculate raw risk. Remember the formula

Probability ★ Impact = Raw Risk

Because both impact and probability have three potential levels, there are a total of nine values. These nine values are divided as follows:

- Low —1 to 3
- Medium—4 to 6
- High—7 to 9

This means that a raw risk rating from one to three is considered low, four to six is ranked as medium, and seven to nine is a high ranking. Although the rankings are evenly distributed, after we place these into a matrix, something becomes apparent that may not have been easily discernable before. Table 9.1 displays these results.

Table 9.1 **Raw Risk Rankings Matrix**

		Low	Medium	High
PROBABILITY	(MULTIPLIER)	1	2	3
High	3	3 – Low	6 – Medium	9 – High
Medium	2	2 – Low	4 – Medium	6 – Medium
Low	1	1 – Low	2 – Low	3 – Low

What you can see by looking at Table 9.1 is that there is only one instance where it is possible to get a high rating. Only a high-probability, high-impact event will result in a high raw risk rating. What is great about this is that a high rating is not diluted. Most findings should not have a high rating. This score should be reserved for only the most urgent and important findings. After a raw risk ranking is calculated, the resulting value along with a policy control level can be used to determine priority.

Before we move on to that step, let's review what has been discussed so far. This is best accomplished by plugging some numbers into our equations and discussing the results. For example, let's assume that during the assessment, it was determined that proper media controls were not in place. Interviews with the cleaning staff revealed that sensitive documents were thrown in the trash and were not properly disposed of. During a walk-through inspection of several areas, you noticed that there were no paper shredders. One of your team members also volunteered to do a little dumpster diving and later presented some documents with sensitive information; others had client information, and even a credit card number was found.

These findings led you and your team to believe that there is a probability of a "3" that a loss of confidential information could have occurred. Your team has also reached the conclusion that if this had happened, the impact probably would not put the organization out of business, but could result in embarrassment, loss of income, or a loss of customers. As such, the team has rated impact as a "2."

Probability $\star$ *Impact* = *Raw Risk* (or) *3* $\star$ *2* = *6*

Control Level

With the raw risk ranking calculations complete, we can move to our second set of calculations. The purpose of this set is to examine the state of the organization's policies and examine the effect this has on our findings thus far. Policy controls are one of the most important security mechanisms. Earlier in the book, we identified three categories of control and 18 classes, as shown in Table 9.2.

Table 9.2   **Categories and Classes of Policy Control**

Management	Technical	Operational
INFOSEC documentation	Identification and authentication	Media controls
INFOSEC roles and responsibilities	Account management	Labeling
Contingency planning	Session controls	Physical environment
Configuration management	Auditing	Personal security
	Malicious code protection	Education training and awareness
	Maintenance	
	System assurance	
	Networking Connectivity	
	Communications security	

Although there are many different states that each of these 18 individual policy classes can exist in, they have been divided into three for ease of analysis. These three states are defined as follows:

- Ratings of "1" should be assigned to policies that are developed and in place but that lack enforcement or are not completely followed. Little work would be required to achieve a level of compliance.

- Ratings of "2" should be assigned to policies that are existent but are somehow deficient. The deficiency can be by any number of factors: It simply hasn't been kept up to date; it may require employees to be trained, or may even require additional technologies to fully implement or correct.

- Ratings of "3" are for situations where no policy exists. A 3 is the highest rating and would be used either when there is no policy or the existing policy is completely out of date or completely fails to address the security risk.

This scale, like the previous two, is highly subjective. Although three possibilities are used here, you could just as easily use a scale with five distinct levels. Other criteria can be used or added to the preceding descriptions as needed. This examination of where we are versus where we need to be is a form of *gap analysis*. Overall, what's important here is to classify your findings in a consistent manner that is documented so that individuals reviewing your findings can follow the process and determine how you arrived at your results.

Calculating the Risk Score

Now let's talk a little about how the risk scale is calculated. The risk score formula is as follows:

*Risk Score = Raw Risk * Level of Control*

How do risk score ratings compare to those of raw risk? There were a total of nine possibilities in our raw risk matrix and three levels of policy control; therefore, the risk score matrix has a total of 27 possibilities. By dividing these into categories of low, medium, and high, we are left with the following values:

- Low—1 to 9
- Medium—10 to 18
- High—19 to 27

The matrix displaying these values can be seen in Table 9.3. As with the raw risk rating matrix, here again it can be seen that the hardest rating to achieve is high risk. A high-risk rating should be used for only the most critical findings.

Table 9.3 **Risk Score Matrix**

Raw Risk		1	2	3
High	9	Medium – 9	Medium – 18	High – 27
	8	Low – 8	Medium – 16	High – 24
	7	Low – 7	Medium – 14	High – 21
Medium	6	Low – 6	Medium – 12	Medium – 18
	5	Low – 5	Medium – 10	Medium – 15
	4	Low – 4	Low – 8	Medium – 12
Low	3	Low – 3	Low – 6	Low – 9
	2	Low – 2	Low – 4	Low – 6
	1	Low – 1	Low – 2	Low – 3

Let's continue this discussion using the previous example of raw risk that resulted in a "6"—medium raw risk rating. During that discussion, we determined that a lack of adequate media controls could pose a risk to the organization. Our findings indicate that there is a media control policy, but because there were no shredders in all locations and users had not been trained to practice effective media control and destruction, the policy was deficient. This led the team to a decision that the level of control be ranked as a "2." *Risk Score = Business Impact × Level of Control or 6 * 2 = 12*

These values would lead us to a final risk score of "12." This correlates to a medium threat value.

The risk score helps quantify the risk discovered during the vulnerability assessment. It also gives you a way to present your findings to management in a way that they can relate to. You should step them through the methodology used to reach your conclusions. Educating them helps them understand how you reached each risk score.

Building the Final Report

With the analysis complete, it's now time to document the results in an official report. The final report is designed to be read by senior management. Its purpose is to help them make operational, technical, and managerial changes. The report should describe threats and vulnerabilities and provide recommendations for controls to reduce risk. The finished document should not read like an audit or investigational report, because that is not what it is. An assessment is a systematic, analytical methodology to assessing vulnerabilities. It is not looking for wrongdoing or to hold individuals accountable for specific actions.

To document your findings and propose solutions, make sure to give those who will be reading the report enough information to make a decision and take action. Writers with a traditional, scientific background often write very precisely, whereas those from other backgrounds sometimes have a more fluid style. No matter what your background is, establish a style that is concise in its approach but allows for more descriptive paragraphs when needed. The last thing you want is for your assessment to not be taken seriously because of a problem with the written report. Common documentation problems include the following:

- Information is hard to scan and grasp quickly.
- Organization is poor or cumbersome.
- Logic leading to conclusions is unclear.
- Conclusions and recommendations are not spelled out.
- Document focus is unclear.
- Sentences are poorly constructed.
- Word choice is imprecise.
- Too much jargon is used.
- Document is poorly constructed.
- Documents are too long.

Avoiding these pitfalls will help ensure that your report gets the time and consideration it deserves. You goal is to communicate effectively the knowledge and information that you have gained by performing this assessment. From a technical context, this report has two major goals:

- It clarifies your findings for the reader.
- It conveys critical information.

Contents of a Good Report

Reports such as the one you are about to prepare put information in an order that enables the reader to reach logical conclusions. The vulnerability assessment should include the following sections:

- Notice
- Executive summary
- Introduction
- Statement of work
- Analysis
- Findings
- Conclusions

Notice

Include a short statement about the confidentiality of the report, such as something similar to the following: "This report contains confidential and proprietary information. Reproduction of this document or unauthorized use is prohibited."

You will want to include this statement on the cover of the report as well as a privacy statement in the footer of each page. After all, you are holding a report that clearly details the organization's vulnerabilities. Although not required, you may also consider including a table of contents. This helps the readers navigate the document. Anything you can do to make the report easier to read will help with its acceptance.

Executive Summary

The section is designed to give the reader a high-level overview of the vulnerability assessment in one to two pages. Executive summaries usually include the following:

- Introduction
- Statement of work performed
- Results and conclusions
- Recommendations

It previews the main points of your report, enabling readers to build a mental framework for organizing and understanding the detailed information in your document. Like it or not, some individuals will not read the entire report. This section will likely be the one that is the most read.

Introduction

The introduction portion of the report is the section that should list all the background information. It should state the purpose of the assessment. Was the assessment performed because of regulatory requirements, due diligences, or in response to a negative event, and so forth. It should also discuss the organization's mission and what information and systems are deemed critical to meet the mission. Finally, it should introduce the team and discuss the skills and expertise that qualified them to perform this assessment.

Statement of Work

This section of the report should contain an overall description of the organization's IT infrastructure and what systems were assessed. It is, in essence, the *methodology*. It defines the scope of work, tasks, and deliverables that you have agreed to produce in the original scoping document. This section should also include network diagrams, system descriptions, physical and logical layouts, and details about users, locations, and third-party connections.

Note

A picture is worth a thousand words. By adding network diagrams, system descriptions, physical and logical layouts, and other diagrams, your readers will have a much better understanding of the network infrastructure.

This is the location where you'll want to include the OICM and SCM. These are the matrixes you developed to establish critical information types and critical systems. For example, suppose the organization being examined is a state agency. This state agency maintains 10 branch offices and has approximately 2,000 employees. Each of the 10 branch offices connects back to the main office for connectivity to services and to access the Internet.

Modernization has become a big driving concern for the state. The agency has made great strides in automating project bidding. The agency has installed systems that manage the bid process and inform the winning company of its selection as the primary contractor. Most projects are performed by contractors, so one of the agency's primary roles is to prepare and maintain project schedules. A discussion with senior state agency officials helped determine the following critical system and information. The agency's OICM is shown in Table 9.4, and its SCM is shown in Table 9.5.

Table 9.4   **Organizational Information Criticality Matrix**

Information type	Confidentiality	Integrity	Availability
Internal documents	Medium	Medium	Low
Customer data	High	Medium	Medium
Contracts	High	Medium	Low
Employee	Medium	Medium	Low
High watermark	**High**	**Medium**	**Medium**

These findings demonstrate that contracts and customer data rank high for the agency. The high watermark is for the confidentiality of this information.

Table 9.5   **System Criticality Matrix**

System type	Confidentiality	Integrity	Availability
Engineering	Low	Medium	Medium
Human Resources	Medium	Medium	Low
Projects	Medium	Medium	Medium
DMZ/Internet	Low	Medium	High
High watermark	**Medium**	**Medium**	**High**

A review of the state agency's SCM shows that availability is the most important system trait. Ideally, these findings should point the team to systems and information that should receive the most in-depth review.

Analysis

This section of the report lists what you found and how you found it. This is the current state of the network. You will want to discuss items of concern that were discovered during the assessment. Because this section follows the statement of work, it should build on what you did during testing. The results of your tests and examinations should be discussed. Overall, this section should stay focused on the importance of security to the organization. It is important to remember to keep your findings balanced. Organizations are not all good nor bad, and the findings shouldn't be either. Comment on what the company is doing right. Even if something hasn't been implemented as a policy but you find one person or department that has developed a method for doing something right, point out this process. Give that person or department praise and even suggest the company use that as a standard. It is good practice to emphasize the good security practices the organization can use to leverage additional security focus for their organization.

If you are not 100% sure about certain findings but believe your findings are correct or require further analysis, you may still include your ideas but you should use words such as "these findings suggest that" or "we are fairly confident that," and so on to indicate the lack of full evidence.

The organization of this material is really your choice. Our preference is to organize it by the 18 classes and categories shown earlier in Table 9.2 or to organize it by impact to the organization. Continuing with the example described in the statement of work, the state agency's documentation was analyzed and ranked as shown in Table 9.6.

Table 9.6 **Risk Scores**

Category	Raw Risk Rating	Total Risk Score
INFOSEC documentation	Low	Low
INFOSEC roles and responsibilities	Low	Low
Contingency plans	Low	Low
Configuration management	Low	Low
Identification and authentication	Medium	Medium
Account management	Medium	Low
Session controls	Low	Low
Auditing	Low	Low
Malicious code protection	Low	Low
Maintenance	Low	Low
System assurance	Low	Low
Networking connectivity	Medium	High
Communications security	Medium	Medium
Media controls	Medium	Medium
Labeling	Medium	Low
Physical environment	Low	Low
Personal security	Low	Low
Education training and awareness	Low	Low

Findings

This section represents the core of this document. It provides detailed recommendations for minimizing the risks that the organization faces. The recommendations must derive logically from the conclusions, be supported both by the conclusions and the data in the discussion, be complete and clearly worded, and be worded so that either a positive or negative response is possible. Give the organization more than one option or possible solution to each vulnerability.

- **Good**—Best option, most expensive. For example, one unit of the organization has direct connection to the Internet through a router. There is no firewall in place. Buying and installing a Cisco PIX would be a good solution to this potential vulnerability. It would also allow services such as HTTP and SMTP to be moved to a DMZ.

- **Cheap**—Mid-level option, less expensive. Using the preceding example, a cheaper solution may be to install a server with Linux IPTables and use it as a proxy to filter ingress and egress traffic. Not as expensive as PIX—Linux is free—but it would require someone with the knowledge and skill to set it up and occasionally monitor.

- **Fast**—Quick and dirty solution, provides a temporary patch. Continuing with the preceding example, you could suggest that an ACL be added to the router. Although it would not provide stateful inspection, it would add additional protection over what is present now.

Your recommendations should be ranked in the order of their critical importance. Items to include in this section of the report include

- Findings
- Category
- Impact
- Details
- Countermeasures

So, how does our example organization fare here? A review of the data from the analysis section indicates that the following six items had medium to high ratings:

- **Identification and authentication**—A review of the identification and authentication policies revealed that although the overall policy structure is acceptable, web users are being authenticated using *base64*. Although good policy has been developed that requires users to identify themselves, it is also important how the user is identified. Base64 authentication over the Web works by prompting the user for a username and password. This information is then transmitted across HTTP, where it is scrambled using Base64 encoding. The key here is that base64 is a coding process, not an encryption process. Because of this, base64 authentication is inherently insecure. It is easy to decode base64 encoded data, so in reality, base64 authentication is essentially sending the password as plain text. Someone would have to sniff the traffic to capture the authentication. This may be somewhat difficult, but by no means is it impossible. The impact of lost authentication credentials could affect the organization, so it is recommended that this method of authentication be replaced with an alternative challenge response protocol such as NTLM. The time and effort involved in this change is minimal.

- **Account management**—We found account management policies to be acceptable. However, during system demonstrations and the interview process, it was discovered that user accounts were not being removed as policy requires when employees leave or move to other departments. It was also discovered that employees were not having old privileges removed when they transferred to other departments. This has resulted in a type of *access creep* in that some employees now have potentially more access than their duties require. This situation could be rectified by providing additional policy training to the IT employees who are responsible for the account management duties.

- **Network connectivity**—Network connectivity policies were found to be deficient. Policy did not clearly define what was allowed and what was not allowed. Some third-party vendors are allowed access to the internal network with few controls and although there is a firewall in place, the rule set is not well defined. These issues could potentially threaten the organization and have been deemed a major risk. We recommend that the individuals responsible for the firewall receive training to better configure it. Also, as an immediate stop-gap measure, some additional controls can be put in place by implementing an *ACL* on the external routers to filter and control traffic.

- **Communication security**—Communication security can be improved by implementing *IPSec* or other technologies to protect data transmissions that may contain sensitive customer information or financial information. Employees who currently access the organization's network offsite do so by dial-in. VPNs should be considered to secure these communications.

- **Media controls**—Although the organization does have media controls in place, there are existing policies that are not being followed. Some dumpster-diving activities during the assessment found sensitive documents that should not have been thrown into the trash. An immediate patch would be to inform employees of existing media control polices, but a more complete solution should include the placement of shredders in all work areas.

- **Labeling**—Directly tied to the media control findings are the issues discovered with labeling. Some of the documents that were discovered to be improperly disposed of were not properly labeled. Interviews indicated that some individuals were confused about labeling and how certain types of documents should be handled and labeled. Revising these policies and providing training to employees could help this situation.

> **Security Baselines**
>
> If you happen to find yourself recommending that an entire security baseline be developed, it's good to
> know that you do not have to take on this task by yourself. SANS and the Center for Internet Security (CIS)
> have developed the SCORE project for just this task. *SCORE* (Security Consensus Operational Readiness
> Evaluation) is a broad-based project that has developed minimum standards and best practice information
> that has been benchmarked for general use by industry at large. Checklists have been developed on every-
> thing from Windows OS, Linux OS, generic web applications, routers, firewalls, and even handheld devices.
> You can take a look at their work by checking out www.sans.org/score.

Conclusions

This section of the report should serve as a wrap-up. It should offer the overall security
stance of the organization and offer a discussion of the benefits of good security practices. The conclusion is the final impression. It is the last opportunity you have to get
your point across to management and leave the reader feeling as if he or she learned
something and is ready to take action. Leaving a paper dangling without a proper conclusion can seriously devalue what was said in the report. Avoid this pitfall.

For our sample organization, what's most important is to address the issues involving
network connectivity. Customer data and contracts could be accessed by individuals who
don't have the need to know, thereby endangering the confidentially and integrity of
these informational assets. Because systems in the *DMZ* and those that contain project
data were ranked as most critical, controls should be put in place to ensure their confidentiality, integrity, and availability.

Determining the Next Step

At this point in the project, you should take a moment to thank everyone who has been
involved. It is important that all members of the team go their separate ways feeling as
positive as possible, knowing that they helped contribute to the bettering of the overall
security of the organization. It may be appropriate to hold a final meeting at which you
thank everyone for their contributions and express enthusiasm that they all played a part
in building a more secure organization. Based on the findings, some of these same individuals may be involved in implementing controls to improve security.

Finally, don't forget that trade-offs must sometimes be made between business objectives and security. Your job here is to make recommendations. Management is ultimately
responsible for determining what is right. These trade-offs may not always be resolved in
favor of security; management must make the decision to accept risk. For example, your
findings might indicate that e-commerce activities put the organization at a greater risk
of attack or denial-of-service. However, this may be weighed against data that indicates
the organization may have a 60% growth in profit by doing business over the Web.
Therefore, management may decide to accept the risk because there is such a high
potential for added growth and revenue. In the end, there is always a trade-off between
security and usability, as shown in Figure 9.2.

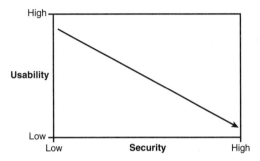

Figure 9.2   Security and usability trade-off.

Accidents, errors, and omissions account for much higher losses than deliberate acts. Some studies indicate that more than 60% of information losses are caused by accidents. Only 35 to 40% are deliberate acts. Of this percentage, most of this activity can be traced to internal sources. That's right—the people you have the most to fear are those closest to you! Therefore, controls that reduce the potential for these harmful effects of insiders should always rank on your list of recommendations. Building good policies and policy enforcement mechanisms is critical. Security against deliberate acts can be achieved only if a potential perpetrator believes there is a definite probability of being detected.

Audit and Compliance

Because security is a process, there is still more work to be done. The recommendations that management accepts will mean more work and more challenges. Each of these solutions has to be applied. Each of these must also be authenticated, tested, and will require reverification of the security posture of your site.

Over time, security policies will become fully implemented and enforced. The real concern then changes from implementing security policies to maintaining them. It's easy to become lax at this point, and if that occurs, policies will start to become obsolete and out-of-date. The real focus will be on compliance and audit. If you're interested in seeing how your polices rank against IOS 17799, the Human Firewall Council has a tool to help you with this task. It is available at http://www.humanfirewall.org/smi/. The Human Firewall Council is a group of professionals who have come together to help educate organizations and individuals on the human issues involved in information security.

Summary

You and your team are near the end of the assessment process. Although there are still some changes to implement, most of the assessment has been completed. This phase started with an analysis of the findings. This was a good opportunity to involve your team in the process and use their input. Just as they were valuable in helping perform the assessment, their skills can be useful in preparing the final report. Hopefully, you have focused attention on the organization's critical systems and information that were identified earlier on in the assessment.

With this information, you will still need a way to rank your findings. Two qualitative tools were introduced here to help in this process. The first was a raw risk score. It can be calculated by multiplying probability times impact. The resulting value can then be used to calculate a total risk score. The risk score is obtained by multiplying raw risk times the level of control. The level of control is the contributing factor that existing policy has on raw risk. Good polices help hold down raw risk, whereas poor policies amplify it.

A total risk score was calculated for each of the 18 categories of policies that were originally introduced in Chapter 5, "Scoping the Project." This provided a way to document the findings so that they are easy for management to digest. The result of this work was compiled into the final report. The report not only serves to document what was performed, but how it was performed and what the findings were. These findings should have focused on remediation efforts that could be implemented quickly and inexpensively and also on solutions that may cost more in time and effort but will provide better long-term security.

> **Note**
>
> Not all recommended controls and solutions will be implemented. Some may not be feasible because of time, cost, technical requirements, or the will of senior management.

What should have been most important about the process is that it served as a learning experience—a chance to learn about the organization, determine the systemic causes that led to vulnerabilities, and solve deficiencies with improved policy, procedures, and training. After all, security is a continuous process that builds on lessons learned. Otherwise, as George Santayana said, "Those who cannot learn from the past are condemned to repeat it."

Key Terms

The following acronyms and terms are used in this chapter. For the explanation and definition purpose of this chapter, these acronyms and terms are defined as follows:

Access creep   The result of employees moving from one position to another within an organization without losing the privileges of the old position but gaining the additional access of the new position. Thus, over time, the employee builds up much more access than he or she should have.

ACL   A table or list stored by a router to control access to and from a network by helping the device determine whether to forward or drop packets that are entering or exiting it.

Base64   A coding process that is used to encode data in some email applications. Because it is not true encryption, it is easily cracked.

DMZ   The middle ground between a trusted internal network and an untrusted, external network. Services that internal and external users must use are typically placed there, such as HTTP.

Gap analysis   The analysis of the differences between two different states, often for the purpose of determining how to get from point A to point B; thus, the aim is to look at ways to bridge the gap.

Impact   Best defined as an attempt to identify the extent of the consequences should a given event occur.

IPSec   Short for IP Security, an extended IP protocol that enables secure data transfer. It provides services similar to SSL/TLS.

Methodology   A set of documented procedures used for performing activities in a consistent, accountable, and repeatable manner.

Policy control   An analysis of the current state of the organization's policies.

Probability   The likelihood of an event happening.

Raw risk   The result of a formula used to calculate risk and vulnerability. IT is calculated as follows: Probability $\star$ Impact = Raw Risk.

Risk score   A way to analyze raw risk. It is calculated by multiplying probability by impact.

SCORE (Security Consensus Operational Readiness Evaluation)   A broad-based project that has developed minimum standards and best practice information that has been benchmarked for general use by industry at large.

Total risk score   A way to analyze total risk. It is calculated by multiplying the raw risk score by the level of control.

10

Post-Assessment Activities

POST-ASSESSMENT ACTIVITIES DEAL WITH REVIEWING the project's summary of findings, assessments, and recommendations that are crafted from the IT infrastructure's risk and vulnerability project final report. Typically, the risk and vulnerability assessment uncovers a multitude of issues, concerns, and security voids inherent in the organization's IT infrastructure and assets. These issues, concerns, and security voids are then assessed based on the organization's defined business drivers, goals, and objectives in parallel with the prioritization or importance of the identified IT systems, applications, and resources that support the organization's business processes and functions.

In many cases, organizations are subject to industry compliancy laws as described in Chapter 3, "Why Risk Assessment." These new compliancy laws define the framework for how organizations are to conduct risk and vulnerability assessments and how an organization must have properly defined security controls, processes, and procedures. As described in Chapter 4, "Risk Assessment Methodologies," conducting a top-down approach for risk and vulnerability assessments requires an existing IT security architecture and framework to be in place. This architecture and framework acts as the yardstick of measurement for how the assessor is to conduct a risk and vulnerability assessment based on a defined set of security controls, processes, and procedures. Many organizations quite simply lack adequate IT security architectures and frameworks that are needed to manage IT infrastructures and IT assets and maintain appropriate levels of confidentiality, integrity, and availability.

This common void is typically the most important post-assessment activity, to create, define, document, and communicate an organization's IT security architecture and framework that may be missing or that has gaps, thus exposing the IT infrastructure and its assets to risk caused by threats and vulnerabilities that are not being addressed by the organization at a policy level. This chapter will define what an IT security architecture and framework is and how it acts as the road map for an organization's overall information security strategies for risk mitigation. Finally, this chapter will discuss how to deal with security breaches and incidents and how to distribute the overall information security roles, responsibilities, and accountabilities throughout the IT infrastructure and the

IT professionals who must now incorporate proper security controls and practices as part of the organization's overall strategy for security of the IT infrastructure and its assets.

IT Security Architecture and Framework

An IT security architecture and framework is a term used to describe an organization's documented information security policies, standards, procedures, and guidelines. Many organizations, after conducting their first risk and vulnerability assessment, come to the immediate realization that they have put little or no effort into the overall security design of the IT infrastructure and its assets. Many organizations still do not have written information security policies, standards, procedures, and guidelines. This can be a frightening realization because the results of a risk and vulnerability assessment project typically are used as the basis for the organization's follow-up business continuity and disaster recovery plans. Executive management is now faced with tough decisions pertaining to information security priorities identified in the assessment report's findings, assessment, and recommendations section. Tactical and strategic recommendations for risk mitigation and enhancing the level of security in the areas that were identified as missing or inadequate must now be prioritized based on risk and exposures identified.

The final assessment and recommendations report for a risk and vulnerability assessment must spell out specifically what new or updated policies, standards, procedures, and guidelines must be documented and adopted throughout the organization to get the organization in alignment with the defined security controls. Many organizations find themselves with serious gaps or voids in their defined and documented security controls. Because of this, it is critical to define in the final assessment and recommendations report what the organization's goals and objectives are for an IT security architecture and framework.

Goals and Objectives

Each organization is unique, but they all share a common foundation in that they need defined goals and objectives for their own IT security architecture and framework. Following are some common goals and objectives for an IT security architecture and framework that an organization may consider:

- To be in compliance with new industry laws, mandates, and regulations that require defined and documented security controls. Properly defined security controls must be documented and implemented throughout the organization, depending upon the requirements of the new law, mandate, or regulation.

- To define a minimum level of acceptable risk for the organization in the seven areas of information security responsibility. This minimum level of acceptable risk must be clearly defined so that the proper security controls can be defined for each area and the IT assets that reside in that area of responsibility.

- To define a comprehensive suite of information security policies that allows the organization to ensure that the confidentiality, integrity, and availability for the IT infrastructure and IT assets is not compromised.

- To demonstrate that information security policies can be used as a powerful proactive tool for running and securing an organization's IT infrastructure and IT assets, thus cost justifying annual funding and support from executive management for information security initiatives.

- To align the organization's minimum acceptable level of risk with the organization's information security policies, standards, procedures, and guidelines.

- To be relevant to the business issues, business drivers, and priorities of the organization in regard to how information security is to be deployed and managed by the organization.

- To be all encompassing for the entire organization with executive management support at the highest level and information security awareness for all employees.

- To be easy to read, understand, and implement under the guidance of the IT organization's chief security officer or designated appointee responsible and accountable for the IT security architecture and framework.

Terminology

When describing an IT security architecture and framework, it is important to define the terminology, definitions, and the hierarchy that will be used throughout this chapter. These terms and definitions are common to IT security architectures and frameworks:

- **Compliance**—There are two kinds of compliance: legal or regulatory compliance as required by new information security laws, mandates, and regulations; and departmental and employee compliance with an IT organization's IT security architecture and framework.

- **Exceptions**—Any exceptions to defined policies, standards, procedures, or guidelines will be listed and described for situations that are beyond the control of the information security organization or beyond the scope of the policy or standards definition.

- **Guidelines**—Guidelines are suggested courses of action to be taken in reference to a policy, standard, and procedure.

- **Procedures**—A procedure defines instructions for installing, monitoring, auditing, or maintaining a particular information security policy, standard, or technical standard.

- **Policy**—An authoritative document supported by executive management that defines how an organization will implement the goals and objectives of the policy in an effort to protect the organization's IT infrastructure and IT assets.

- **Requirements**—Requirements are the elements of a standard, whether it is an actionable item or a technical definition or description for how information security hardware, software, or configurations are to be implemented in the IT infrastructure.

- **Standard**—A document that defines a common organizational method or approach as an actionable item to a specific policy. A standard represents the elements of a policy that must be followed to ensure the confidentiality, integrity, and availability of the IT infrastructure and its assets.

- **Technical standard**—A document that defines configurations and what hardware and software are authorized to connect and operate on the organization's IT infrastructure. A technical standard refers to the use and implementation of specific hardware, software, and/or configurations for information security customer premise equipment (CPE) based on predefined technical requirements that must be adhered to throughout the IT infrastructure.

Defining the Structure and Hierarchy

How an IT organization structures and documents its policies, standards, procedures, and guidelines requires careful analysis and design. Information technology and security personnel responsible for managing and maintaining the IT infrastructure's security must clearly understand the duties, tasks, roles, responsibilities, and accountabilities. One such information security policy structure was defined by the META Security Group, now part of the Gartner Group through acquisition. This information security policy structure is based on the following five foundational elements:

- **Risk Management Basis**—Creation of the organization's information security policies is driven by risk management and the mitigation of risks to threats and vulnerabilities. This aligns the IT security architecture and framework to the IT infrastructure's defense-in-depth strategy to combat against threats and vulnerabilities.

- **Hierarchical Policy Structure**—A hierarchical structure allows for clear and concise definitions and keeps the policy high-level, where the standards, procedures, and guidelines are more detailed and can define the roles, responsibilities, and accountabilities of IT security professionals and IT staff.

- **Guideline Definition**—A guideline provides a framework for how the information security policies and standards are to be implemented throughout the IT infrastructure and organization. These guidelines in turn provide the flexibility and roadmap for how a department within an organization is to implement the policies and standards.

- **Threat and Vulnerability Policies**—Risk management must address threats and vulnerabilities through the creation of policies that address these issues directly. Organizations must have specific threat and vulnerability policies to properly combat against the risks that are inherent with IT infrastructures and assets.

- **Policy Interpretation**—Policies are not open to interpretation and must be consistent and understood by all departments in an organization. Any discrepancies or exceptions to the IT organization's policies must be reviewed and assessed uniquely by the Change Control Board and in accordance with the organization's

Change Management Policy or the Chief Security Officer or equivalent party responsible and accountable for the organization's overall information security.

When creating a structure and hierarchy for an IT security architecture and framework, it is best organized from a risk management perspective because it aligns the policies, standards, procedures, and guidelines specifically to mitigate risk caused by threats and vulnerabilities to the IT infrastructure and its assets. The results of the IT organization's risk assessment will form the foundation for what policies, standards, procedures, and guidelines are needed to ensure the confidentiality, integrity, and availability of the organization's IT infrastructure and assets. The recommended information security architecture and framework should be based on the risk management goals and objectives that are aligned with the organization's business drivers, priorities, and requirements. Risk is a function of threat, vulnerability, and asset value and exists if a threat can exploit an actual vulnerability and adversely impact an IT asset or data asset. It is important to note that risk can never be completely eliminated; however, it can be managed through proper security controls, measures, and frameworks for securing the IT infrastructure and its assets.

The risk management approach to information security involves identifying, assessing, and appropriately mitigating vulnerabilities and threats that can adversely impact the organization's IT infrastructure and assets. This risk management approach for an IT security architecture and framework is depicted in Figure 10.1.

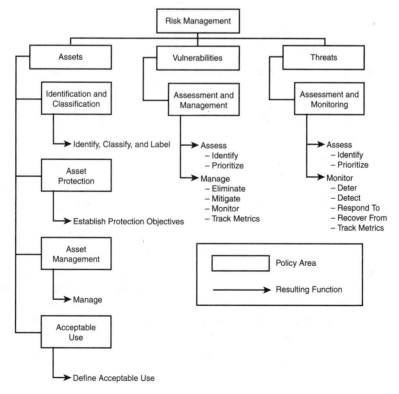

Figure 10.1   Risk management and relationship to threats and vulnerabilities.

Classifying IT Assets

Under this risk management approach, IT assets, threats, and vulnerabilities are juxtaposed so that risk mitigation can be addressed for known threats and vulnerabilities to the IT assets currently owned by the organization. IT assets can be classified, for example, into priorities such as Critical, Major, and Minor. A critical IT asset is the most important to the organization and a minor IT asset is the least important to the organization.

By classifying IT assets, an organization can identify its mission-critical IT assets first and prioritize its information security countermeasures and investments second. This type of prioritization is commonplace in organizations that have a limited budget for information security initiatives or must prioritize the design and deployment of information security controls and security countermeasures because of limited resources and funds.

Classifying Data Assets

Another example of asset classification or categorization is the creation and implementation of a *data classification standard*. A data classification standard requires an organization to define categories for its information assets, thus creating the need for different levels of security for those data assets throughout the IT infrastructure based on its classification and where it is located in the IT infrastructure. The following is a sample data classification standard that classifies and categorizes requirements for information security for the data itself.

Sample Organizational Data Classification Standard

SECRET: This classification applies to data that is required by law, mandate, statute, or regulation and is sensitive in nature, requiring special precautions to prevent unauthorized viewing. Unauthorized disclosure of this data carries a critical threat to the organization or the owner of the data. Disclosure of data in this category must be made by the data owner in accordance with defined policies as defined by the data owner. Users who use and access SECRET data require the IT infrastructure to have the utmost in information security controls from where the SECRET data is housed, transported through the IT infrastructure, and ultimately where the end user accesses this data.

CONFIDENTIAL: This classification applies to data that is sensitive in nature, which requires special precautions to prevent unauthorized viewing but is not required by law, mandate, statute, or regulation. Unauthorized disclosure of this data carries a major threat to the organization or the owner of the data. Disclosure of data in this category must be made by the data owner in accordance with defined policies as defined by the data owner. Users who use and access CONFIDENTIAL data require the IT infrastructure to have an appropriate level of information security controls from where the CONFIDENTIAL data is housed, transported through the IT infrastructure, and ultimately where the end user accesses this data.

INTERNAL USE: This classification applies to information that is intended for use within the organization only. Although data in this category is not protected by statute, its disclosure could adversely impact the organization, its business partners, and/or its customers. Disclosure of data in this category must be made by the data owner and in accordance with defined policies defined by the data owner. Users who use and access INTERNAL USE data require the IT infrastructure to have an appropriate level of information security controls from where the INTERNAL USE data is housed, transported through the IT infrastructure, and ultimately where the end user accesses this data.

PUBLIC USE: Data in this classification can be disclosed to anyone for any reason without any negative impact to the organization, its business partners, and/or its customers. Users who use and access PUBLIC USE data typically do not require any information security controls to secure or protect this kind of data with the exception of where the PUBLIC USE data is housed and how it is transported through the IT infrastructure before it leaves the organization's IT infrastructure. Examples of PUBLIC USE data include websites and the informational content typically found on nonsecured websites that users can freely access. Access to secured informational content on websites may require end users to fill in personal or privacy information, thus requiring the owner of the website to use web encryption techniques, such as SSL-128 bit encryption, to protect the confidentiality of the end user's privacy information prior to transport over the public Internet.

After a data classification standard is defined for an organization, the appropriate asset protection goals and objectives can be defined in accordance with the different classifications or categories. IT asset protection goals and objectives can then be aligned properly. After these goals and objectives are defined, appropriate levels of information security techniques and technologies can be designed to provide the level of security needed to support the data classification standard. After these information security techniques and technologies are purchased and implemented by the organization, asset management can take place. Management of IT assets and information assets can commence through the creation and implementation of sound asset management procedures and guidelines.

Finally, the creation and deployment of acceptable use policies for the organization's IT assets and information assets can be defined. They should be monitored and managed by the IT organization's information security personnel responsible and accountable for ensuring that its policies, standards, procedures, and guidelines are followed. This risk management approach to mitigating threats and vulnerabilities is depicted in Figure 10.2 and represents a continuous life cycle to properly mitigate risk.

Hierarchical IT Security Architecture and Framework

By creating and implementing a hierarchical IT security architecture and framework, an organization can align and link policies with the organization's risk management strategy that incorporates standards, technical standards, procedures, and guidelines. Figure 10.3 depicts this hierarchical policy structure that allows for organized and clearly defined goals and objectives so that the organization can implement and enforce them throughout the IT infrastructure. Through the defining of a hierarchical structure, elements at lower levels in the framework are directly linked with the risk management strategy and business objectives of the organization.

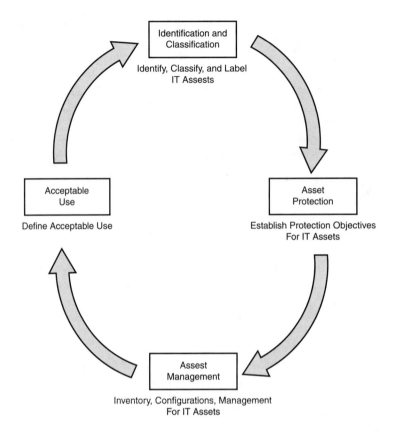

Figure 10.2   Risk management approach to mitigating threats and vulnerabilities.

This hierarchal IT security architecture and framework structure consists of the following elements:

- The organization's IT security architecture and framework must include goals and objectives for securing the IT infrastructure and its assets.

- At the highest level, information security policies are required to define what information security goals and objectives are to be addressed and handled by the organization.

- In support of the information security policies, standards and technical standards are required that provide for measurable or auditable guidance in each policy area. Note that a policy can have more than one standard associated with it.

- For proper implementation, procedures and guidelines are required that describe how to implement the standards and technical standards.

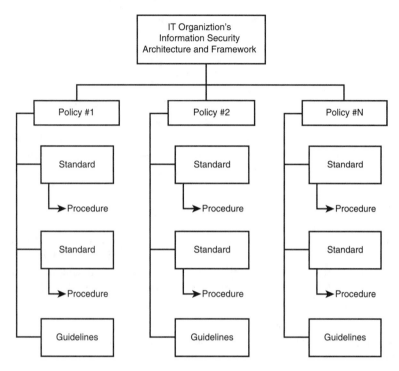

Figure 10.3   Hierarchical IT security architecture and framework structure.

Sample IT Security Architecture and Framework

Information security policies are created to provide a universal definition for how the IT infrastructure and assets must be implemented with solution-specific standards, procedures, and guidelines as defined by the organization. A typical IT security architecture and framework based on risk management includes the following elements at the policy definition level:

- **Asset Identification and Classification**—The organization's IT assets and resources must be appropriately documented, labeled, inventoried, and categorized according to the asset identification and classification specifications and parameters defined in each of the referenced standards.

- **Asset Protection**—The organization's IT assets must be protected based on the defined standards, procedures, and guidelines to ensure the confidentiality, integrity, and availability of the organization's IT assets and resources.

- **Asset Management**—The organization's IT assets must be properly managed with established procedures and guidelines to ensure the confidentiality, integrity, and availability of the organization's IT assets and resources. Asset Management includes Change Control Procedures and Guidelines as defined by the Change Control Board of the organization.

- **Acceptable Use**—The organization's acceptable use policies require all employees, contractors, and third parties to read, sign, and comply with the organization's Acceptable Use Policies (AUPs). AUPs are typically drafted to encompass Internet access, Internet etiquette, electronic mail usage, and access to the organization's IT resources, systems, and assets prior to gaining access.

- **Vulnerability Assessment and Management**—The organization's IT infrastructure and assets must undergo a vulnerability assessment as per the defined policies of the organization. In addition, management policies must be periodically assessed to properly identify and prioritize technical, organizational, procedural, administrative, or physical security weaknesses to maintain the confidentiality, integrity, and availability of the organization's IT assets.

- **Threat Assessment and Management**—Threat assessment and management must be implemented within the seven areas of information security responsibility in an effort to take a proactive role in the monitoring and containment of threats from unauthorized users who access the organization's IT infrastructure and assets.

- **Security Awareness and Training**—The organization's employees, contractors, and third parties must participate and take the information security awareness training program to ensure proper understanding of the policies, standards, procedures, and guidelines for the organization.

This risk-management-based IT security architecture and framework is depicted in Figure 10.4.

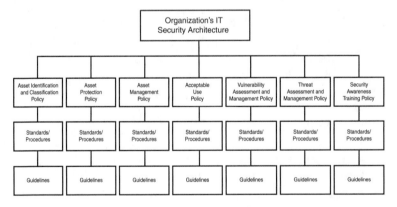

Figure 10.4   Risk-management-based IT security architecture and framework.

Roles, Responsibilities, and Accountabilities

Change is not an easy process for IT organizations, especially when that change pertains to the security of IT infrastructure components and deals with end users. Implementing change and getting acceptance or buy-in for the roles, responsibilities, and accountabilities for information security is paramount. This is critical because of the *separation of duties*, given the seven areas of information security responsibility. This separation of duties is the result of a *defense-in-depth* approach to securing the IT infrastructure, where the duties, tasks, roles, responsibilities, and accountabilities are distributed in a layered fashion across the organization. Security controls, procedures, and guidelines must be fully understood to mitigate risk.

The staffing and information security expertise that is needed to support the roles, tasks, responsibilities, and accountabilities throughout the IT infrastructure encompasses many areas in information technology. The seven areas of information security responsibility require full cooperation and understanding of each person's responsibilities and accountabilities in the information security chain of defense. Many organizations lack the experience and expertise in information security and are forced to either get the proper training or obtain assistance from consultants to fulfill the new roles, tasks, responsibilities, and accountabilities. To adequately address the information security requirements of an IT organization, specific expertise in the seven areas of information security responsibility is required:

- **User area**—This area refers to the organization's acceptable use policies (AUPs) and that employees, consultants, contractors, and third parties must sign the AUPs to be granted access to the organization's IT resources.

- **Workstation area**—This area refers to the end user's desktop devices, such as a computer, VoIP telephone, or PDA device. Workstation devices require a significant amount of vulnerability and software patch management to maintain the integrity of the device.

- **LAN area**—This area refers to the physical and logical local area network technologies (for example, 100Mbps switched Ethernet, 802.11 family of wireless LAN technologies) used to support workstation connectivity to the organization's network infrastructure.

- **LAN-to-WAN area**—This area refers to the organization's internetworking and interconnectivity point between the LAN and the WAN network infrastructures. Routers, firewalls, demilitarized zones (DMZs), and intrusion-detection systems (IDS) are commonly used as security monitoring devices.

- **Remote access area**—This area refers to the authorized and authenticated remote access procedures for users to remotely access the organization's IT infrastructure, systems, and data.

- **WAN area**—Organizations with remote locations require a wide area network connection. Organizations typically outsource WAN connectivity from service providers for end-to-end connectivity and bandwidth. This area typically includes routers, circuits, switches, firewalls, and equivalent gear at remote locations.

- **Systems/applications area**—This area refers to the hardware, operating system software, and application software. IT servers, systems, applications, and data assets are typically hosted in a data center and/or in computer rooms.

Tip

Many organizations require information security staff augmentation or outsourced, managed security services because of a lack of qualified information security resources. Training internal employees in information security or hiring information security consultants is certainly one way to obtain some information security knowledge. This strategy coupled with outsourcing managed security services is commonplace given the complexity of information security. Today, many organizations outsource elements of their information security responsibilities to managed services providers who specialize in outsourced security monitoring and assessment services.

Seven Areas of Information Security Responsibility

Specific to these seven areas of information security responsibility are the following requirements for IT personnel regarding roles, tasks, responsibilities, and accountabilities:

User Area

- **Roles/Tasks**—This area pertains to granting authorized access to the organization's IT infrastructure, resources, and assets for employees, contractors, and other third parties who must review, sign, and execute the organization's AUPs for Internet access, email usage, and access to the organization's computer resources.

- **Responsibility**—The responsibility for obtaining the appropriate AUPs prior to commencing any work and access to the organization's IT infrastructure, resources, and assets lies with the organization's human resources department.

- **Accountability**—The organization's human resources department is typically accountable for obtaining, verifying, and auditing each employee's, contractor's, or other third party's properly submitted AUPs and agreements.

Workstation Area

- **Roles/Tasks**—This area pertains to maintaining and updating user workstations and devices (hardware, software, firmware, operating systems, software patches, memory, and so on) that are authorized and approved for access and connectivity to the organization's IT infrastructure. Specifically, workstation operating systems, antivirus software updates, and other workstation configuration standards must be kept current and validated to maintain the integrity of the end user's workstation. Workstation client software used for remote access and security is also part of this area.

- **Responsibility**—The responsibility for maintaining and updating the user workstations and devices is the responsibility of the IT support personnel for that department or the IT organization's workstation technicians. Technology standards must be followed to maintain the integrity of the organization's workstations.

- **Accountability**—Each department's IT manager or the IT organization's director of desktop technology will be held accountable for verifying, validating, and updating the organization's workstation configurations, identifying gaps or deficiencies, and ensuring that any deficient workstation, operating system, software patches, and antivirus software updates are updated and made compliant to the IT organization's policies and standards.

LAN Area

- **Roles/Tasks**—This area pertains to the physical local area network infrastructure elements, wiring, hubs, switches, wireless access points, and the physical connection to the departmental or building local area network systems. In addition, this area pertains to the logical workstation-to-LAN connection via an authorized logon UserID and password for access to the departmental LAN server. This is also typically the first level of authentication required for end users to access the organization's IT infrastructure.

- **Responsibility**—Maintaining, updating, and providing physical connectivity for workstation devices to a departmental LAN system is the primary responsibility of the IT organization's LAN or networking department. This responsibility includes the workstation wiring, LAN hub or switch port access, and physical connectivity or wireless access point connectivity to the departmental or system LAN server. Maintaining, updating, and providing ongoing support for LAN server system administration is the responsibility of the respective IT organization's LAN system administrators or LAN managers.

- **Accountability**—The accountability for maintaining, updating, and providing ongoing technical support for the LAN area and complying with the IT organization's policies and standards pertaining to LAN and network technology lies with the IT organization's director of LAN or network technology.

Remote Access Area

- **Roles/Tasks**—This area pertains to the organization's end users who must remotely access the IT infrastructure via an authenticated connection through the Internet, dial-up, or other means of connectivity (for example, authorized users from home or other remote location). In addition, this area pertains to the logical workstation-to-network connection via an authorized logon UserID and password for access to state-owned resources and systems. Remote workstations that require client software for VPN support and/or intrusion-detection monitoring are also part of this area.

- **Responsibility**—The responsibility for defining the security requirements and standards for authorized remote access resides with the IT organization's WAN department. Remote access responsibilities include implementing, maintaining, updating, and providing ongoing support for remote access system administration, authentication, and availability.

- **Accountability**—Accountability for defining and evaluating remote access standards and technologies, as well as implementing, supporting, and ensuring that the IT organization's policies and standards are followed, lies with the director of WAN or network technology.

LAN-to-WAN Area

- **Roles/Tasks**—This area pertains to the router, firewall, and intrusion detection monitoring device (if applicable) that interconnects the LAN to the WAN. Router configuration, firewall configuration, design of a DMZ, system monitoring, intrusion detection monitoring, and ongoing system administration for the router, firewall, and intrusion detection system are part of this area.

- **Responsibility**—The responsibility for the IT organization's routers, configuration, and maintenance resides within the WAN department. The responsibility for all firewall configuration and monitoring and intrusion detection devices resides with the IT organization's IT security department (if applicable); otherwise, this responsibility typically resides with the WAN department.

- **Accountability**—The accountability for maintaining, updating, and providing ongoing technical support for routers, firewalls, and intrusion-detection monitoring and ensuring that this area is in compliance with the IT organization's policies and standards lies with the director of IT security or the director of WAN or network technology.

WAN Domain

- **Roles/Tasks**—This area pertains to the wide area network that is to be deployed throughout the organization to interconnect its remote sites to a common network infrastructure. The wide area network comprises backbone circuits, NAP and POP switches, routers, firewalls, and end site devices (routers, CSU/DSUs, codecs, and so on) that will be installed at identified end-site locations.

- **Responsibility**—Typically, a service provider provides the wide area network connectivity and in some cases a completely outsourced wide area network including CPE equipment and the management of the WAN and CPE equipment. If this is the case, *Service Level Agreements* (*SLAs*) are commonly used to define the service provider's responsibilities as they pertain to network bandwidth, performance, and the confidentiality, integrity, and availability of the WAN. Service providers typically provide a single point of contact as well as escalation procedures for circuit failures and outages. The IT organization's director of WAN or network technology is usually responsible for managing the relationship with the service provider.

- **Accountability**—The accountability for managing the WAN service provider lies with the IT organization's director of WAN or network technology. The service provider, through documented SLAs, is responsible for maintaining, updating, and providing ongoing technical support, monthly network management reports, and SLA guarantees for all circuits, switches, routers and firewalls (outsourcing the configuration and management of firewalls may apply). Review of these monthly reports is the responsibility of the IT organization's director of WAN or network technology.

Systems/Applications Domain

- **Roles/Tasks**—The systems and application area consists of hardware, systems, application software, database software, and data. This area includes hardening the operating system software, configuring the servers and applications, and implementing security countermeasures. This domain typically encompasses all server platforms (mainframe, Unix, and Microsoft), as well as systems and applications that reside in the IT organization's data center.

- **Responsibility**—The IT organization's systems and application system administrators and applications developers are responsible for maintaining and managing the hardware and systems software for the organization's production systems and applications. This responsibility includes establishing tools and techniques for ensuring the confidentiality, integrity, and availability of the hardware and systems software.

- **Accountability**—The accountability for the organization's production systems and applications lies with the director of systems and the director of application development. The accountability for security of the systems and applications typically lies with the director of IT security and the data owner. The accountability for the production system's and application's compliancy to the IT organization's policies and standards lies with the director of LAN or network technology.

Many IT organizations are struggling to augment or educate their current IT staff in information security practices, procedures, and guidelines. Traditional IT job descriptions are being expanded to include the roles, tasks, responsibilities, and accountabilities unique for information security. In some cases, organizations are creating entire IT security departments within their existing IT organization. Other organizations put the IT security department outside of the IT organization and have them report directly to the chief security officer (CSO) and not the chief information officer (CIO). Training and certifying IT professionals in information security is paramount. Without the proper background, knowledge, and experience in information security, creation and implementation of an IT security architecture and framework is a difficult task. In addition, training the end users to be more security conscious is not an easy task and requires constant reminders and education to bring the security consciousness of the organization to a consistent level.

Security Incident Response Team (SIRT)

Many organizations are not prepared to deal with security breaches and security incidents. One of the most important post-assessment activities is to define how the organization will handle security breaches and security incidents. This requires preplanning and an understanding of how to handle the situation and physical evidence in the event that the organization pursues criminal charges. Assessment and management of threats must be identified and prioritized for the organization's IT assets and data assets. After threats are identified for the organization's IT assets and data assets, monitoring the security of the IT infrastructure, IT assets, and data assets can be defined and implemented. Monitoring threats requires documented operational procedures that specify how security and network management personnel are to examine system audit logs, review intrusion detection system logs, and react to security breaches or incidents. Reaction or response to real-time security breaches or incidents is typically handled by the organization's internal Security Incident Response Team (SIRT).

Security Incident Response Team (SIRT)

Security Incident Response Team (SIRT)—This responsibility is the equivalent of a security Tiger Team that will take full responsibility for addressing and handling all critical security breaches and incidents that are logged and identified by the organization's Network Operations Center (NOC) or Security Operations Center (SOC). Given the nature and sensitivity of critical security breaches and incidents, the SIRT shall have full authority and jurisdiction to pull resources and obtain information from any of the seven areas of information security responsibility or end users and their workstations directly if the security breach or incident was conducted by an internal employee.

The SIRT's primary role and responsibility is to lead the efforts of a consolidated SIRT response effort for identified and documented critical security breaches and incidents. This responsibility is a 24×7×365 operational and support task that must be reactive to critical security breaches and incidents as they occur. Typically, the SIRT will not be called upon unless a critical security breach or security incident is identified and documented by the organization's NOC or SOC.

SIRTs are usually composed of an organization's IT and IT security personnel, human resources, legal, the data owner, and executive management. Typically, organizations require that the SIRT members sign a Confidentiality Agreement to maintain the privacy of the SIRT data collection and information gathering, especially if the incident is of a criminal nature and conducted by an internal employee. It is recommended that the SIRT team be led by the organization's IT security department or designated officer or official given their expertise in handling forensic analysis and conducting such an investigation. SIRTs typically are given the highest authority and responsibility to pull one designated resource from each of the seven physical domains as deemed necessary, depending upon the scope of the security breach or incident. Executive management support and approval to pull these designated resources together for the SIRT team is required. Refer to Appendix E for a sample SIRT Incident Report template.

SIRTs are required to conduct forensic analysis, maintain the integrity of the breached IT asset or systems, and provide assistance with law enforcement and legal officials to collect evidence and data needed to conduct an investigation. In some cases, criminal charges are warranted if the security breach or incident is in violation of a law, mandate, statute, or regulation.

SIRT Response Procedures

An important post-assessment task is to define an appropriate SIRT response procedure for the organization. The following is a sample procedure definition for an organization's SIRT. This procedure definition is typically implemented to handle critical security breaches and incidents such as a new virus spreading rapidly throughout the IT infrastructure. These procedures are as follows:

1. A security breach or incident is called into the NOC or SOC on which the trouble ticket is classified as CRITICAL.

2. For all CRITICAL or MAJOR security breach/incident trouble calls, document and describe the problem on the trouble ticket and provide the necessary contact information for the affected end users or IT assets.

3. Page the SIRT team leader immediately upon logging of the trouble call and creation of the trouble ticket and inform the team leader of the incident.

4. The SIRT team leader is to identify the scope of the security breach or incident and immediately contact the necessary SIRT team participants depending on the scope of the problem, if deemed necessary. If any non-SIRT team members are required, ensure that the new participant completes the Confidentiality Agreement prior to involvement. The SIRT team leader must create a preliminary action plan based on the nature of the security breach or incident.

5. The SIRT team leader is to contact the CSO/CIO/CEO and inform him/her of the nature and scope of the CRITICAL or MAJOR security breach or incident and review the preliminary action plan prior to commencement.

6. The SIRT shall commence with a security incident response based on the guidelines presented in the SIRT report. This may or may not require physically or logically disabling the system or servers that are affected. During the investigation period, the SIRT must document everything based on known information under the assumption that the data collected could be used as evidence in a court of law. The SIRT must be careful not to alter, taint, or manipulate the IT assets that the security breach or incident affected.

7. After the incident, the SIRT must prepare a security incident report with relevant details, SIRT meeting minutes, and any recommendations for action items. Copies of logs, intrusion detection logs, systems or server access information, and copies of reports from other areas should be included in the incident report.

8. After the incident, the SIRT must be prepared to describe what happened, why it happened, and what can be done to prevent a reoccurrence of the security breach or incident prior to placing the system or servers back in production after the system and its application data has been fully recovered. The SIRT must present its recommendations to the CIO/CSO/CEO and the affected IT asset owner prior to placing the IT assets back into production.

9. The SIRT and its incident report must remain confidential and made known only to the CIO/CSO/CEO and other pertinent officials on a need-to-know basis. If legal action or charges are to be made, the SIRT incident report may become part of the physical evidence used in a court of law. Refer to Appendix E for a sample SIRT Incident Report template.

Security Workflow Definitions

Many organizations lack the proper *security workflow definitions and procedures* for their NOC and/or SOC operations personnel. This is a common weakness found in many organizations that first conduct a risk and vulnerability assessment on their IT infrastructure and IT assets. These workflow definitions and procedures provide the road map for how to handle information security breaches and incidents throughout the organization. The organization's final assessment and recommendations report typically will define and make recommendations for how security workflow definitions and procedures are to be defined for the organization, depending upon the internal IT and IT security resources available.

Recommendations for security workflows and definitions should describe the interaction and communication that is needed among the different departments, roles, responsibilities, and accountabilities throughout the organization. The goals and objectives of these security workflows and definitions are as follows:

- To define the roles and responsibilities for security monitoring, auditing, and SIRT involvement within each of the seven areas of information security responsibility as defined in Chapter 3, "Why Risk Assessment."

- To define categories or classes of security breaches and incidents that correlate to the level of response that must be provided within each of the seven areas of information security responsibility.

- To define the interaction and communication between the defined organizational structure for all seven areas of information security responsibility.

- To define who is to be held accountable for specific security responsibilities within each of the seven areas of information security responsibility.

An example of a security workflow definition is how to handle security breaches and incident calls into the NOC or SOC for the organization. This is depicted in Figure 10.5.

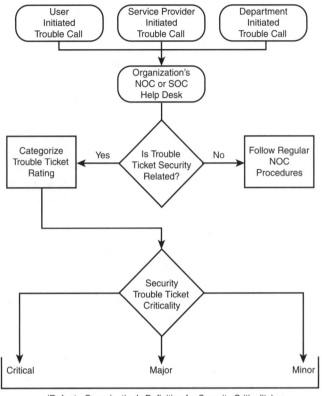

Figure 10.5   Security workflow definition for handling security-related trouble tickets.

Security Workflow Procedures

The following defines the procedures for the handling of security breaches and incident-related trouble calls:

1. All security-related breaches and incidents throughout the organization are to be called into the NOC or SOC help desk for proper documenting and trouble-ticket assignment.

2. End users, service providers (if applicable), and departments within the organization must interface and interact with the NOC or SOC help desk to capture, document, and process all security related breaches, incidents, or actions that are required.

3. Upon contact with the NOC or SOC help desk, the help desk technician will respond to the call and determine whether the call is security related. If not, the

call is processed according to existing NOC procedures. If the call is security related, a criticality determination will be conducted, depending upon the severity of the security breach or incident.

4. After it is documented and logged, to determine the severity of the trouble call the security trouble ticket must immediately be classified as CRITICAL, MAJOR, or MINOR as per the organization's definition for problem severity.

After a trouble call is logged and documented with the appropriate contact information and problem description, classification of the trouble call is imperative to provide the appropriate level of response. The organization's NOC or SOC help desk must be properly trained to handle security-related trouble calls with special care and attentiveness, especially if it is a security breach or incident and not a configuration management request.

Security trouble calls will be categorized based on their level of severity. Typically, all other security related breaches and incidents will be classified based on their severity or classification definition. Classification of the level of severity for security breaches or incidents is typically documented as an organizational standard within an IT security architecture and framework. A sample classification of severity for security breaches or incidents is shown in Figure 10.6.

Critical	Major	Minor
Level 1 Immediate SIRT Team Dispatch Until Problem Isolated and Contained	Level 2 Immediate Telephone Response and < 4 Hour Fix Time	Level 3 Immediate Telephone Response and < 8 Hour Fix Time
Security Breach/Incident Identification: • Generate Trouble Ticket and Document the Incident	Security Breach/Incident Identification: • Generate Trouble Ticket and Document the Incident	Security Breach/Incident Identification: • Generate Trouble Ticket and Document the Incident
Problems Defined as Critical: - CIO or CSO Initiated Trouble Call -Wide-scale virus threat -Major application or system compromised -Financial or transaction processing system compromised -3rd Offense of User violation of the organization's AUP or Confidentiality Agreement -RESTRICTED data and/or systems have been compromised -Intrusion Detection System Flags an Unauthorized User Penetration or Access	Problems Defined as Major: - Department Director Initiated Trouble Call -Entire LAN or department's workstations effected by virus -2nd Offense of User violation of the organization's AUP or Confidentiality Agreement -Agency application or system compromised -CONFIDENTIAL data and/or systems have been compromised -Intrusion Detection System Flags an Unknown User Penetration or Access	Problems Defined as Minor: -User Initiated Trouble Call -Single workstation affected by virus -1st Offense User violation of the organization's AUP or Confidentiality Agreement -INTERNAL data and/or systems have been compromised -Firewall filter or configuration needs to be implemented due to inability of User to get through, etc.

Figure 10.6   A sample security breach/incident severity classification.

Vulnerability Management

In addition to monitoring and managing threats, assessment and management of vulnerabilities is the other major void that is commonly found post-assessment on an IT infrastructure. Conducting risk and software vulnerability assessments and management is a continuous life cycle that requires documented procedures for conducting assessments on the IT infrastructure and the IT assets that are vulnerable. Vulnerability assessments require strategies for handling software vulnerabilities throughout the organization, which accounts for a majority of the server and workstation vulnerabilities given the vulnerabilities found in operating system software for servers and workstations.

The software vulnerability window must always be kept in line with the organization's defined *Software Vulnerability Standard* for minimizing the vulnerability window caused by software vulnerabilities. An enterprise software vulnerability management strategy coupled with a software patch management solution is required. An automated software patch management system and solution may be required for organizations that have large quantities of production servers and workstations.

Automating Software Patch Management

Automating an organization's software patch management solution requires careful planning and use of a patch management automation tool. Tracking, monitoring, and validating compliancy with the organization's minimum acceptable level of risk for software vulnerabilities is a full-time and ongoing responsibility. Because software vulnerabilities rank high in many organizations that conduct a risk and vulnerability assessment, many organizations must first define a policy for minimization of the vulnerability window and how the organization is going to validate compliancy throughout the enterprise.

The following defines an approach for handling software patches throughout the organization:

1. Create a Software Vulnerability Policy to define the organization's vulnerability window and standards, procedures, and guidelines for tracking, monitoring, and reporting on known software vulnerabilities.

2. Conduct a GAP analysis of known IT assets (servers and workstations) and their known software vulnerabilities:

   - Create a report of any new GAPs on production servers and workstations and prioritize them.

   - Assess whether to deploy the software patch on production servers or workstations, especially if testing and validation is required (this is highly recommended) prior to deployment of the software patch update.

   - Obtain approval from the organization's Change Control Board prior to deployment of the software patch.

3. Set patch update deployment schedule.

4. Execute the software patch update deployment on identified workstations and servers.

5. Confirm that the software patch update was accepted and received by the affected servers and/or workstations.

6. Verify that the software vulnerability and gap is closed for the affected servers and/or workstations.

7. Continuously monitor, track, and report on the organization's software vulnerabilities.

8. Repeat process.

The results of a risk and vulnerability assessment typically require the organization to prioritize what vulnerabilities need to be addressed first by the organization. Many organizations are faced with limited budgets and thus must prioritize how they will spend funds on security initiatives and security countermeasures for identified threats and vulnerabilities. This is not an easy task and must be conducted with the security of the entire organization in mind. Then the organization can formulate a vulnerability management strategy that typically requires the elimination, mitigation, monitoring, and tracking of metrics.

Enterprise Vulnerability Management

Enterprise vulnerability management is a recurring process and requires documented procedures and guidelines so that compliance and conformance to the organization's policies and standards can be implemented properly. Vulnerability management typically contains the following processes:

- **Discovery**—Perform an IT infrastructure and IT asset threat and vulnerability investigation.
- **Prioritize**—Prioritize those vulnerabilities on production IT infrastructure assets based on their criticality to the organization and the Data Classification Standard.
- **Mitigate**—Mitigate vulnerabilities via configuration updates, software patch updates, asset shielding behind firewalls, and/or patch installations.
- **Maintain**—Conduct ongoing configuration management and provisioning.
- **Monitor**—Continuously monitor the IT infrastructure and its IT assets by implementing procedures and guidelines for security management, reporting, and auditing.
- **Baseline**—Conduct periodic baseline definitions for the IT assets, systems, and devices via assessments and continuous monitoring for security and software integrity.

Training IT Staff and End Users

The most important post-assessment activity is to train the IT staff on their new information security responsibilities and accountabilities and the end users on the importance of information security. Given the roles, tasks, responsibilities, and accountabilities defined in this chapter, many IT organizations are faced with two training initiatives: training their IT staff and training their end users. Training the IT staff requires a careful examination of the seven areas of information security responsibility. This training should include information security as well as professional certifications, such as the CISSP® Professional Certification offered by the International Information Systems Security Certification Consortium known as (ISC)^2 or through the Global Information Assurance Certification (GIAC), which offers in-depth training in all the key areas of security.

Training the end users typically requires security awareness training for new employees during their employment orientation. Review of the organization's AUPs and security awareness training program are usually prerequisites for new employees, contractors, or third parties prior to granting them access to the IT infrastructure's resources, systems, and applications.

When conducting a risk and vulnerability assessment, one of the things that should be investigated is the qualifications, experience, and capabilities of the IT staff in regard to information security and being able to design, implement, and ensure the confidentiality, integrity, and availability of the IT infrastructure and its assets. Through interviews, examination of current practices, and review of the IT staff's experience in information security, specific recommendations can be made to enhance the knowledge and skill sets of the organization's IT staff. Given the roles, tasks, responsibilities, and accountabilities defined in this chapter, a gap analysis should be conducted on the seven areas of information security responsibility and the current human resources, IT, and IT security staff in an effort to identify any gaps or voids in roles, responsibilities, and accountabilities for the organization. This gap analysis is critical because without properly trained IT staff in information security practices and techniques, implementation of the IT security architecture and framework cannot be done with internal resources. The organization is forced to hire outside information security consultants or outsource portions of its information security responsibility to managed security service providers.

The methodology and approach for identifying the training needs of current IT staff is as follows:

- Define the roles, tasks, responsibilities, and accountabilities for information security in the seven areas of information security responsibility.

- Interview the human resources staff and appropriate IT staff who are currently responsible and accountable for implementation of the IT security architecture and framework and the procedures and guidelines in each of the seven areas of information security responsibility.

- Review the IT staff's current job descriptions and identify any gaps, voids, or missing elements in regard to the roles, tasks, responsibilities and accountabilities for information security.

- Prioritize the gaps and voids in the IT staff's knowledge and background in the seven areas of information security responsibility.

- Create a training strategy and budget that will allow the organization to educate, train, and certify its own internal IT staff in information security practices and techniques or create a budget to hire outside information security consultants to help fill in the gaps and voids as an interim solution prior to training internal IT staff.

- Commit to continuous information security education and training for the organization's IT staff, particularly as new systems, applications, and countermeasures are designed and implemented throughout the IT infrastructure.

- Verify and validate that the organization's IT staff are getting the appropriate level of training and knowledge through professional certifications such as the CISSP® professional certification for information security professionals or GIAC.

- In concert with human resources, update the roles, tasks, responsibilities, and accountabilities of the IT staff's job descriptions and annual performance review criteria so that information security is brought to the forefront of the organization's IT staff's priorities.

- Review the education, training, and certification strategy along with human resource development and annual performance review changes so that the IT staff is now information-security ready and motivated.

Developing and delivering an organizational security awareness training program requires a strategy for how best to deploy the knowledge and awareness in concert with the organizations information security policies and standards. In most cases, security awareness training is best delivered via videotape or via an online, e-Learning platform if the organization's end user population is large and distributed in many remote locations. The security awareness training program should focus on the AUPs, policies, standards, procedures, and guidelines that the IT organization wants to deploy throughout the organization. In addition, the security awareness training should stress the importance of each employee's, contractor's, or third-party individual's responsibility and accountability for ensuring the confidentiality, integrity, and availability of the organization's IT infrastructure and its assets.

In concert with the organization's security awareness and training policy for all employees, contractors, and third-party individuals, an organization should define consistent goals and objectives throughout the enterprise. The security awareness and training policy goals and objectives should include the following:

- Develop a comprehensive security awareness program based on the organization's security awareness and training policy for different audiences, including IT, human resources, IT directors and managers, employees, contractors, and third-party individuals.

- Develop a unique information security training program that consists of training the organization's IT and human resource directors and managers, employees, contractors, and third-party individuals who have specific roles, tasks, responsibilities, and accountabilities pertaining to the policies, standards, technical standards, procedures, and guidelines as defined by the organization's IT security architecture and framework.

- Deliver periodic information security awareness programs and initiatives that educate and make the organization's employees, contractors, and third-party individuals aware of the organization's IT security architecture and framework for ensuring the confidentiality, integrity, and availability of the IT infrastructure and assets.

- Align the information security roles, tasks, responsibilities, and management accountability to the seven areas of information security responsibility and train those individuals for their new responsibilities and accountabilities.

- Make it easy to deliver, track, and audit all employees, contractors, and third-party individuals who take the security awareness training programs. Tracking the security awareness training and the signed AUPs of the employees, contractors, and third-party individuals must be simple and easy to correlate.

Typically, security awareness training is targeted to the end users and the systems and applications that they access on a day-to-day basis, whereas security awareness training for IT staff is more technical and focused on the information technology goals and objectives. Common topics for information security awareness usually incorporate elements of the information security standards that are part of the organization's IT security architecture and framework definition. Security awareness training can be derived from the organization's IT security architecture and framework. By focusing on the policies and standards, an organization can address the security awareness and information security topics in its security awareness training program and campaign.

Summary

Now that the organization's risk and vulnerability assessment is completed, many organizations are left with gaps and voids in the overall security of their IT infrastructure and assets as defined by the organization's goals and objectives and minimum acceptable level of risk for the seven areas of information security responsibility. These gaps and voids are compounded with the lack of experience and capabilities of the organization's IT staff given their expanded information security roles, tasks, responsibilities, and accountabilities that they must now take ownership of to ensure the confidentiality, integrity, and availability of the IT infrastructure and assets.

IT organizations must create and implement an IT security architecture and framework to get a handle on how to implement the security goals and objectives of the organization. This IT security architecture and framework must then be communicated to the IT staff, the managers that are held accountable for ensuring the confidentiality, integrity, and availability, and the end users who work for the organization. Without a collective and all-encompassing plan for communicating the organization's information security policies, standards, procedures, and guidelines, creating the IT security architecture and framework is moot.

Obtaining buy-in and acceptance for an IT security architecture and framework must start with the IT organization and IT staff that are responsible and accountable for information security. This typically requires changing and updating the job descriptions or creating new ones so that the organization can hire trained, certified, and qualified information security professionals for its IT staff. IT managers must work with the human resources department in an effort to upgrade current job descriptions as well as create new ones to support the information security initiatives and programs that the results of the risk and vulnerability assessment and recommendations report identified and prioritized. After this is done, organizations stand a better chance of making an impact on the information security of the IT infrastructure and assets.

Many organizations expand the roles, tasks, and responsibilities of their IT staff and merely add it to their already overloaded workload and responsibilities. This is not an effective strategy to ensure that information security initiatives and priorities are implemented properly. Obtaining buy-in and acceptance must start with the IT organization and then must permeate to the end users in an effort to get a collective and all-encompassing information security campaign moving in an organization.

Key Terms

Acceptable Use Policy (AUP)   A policy that defines what employees, contractors, and third parties are authorized to do on the organization's IT infrastructure and its assets. AUPs are common for access to IT resources, systems, applications, Internet access, email access, and so on.

Change Control Board   A governance organization or committee that consists of executive management in regard to changes, modifications, or updates to the IT infrastructure and its assets.

Change Management Policy   A policy that is defined by a Change Control Board to manage, review, and approve changes to the IT infrastructure and its assets. Typically, changes that impact the IT infrastructure and its assets must obtain approval of the organization's Change Control Board.

Data Classification Standard   A standard that defines an organization's classification of its data assets. Typically, a data classification standard will dictate the level of minimum acceptable risk within the seven areas of information security responsibility.

Defense-in-Depth   A term used to describe a layered approach to information security for an IT infrastructure.

IT Security Architecture and Framework   A term used to describe a hierarchical definition for information security policies, standards, procedures, and guidelines.

Minimum Acceptable Level of Risk   The stake in the ground that an organization defines for the seven areas of information security responsibility. Depending on the goals and objectives for maintaining confidentiality, integrity, and availability of the IT infrastructure and its assets, the minimum level of acceptable risk will dictate the amount of information security countermeasures that are needed to be in compliance with this definition.

Network Operations Center (NOC)   An organization's help desk or interface to its end users where trouble calls, questions, and trouble tickets are generated.

Security Operations Center (SOC)   An organization's or service provider's help desk or interface to its end users or customers where trouble calls, questions, and trouble tickets pertaining to security issues, breaches, and incidents are forwarded.

Security Workflow Definitions   Given the defense-in-depth, layered approach to information security roles, tasks, responsibilities, and accountabilities, a security workflow definition is a flowchart that defines the communications, checks and balances, and domain of responsibility and accountability for the organization's IT and IT security staff.

Separation of Duties   Given the seven areas of information security responsibility, separation of duties defines the roles, tasks, responsibilities, and accountabilities for information security uniquely for the different duties of the IT staff and IT security staff.

Service Level Agreements (SLAs)   A contractual agreement between an organization and its service provider. SLAs define and protect the organization in regard to holding the service provider accountable for the requirements as defined in an SLA.

Software Vulnerability Standard   A standard that accompanies an organization's Vulnerability Assessment and Management Policy. This standard typically defines the organization's vulnerability window definition and how the organization is to provide software vulnerability management and software patch management throughout the enterprise.

Security Assessment Resources

APPENDIX A CONTAINS A LIST OF SITES that maintain security standards, general security websites, and security tool sites.

Security Standards

The standards detailed here were developed to help evaluate and establish system assurance and measure and assess security. Trust gives us some assurance that these systems will operate in a given and predictable manner and that our IT infrastructure is secure.

Common Criteria (CC) for IT Security Evaluation

The CC is used for evaluation of Information Technology (IT) security systems. IT contains both functional requirements and assurance requirements.

The three links that follow are for sites in the United States, Canada, and the United Kingdom. Each provides more information about Common Criteria and its application.

http://csrc.nist.gov/cc/
http://www.cse-cst.gc.ca/en/services/common_criteria/common_criteria.html
http://www.cesg.gov.uk/site/iacs/index.cfm?menuSelected=1&displayPage=1

FIPS PUB 140-1 and 140-2

FIPS 140-1 describes security requirements for U.S. federal government purchases. FIPS 140-2 specifies security requirements to be satisfied by a cryptographic modules used within security systems. These publications are sponsored by the U.S. Department of Commerce and the National Institute of Science and Technology.

ISO17799

ISO17799 is a comprehensive set of controls comprising best practices in information security. Its predecessor was British Standard for Information Security Management (BS 7799). Read more about it at
www.iso-17799.com

GAO Risk Assessment Process

The document, Basic Elements of the Risk Assessment Process GAO 00-33, is available at the following link:
http://www.gao.gov/cgi-bin/getrpt?GAO/AIMD-00-33

OSSTMM

Open Source Security Testing Methodology Manual. To learn more about the OSST-MM, visit the following link:
http://www.isecom.org/osstmm/

DoD Rainbow Series

Although most have been superceded by the CC, the Rainbow series of documents still offer some useful information. These standards can be found at
http://csrc.nist.gov/secpubs/rainbow

NIST

The following is a list of security-related National Institute of Standards and Technology (NIST) documents that can be obtained by accessing the NIST website at
http://csrc.nist.gov/publications/nistpubs

SP 800-2	Public-Key Cryptography
SP 800-3	Establishing a Computer Security Incident Response Capability (CSIRC)
SP 800-4	Computer Security Considerations in Federal Procurements: A Guide for Procurement Initiators, Contracting Officers, and Computer Security Officials
SP 800-5	A Guide to the Selection of Anti-Virus Tools and Techniques
SP 800-6	Automated Tools for Testing Computer System Vulnerability
SP 800-7	Security in Open Systems
SP 800-8	Security Issues in the Database Language SQL
SP 800-9	Good Security Practices for Electronic Commerce, Including Electronic Data Interchange
SP 800-10	Keeping Your Site Comfortably Secure: An Introduction to Internet Firewalls
SP 800-11	The Impact of the FCC's Open Network Architecture on NS/EP Telecommunications Security
SP 800-12	An Introduction to Computer Security: The NIST Handbook
SP 800-13	Telecommunications Security Guidelines for Telecommunications Management Network

SP 800–14	Generally Accepted Principles and Practices for Securing Information Technology Systems
SP 800–15	Minimum Interoperability Specification for PKI Components (MISPC), Version 1
SP 800–16	Information Technology Security Training Requirements: A Role- and Performance-Based Model (supersedes NIST Spec. Pub. 500–172)
SP 800–17	Modes of Operation Validation System (MOVS): Requirements and Procedures
SP 800–18	Guide for Developing Security Plans for Information Technology Systems
SP 800–19	Mobile Agent Security
SP 800–20	Modes of Operation Validation System for the Triple Data Encryption Algorithm (TMOVS): Requirements and Procedures
SP 800–21	Guideline for Implementing Cryptography in the Federal Government
SP 800–22	A Statistical Test Suite for Random and Pseudorandom Number Generators for Cryptographic Applications
SP 800–23	Guideline to Federal Organizations on Security Assurance and Acquisition/Use of Tested/Evaluated Products
SP 800–24	PBX Vulnerability Analysis: Finding Holes in Your PBX Before Someone Else Does
SP 800–25	Federal Agency Use of Public Key Technology for Digital Signatures and Authentication
SP 800–26	Security Self-Assessment Guide for Information Technology Systems
SP 800–27	Engineering Principles for Information Technology Security (A Baseline for Achieving Security)
SP 800–28	Guidelines on Active Content and Mobile Code October 2001
SP 800–29	A Comparison of the Security Requirements for Cryptographic Modules in FIPS 140-1 and FIPS 140-2
SP 800–30	Risk Management Guide for Information Technology Systems
SP 800–31	Intrusion Detection Systems (IDS)
SP 800–32	Introduction to Public Key Technology and the Federal PKI Infrastructure
SP 800–33	Underlying Technical Models for Information Technology Security
SP 800–32	Introduction to Public Key Technology and the Federal PKI Infrastructure
SP 800–33	Underlying Technical Models for Information Technology Security
SP 800–34	Contingency Planning Guide for Information Technology Systems

SP 800-38A	Recommendation for Block Cipher Modes of Operation—Methods and Techniques
SP 800-40	Procedures for Handling Security Patches
SP 800-41	Guidelines on Firewalls and Firewall Policy
SP 800-44	Guidelines on Securing Public Web Servers
SP 800-45	Guidelines on Electronic Mail Security
SP 800-46	Security for Telecommuting and Broadband Communication
SP 800-47	Security Guide for Interconnecting Information Technology Systems
SP 800-51	Use of the Common Vulnerabilities and Exposures (CVE) Vulnerability Naming Scheme
SP 800-55	Security Metrics Guide for Information Technology Systems
SP 800-58	Security Considerations for Voice Over IP Systems
SP 800-61	Computer Security Incident Handling Guide
SP 800-78	Cryptographic Algorithms and Key Sizes for Personal Identity Verification

General Security Websites

The sites listed next are of general security interest. These organizations offer many resources to help build effective security.

Carnegie Mellon CERT

www.cert.org

International Information Systems Security Certification Consortium (ISC²)

www.isc2.org

Infosec security portal

www.infosyssec.com

InfraGard (FBI and business security partnership program)

www.infragard.net

Information Systems Security Association

www.issa.org

National Infrastructure Protection Center

www.nipc.gov

SANS develops and maintains a large collection of research documents about various aspects of information security.

www.sans.org

Security Tool Websites

Having the right tool can make the testing and analysis of infrastructure security much easier. Listed next are some sites that maintain various security tools:

DumpSec is a GUI Windows-based enumeration tool that can provide account information, RID information, open shares, and more. The link is shown as follows:

www.somarsoft.com

A nice list of bootable Linux CDs is available at the following address. Many of these have really good distributions of tools preconfigured and ready to go that will be of aid to those doing security work.

www.frozentech.com/content/livecd.php

Cain and Abel is a GUI Windows-based password cracking and enumeration tool that is free to download at

www.oxid.it

NetStumbler is the leading wireless scanning tool used to identify and enumerate 802.11 wireless networks. You can download it at

www.netstumbler.org

Nmap is an open source Windows and Linux scanning tool. To learn more about it or download the tool, visit the following link:

www.insecure.org

SuperScan is a Windows scanning tool for TCP and UDP. It's available for free from Foundstone at

www.foundstone.com/resources/freetools.htm

Scanrand is another useful security tool that is free to download from the following url:

www.lurhq.com/scanrand_dissected.pdf

TCH-Amap is a valuable scanning tool that is free to download at

http://thc.org/thc-amap/

John the Ripper is a Linux and Windows password-cracking tool that can be used to audit the strength of your passwords. It can be downloaded from

www.openwall.com/john

SNORT is a great open source IDS tool available for Windows and Linux. SNORT can be downloaded at the following site:

www.snort.org

Packetyzer is Ethereal with a new interface. It's free to download from:

www.networkchemistry.com/products/packetyzer

Rainbowcrack is a password-cracking tool that works off of the fast time-memory trade-off technique. You can download it at

www.antsight.com/zsl/rainbowcrack

Ophcrack is another password-cracking tool that uses the fast time-memory trade-off technique. You can download it from the following site:

http://lasecwww.epfl.ch/~oechslin/projects/ophcrack/

Nessus is one of the premiere open source scanning tools. You can download it from the following site:

www.nessus.org

Metasploit is an exploit and vulnerability assessment tool. You can download it at:

www.metasploit.com

B

Security Assessment Forms

THIS APPENDIX PROVIDES SAMPLE TEMPLATES that you can use to aid in the assessment process.

Information Request Form

The information request form (as shown in Table B.1) will provide you with information that helps define the size and scope of the assessment. If you can't gather all this information before the initial meeting, that's okay because after management has given the project the green light, you'll have the additional support to gather more information.

Table B.1 **Information Request Form**

Contact Name	
Phone Number	
Cell Phone	
Email	
Mail Stop	
Administrative	**For this section, please describe administrative aspects of your organizational environment.**

What is the core mission of the organization?

How many locations does the organization have?

Does the assessment encompass all locations or just a limited number of sites?

What event is driving this assessment?

Does the organization have existing security policies and procedures?

Does the organizations have physical controls in place to control the movement of employees and visitors?

Do any vendors or corporate partners have access to the network?

Are any IT services outsourced, and if so, which ones?

Technical   **For this section, please describe technical aspects of your organizational environment.**

How many servers are located at each site?

What OSs are in place for these servers?

How many workstations are located at each site?

What OSs are in place for these workstations?

What networking protocols are used?

Are there any mainframes?

How many connections are there to the Internet?

What services are made available externally?

What services are made internally?

Is wireless technologies used?

Is VoIP used?

What types of redundant systems are in place?

Security   **For this section, please describe the security aspects of your organizational environment.**

What type of encryption technologies are used?

Is there a VPN?

Is authentication centralized?

What type of authentication systems are used?

How is access controlled?

What type of firewalls are used?

Is there an IDS/IPS in place?

Legal   **For this section, please describe the legal aspects of your organizational environment.**

What state, provincial, and federal laws must the organizations comply with?

HIPAA

GLB

SOX

Family Education Rights and Privacy Act

National Institute of Standards and Technologies

Document Tracking Form

It is best to appoint one person to collect and distribute all policies and documents requested. A simple form as shown in Table B.2 can ease the administration of this task.

Table B.2   **Document Tracking Form**

Title	Custodian	Date Requested	Date Received	Date Returned, Archived, or Destroyed

Critical Systems and Information Forms

Having an inventory of existing equipment and being able to track the organization's documents is just part of the task. If the organization has not provided you with information on critical information and systems, you will have to work with them to determine these items. The Organization Information Criticality Matrix (OICM) is shown in Table B.3 and the Systems Criticality Matrix is shown in Table B.4.

Table B.3   **Organization Information Criticality Matrix (OICM)**

OICM	Confidentiality	Availability	Integrity

High Watermark

Table B.4 **Systems Criticality Matrix (SCM)**

SCM	Confidentiality	Availability	Integrity

High Watermark

Level II Assessment Forms

The following forms, as shown in Tables B.5, B.6, and B.7, can be used when assessing servers and during system demonstrations.

Table B.5 **Password Controls**

Password Action	Recommended Value	Actual Value
Enforce password history	10 days	
Maximum password age	30 days	
Minimum password age	1 day	
Minimum password length	7 characters	
Passwords must meet complexity	Enabled	
Account lockout threshold	After 3 attempts	

Table B.6 **Audit Controls**

Auditing	Recommended Value	Actual Value
Audit system events	Success and failure	
Audit process tracking	None	
Audit privilege use	Failure	
Audit account logon events	Failure	
Audit account management	Success and failure	
Audit directory service access	None	
Audit logon events	Failure	
Audit object access	Success	
Audit policy change	Failure	

Table B.7 **Access Options and Controls**

Access Options	Recommended Value	Actual Value
Rename administrator account	Rename	
Audit the use of backup and restore privilege	Enabled	
Shut down system immediately if unable to log security audits	Enabled	
Do not display last username	Enabled	
Display message text for users attempting to log on	Enabled	
Message title for users attempting to log on	Enabled	
Prompt user to change password before expiration	1 week	
Network access: Do not allow anonymous enumeration of SAM accounts	Enabled	
Can shares be accessed anonymously	No	
Force logoff when logon hours expire	Enabled	
Suspend session time	30 minutes	
Do not display last username	Enabled	
Restrict floppy, CD-ROM, and USB ports	Enabled	

C

Security Assessment Sample Report

THIS APPENDIX PROVIDES A TEMPLATE EXAMPLE, as shown in Table C.1, that can be used for a final report. This template outlines the information, data, and procedures for documenting a security assessment so that the results can be provided to management. The report template contains the following sections:

- Notice
- Executive summary
- Introduction
- Statement of work
- Analysis
- Conclusions

Note that this is an example; each organization should modify this template to meet its own existing needs. Below the template you will find guidelines and information on what each section should contain.

> **Note**
> The template example shown in the appendix is also available on the book's CD.

Table C.1   **Security Assessment Sample Report**

Section	Contents
Notice	Contains confidentiality notice.
Executive summary	Brief overview of the assessment and its findings.
Introduction	Discusses organization, locations, mission, and employees.
Statement of work	Defines the "what" and "how" of the assessment.
Analysis	Details what you found and how you found it.
Conclusions	Outlines what changes should be made to improve security.

Notice

"This report contains confidential and proprietary information. Reproduction of this document or unauthorized use is prohibited." This statement should be included on the cover of the report as should some type of similar statement on each page. After all, you are holding a report that clearly details the organization's vulnerabilities.

Executive Summary

The Executive Summary should give a brief overview of the assessment and your findings. The pages of the Executive Summary should be numbered i, ii, and so on, and it should be the first thing to appear after the cover page of the report. The Executive Summary is basically divided into several paragraphs. These should include

1. A brief overview of the organization. Include the mission and purpose of the organization, who their customers are, and how many people are employed at what locations.

2. Information as to why the vulnerability assessment was performed. What drove this project? Was it to demonstrate due diligence; comply with state, provincial, or federal laws; or because of a breach in security? There should also be information listing the dates of the assessment, the purpose, and the methodology used.

3. A listing of what systems, networks, or controls were assessed. Describe how these systems are used, their criticality in the organization, and how the IT infrastructure is designed.

4. The findings, discoveries, and recommendations should be briefly discussed next. This should be just a quick, high-level overview of what was discovered. Remember that recommendations are voluntary and that senior management is ultimately responsible to decide what changes should or should not be implemented.

5. The final paragraph of the Executive Summary should list the personnel who helped with the project; you should be sure to acknowledge everyone involved.

Introduction

In many ways, the introduction restates what has been briefly covered in the Executive Summary. Therefore, the first one or two paragraphs should discuss the organization, its locations, mission, employees, and the items that were assessed.

Again, why was the assessment performed? The reasons might be due diligence; compliance with state, provincial, or federal laws; a breach in security; or other factors—the level of urgency will vary. So you will want to be sure to keep this in mind when detailing the project. Include what types of information the vulnerability assessment team gathered and how they gathered it.

Statement of Work

This section of the report should address the "what" and "how" of the assessment. You will want to review the final scope of the assessment. No matter how it started, there is always the possibility that during the assessment some project creep occurred.

Describe what systems or networks were examined, what they are used for, and how they were examined. Was only a level I assessment performed in which documentation was reviewed? Was a level II assessment performed, with some scanning and hands-on testing? Or was a level III assessment performed with in-depth penetration testing? You will want to list all these details here. Include such things as the types of policies that were reviewed, the number of servers and workstations examined, and the hardware platform, software, firewalls, and other items that help list and specify what exactly was tested and how. Any of these systems or devices that connect externally should be described, as should the security levels related to this connection.

Discuss which individuals performed which tests. What equipment and methods were used to perform these tests? Most likely there were system demonstrations and interviews. This information should also be mentioned. Stick to numbers and systems here. An assessment is not an audit, so individuals shouldn't be mentioned.

Analysis

This section of the report lists what you found and how you found it. This is the current state of the network. You will want to discuss items of concern that were discovered during the assessment. Because this section follows the statement of work, it should build on what you did during testing. The results of your tests and examinations should be discussed. Overall, this section should stay focused on the importance of security to the organization. It is important to remember to keep your findings balanced. Organizations are not all good or bad, and the findings shouldn't be, either. Comment on what the company is doing right.

Discussion of findings should list several sentences that briefly detail each problem. It can be organized in a table by findings and show the impact to the organization, such as high, medium, or low, as well as a solution. Or it can be organized by class and category, such as management findings, operational findings, and technical findings.

Recommendations

Recommendations should be clearly stated. This section is the most important part of the document. Your recommendations should be derived logically from the analysis of the data and be verifiable. Just remember that no organization will ever be 100% risk free. There is always the need to balance the cost of protection against the level of risk. If it is too costly or impractical to remove a vulnerability, you should say so, but include other recommendations or courses of action.

Conclusions

This is it; this section is where you should clearly state your conclusions. Although this is certainly the place to list what's wrong and what needs to be fixed, you'll also want to discuss what works and what is being done right. What are your findings and what is the organization's overall level of security? You will be making the conclusions; however, it will be up to those responsible for the systems to determine what to implement. Because money is always an issue, you should recommend several options. If the best solution isn't feasible because of the budget, the organization can implement other stop-gap solutions to improve the situation from its current state.

Tip

If necessary, include an appendix that lists the tests that were performed and their results. If it's a large amount of detailed data, you may want only to reference it here and supply those details by including a CD with the original data files.

D

Dealing with Consultants and Outside Vendors

AFTER THE DECISION HAS BEEN MADE TO CONDUCT an internal risk and vulnerability assessment, deciding how to proceed and whether to conduct the risk and vulnerability assessment with internal resources or external resources is the next decision. Conducting a risk and vulnerability assessment with internal resources can be done by organizations that have the resources and skills needed to conduct an objective risk and vulnerability assessment. Using internal employees to conduct an internal risk and vulnerability assessment may result in prejudice and a nonobjective perspective when it comes to assessing and recommending specific remedies or courses of action to mitigate or remediate known risks, threats, and vulnerabilities. Conducting a risk and vulnerability assessment with an outside consultant or vendor will allow for an objective and unbiased assessment and recommendation.

This appendix provides an overview of how to procure outside consultants or vendors, what to include in the proposal or statement of work, and how to evaluate consultants and vendors who are responding to the proposal or statement of work to conduct a risk and vulnerability assessment on the organization's IT infrastructure and assets. This appendix provides the reader with an overview of the different procurement methods that can be utilized when contracting with an outside consultant or vendor. In addition, this appendix provides some useful tips and approaches to ensure that the outside consultant or vendor provides the tasks and deliverables as per the proposal or statement of work document.

Some organizations may want to hire a consultant to write the actual proposal or statement of work for conducting an objective risk and vulnerability assessment. In this case, the consultant should not be allowed to respond to the proposal or statement of work given that they have an unfair advantage because of their intimate familiarity with the IT infrastructure and assets. Other organizations will craft a proposal or statement of work and solicit proposal responses to make a sound business decision pertaining to the hiring of an outside consultant or vendor to perform the objective risk and vulnerability assessment. The creation of selection criteria for hiring an outside consultant is then evaluated so that a contract award can be made.

This appendix will focus on the later process in which organizations craft their own proposals and statement of work documents to solicit bids and proposal responses for conducting a risk and vulnerability assessment service offering.

Procurement Terminology

Depending on the type of organization, procurement laws, mandates, and regulations may apply given the organization's jurisdiction. Most laws require that the U.S. federal government, state governments, county, and municipal governments purchase products or services especially in public bidding and procurement situations such as Invitation to Bids, Request for Proposals, or Request for Quotations. This is also true of the Canadian federal government and provincial governments within Canada. Most corporations, whether privately held or publicly traded, are not subject to procurement laws, mandates, or regulations. When purchasing professional services, be sure to work with your purchasing department to understand the purchasing and procurement procedures that must be followed when procuring professional services of any kind.

The following presents some terminology that the reader must become familiar with when dealing with purchasing or procurement of consulting services for conducting a risk and vulnerability assessment service.

- **Letter of Understanding (LOU)**—This is an informal letter that is typically attached to a purchase order for procurement of services as described in the LOU. It is a nonbinding, noncontractual engagement letter that describes the tasks and deliverables and terms and conditions for the consulting engagement. The LOU is used by consulting firms and independent consultants who desire to work for clients in this nonbinding, noncontractual language style letter. The LOU typically generates a purchase order on which the LOU and the tasks and deliverables are clearly defined.

- **Invitation to Bid (ITB)**—This is a formal procurement document and procedure that solicits bids from consultants and vendors who desire to respond to the ITB. An ITB is typically required by law or mandate in certain states, provinces, counties, or municipalities that require a formal bid process to purchase products or services that exceed a certain dollar value. For example, an ITB may be required to procure products or services if the value is greater than $15,000.00 U.S.D or $15,000.00 C.D.

- **Request for Information (RFI)**—An RFI is an excellent method for obtaining additional information, requirements, and tips for crafting a formal ITB or RFP document. The RFI is an excellent vehicle for asking technical and nontechnical questions of consultants and vendors to which the organization can learn from and craft a more detailed and specific ITB or RFP for the procurement of consulting services for conducting a risk and vulnerability assessment project. Creating and submitting an RFI is typically done in accordance with procurement laws, mandates, and regulations (if any). An RFI is merely a tool to ask technical and non-technical questions to the consultant and vendor community pertaining to how best to approach a risk and vulnerability assessment for the organization. The answers to the RFI can then be reviewed and assimilated into the final requirements and description of the tasks and deliverables that are desired by the organization.

- **Request for Quotation (RFQ)**—This is a formal procurement document and process that is typically used in situations where consultants or vendors are already on an approved consultant or vendor list for providing IT and IT security professional services. Many state, provincial, and county governments use the RFQ for purchasing and procuring products and services from existing state and county government contract vehicles. RFQs are then submitted to approved consultants and vendors for products and services that are already on the approved state, province, or county government bid list. Tasks and deliverables are provided in the RFQ and pricing is provided by adding the hourly rates for professional services from the state government and/or county government contracts for professional services. RFQs help streamline the procurement process and typically are used by state, provincial, and county governments when procuring products and services with state, provincial, and county-approved contract vehicles.

- **Request for Proposal (RFP)**—This is typically the most expensive and time consuming of all the formal procurement procedures and is used for large-scale and high-dollar value purchases for products and services. An RFP is typically required by law or mandate for U.S. and Canadian federal government, state, and provincial governments, county governments, and municipal governments that require a formal bid process to purchase products or services that exceed a certain dollar value or that are large in scale and extend into more than one fiscal year. The RFP process typically follows a sequential procurement procedure as defined by federal, state, provincial, county, and municipality procurement laws, mandates, and regulations. This detailed process is what makes the RFP procurement process the most expensive and time consuming for an organization. These steps are described later in this appendix.

- **Statement of Work (SOW)**—A statement of work document (SOW) is a document that defines the scope of work, tasks, and deliverables that are to be completed for the professional services engagement. A SOW must be clearly written and understood by both parties; it describes in detail what project tasks consist of and what project deliverables will be provided throughout the life of the project. An SOW can be attached to a purchase order for direct purchasing or can be inserted into a larger procurement document such as an LOU, ITB, RFQ, or RFP.

Typical RFP Procurement Steps

The RFP procurement process is the most detailed procurement procedure that an organization can utilize for the purchase of professional services such as a risk and vulnerability assessment. Depending on the size and scope of the procurement, an RFP procurement process can last months or more than a year if specific procedures and guidelines have to be followed and contract negotiations stall. Deciding on the structure, format, and the actual writing of the RFP document is a very time-consuming effort that typically requires technical and nontechnical support from the RFP project team members. Then the RFP document requires extensive review, editing, and quality assurance so that RFP addendums can be minimized. The more clear and concise the RFP document is, the easier it is for consultants and vendors to respond to the RFP document.

The goal and objective of an RFP procurement process is to develop a detailed but clearly understood RFP document so that the consultant or vendor companies responding can provide cost-competitive RFP responses without violating any procurement laws, mandates, and regulations that may warrant official protest from other RFP respondents. The RFP procurement process includes the following steps:

- **Assemble an RFP Project Team**—Prior to the creation or development of the RFP document, the purchaser or organization purchasing the product or service must be identified and an RFP project team must be created, consisting of an RFP project team leader, a purchasing representative, IT security professionals, and other pertinent technical and nontechnical resources that will assist in the requirements definition, technical and nontechnical descriptions, and the overall structure and format of the RFP document itself.

- **Development of RFP Structure and Format**—Most RFPs are structured and formatted to have a Technical Response section and a Cost Proposal section with separate evaluation criteria for both sections. Federal, state, provincial, county, and municipal governments typically have RFP document templates that are organized according to the procurement laws, mandates, and regulations that must be followed.

- **Assemble the RFP Evaluation Team**—The selection and identification of a qualified RFP evaluation team composed of nontechnical business professionals and technical IT and IT security professionals is critical to ensure an accurate and effective RFP evaluation for the technical and nontechnical sections of the RFP response. In many cases, if a consultant or vendor assisted the organization with the RFP creation and procurement process, they may be precluded from participating in the RFP evaluation process, depending upon procurement rules and guidelines that must be followed.

- **Creation of RFP Evaluation Methodology**—This is one of the most difficult elements of the RFP document to create. Figuring out how the organization is to evaluate the RFP responses is the most important element to provide a fair and equitable evaluation of all RFP responses that are submitted. Many organizations must comply with procurement and purchasing laws, mandates, and regulations, so always confirm whether your organization is under strict guidelines. Many RFP evaluation methodologies are based on a weighted scale and point system that the RFP evaluators review and score for each element in the technical and nontechnical sections of the RFP response.

- **Creation of RFP Bid Documents**—Many pieces of an RFP document must be defined and documented. These pieces are listed in this bulleted list. Creation of the RFP bid documents under procurement law, mandates, and regulations requires the utmost in confidentiality and zero communications with the consultant and vendor community. Failure to comply with procurement laws and procedures can disqualify a consultant or vendor from participating in the RFP process. Many organizations hire outside consultants to assist in the creation of the RFP bid documents, especially if technical or security-related requirements exist. Other organizations rely on the RFP project team to author sections of the RFP document that they have specific expertise in writing.

- **Creation of RFP Instructions**—The RFP instructions must clearly describe and define the procurement laws and procedures that must be followed throughout the RFP process. The RFP instructions must be clearly written to minimize any questions or confusion the consultants or vendors may have regarding the RFP process. The RFP instructions will include specific RFP project timelines, instructions for communicating questions and for obtaining RFP addendums, RFP submittal instructions, and other information pertaining to how to properly respond and submit an RFP response without violating any procurement laws.

- **Creation of RFP Mandatory and Technical Requirements**—Creating the RFP's mandatory minimum and technical requirements for a risk and vulnerability assessment is the most important part of the requirements definitions. In many cases, the purpose for conducting a risk and vulnerability assessment is to provide justification for spending funds on security for the IT infrastructure and assets. In other cases, the purpose of conducting a risk and vulnerability assessment is to assist an organization in defining an IT security architecture and framework based on the gaps and voids that are identified during the assessment. Many IT organizations need to conduct a risk and vulnerability assessment so that the organization can ensure the availability, integrity, and confidentiality of its IT infrastructure and assets. Creation of the RFP's mandatory minimum requirements and technical requirements are critical in order to eliminate organizations that are not financially sound, technically capable, or that require subcontractors to perform a majority of the work instead of having the expertise internal to the consulting or vendor company.

- **Public Announcement of RFP Bid Process/Prebid Conference**—Public procurements such as an RFP for risk and vulnerability assessment services require a public announcement or advertisement in a newspaper. Usually a newspaper advertisement or announcement is used to notify the consultant and vendor community that an RFP is to be released. For complex risk and vulnerability assessments, a prebid conference may be announced to share with the vendor community information about the upcoming RFP document.

- **Release of Official RFP Bid Document to Public**—This is the official date that the RFP bid document will be released to the general public.

- **Intent to Submit an RFP Response**—Many organizations require that any consultant or vendor that intends on submitting a formal RFP response must indicate their intent to submit a Response by a certain date and time. This allows the organization to focus its attention on those consultants and vendors that indicate they are responding to the RFP. All other consultants and vendors are not considered eligible to respond to the RFP after the deadline is passed for indicating the consultant's or vendor's intent to submit an RFP response.

- **Conduct RFP Bidder's Conference #1**—Typically, three to four weeks after the RFP is publicly released, the purchasing organization conducts an RFP bidder's conference where consultants and vendors can ask questions pertaining to the RFP document and the RFP process itself. This is the only allowed forum for consultants and vendors to ask questions. Typically, answers are provided verbally at the conference; however, all questions and answers are documented and provided to all RFP participants in the form of an official RFP addendum.

- **Prepare and Release RFP Bidder's Conference Addendum(s)**—The RFP may have more than one addendum as a result of the questions asked at the RFP bidder's conference and submitted in writing formally as per the RFP's question submittal instructions. All official correspondence to the consultants and vendors responding to the RFP is done through the RFP addendum.

- **Conduct RFP Bidder's Conference #2 (Optional)**—In the event that a second RFP bidder's conference is required, the organization announces a second conference where formal questions and answers can be provided via the RFP addendum.

- **RFP Response Submittal Due Date**—This is the due date, due time, and submittal address or location for all official RFP responses. Failure to follow the RFP submittal instructions may result in the RFP response being disqualified and not even evaluated. Following the RFP submittal instructions exactly as they are defined is the only way to ensure that the RFP response will be officially accepted by the purchasing organization.

- **RFP Public Announcement of Received RFP Responses**—Upon receipt of submittals and the expiration of the deadline for RFP submittals, the purchasing organization publicly announces which companies submitted an RFP response.

- **RFP Evaluation Process Commences with RFP Mandatory Minimum Requirements Review**—This is a quiet period in which the purchasing organization and the consultants and vendors that submitted an RFP response are not allowed to communicate with one another except through the RFP's submittal instructions for questions and answers, which is done through the RFP addendum. Typically, the RFP's Mandatory Requirements section is reviewed first for the RFP response's compliance with following the submittal instructions. Failure to follow the submittal instructions and RFP mandatory requirements may disqualify the RFP completely. This is critical to understand because nobody wants an RFP response, which is very time consuming to create, to be thrown out and disqualified because of a technicality or failure to meet all of the RFP's mandatory minimum requirements.

- **RFP Evaluation Process Continues with Scoring Sheets Filled In and Tabulated**—After the RFP's mandatory minimum requirements are met, that RFP's technical requirements responses can be examined and analyzed by the RFP evaluation team members. Whether this is a qualitative or quantitative RFP evaluation, each RFP evaluator must evaluate the RFP responses from his or her own perspective and understanding of the project. Typically, RFP evaluators are required to fill in RFP response sheets with scores based on a predefined yardstick. In some cases, a weighted scoring factor may put more value on certain requirements and less value on other requirements as they are evaluated by the RFP evaluators.

- **RFP Contract Award Public Announcement**—When all RFP responses have been completed, tabulated, and compared, the purchasing organization, after careful review and quality assurance of the RFP evaluations, makes an intent to award a contract for the risk and vulnerability assessment. This intent to award is merely that—an intent to award a contract pending contract negotiations and finalization.

- **RFP Contract Protest Period**—For public procurements, a period of protest usually commences after a public announcement is made of the intent to award a contract. Depending on any applicable procurement laws, the protest period starts from the date of intent to award a contract to a specified time that the other consultants and vendors may protest if they can prove or justify that a procurement violation or error in the awarded consultant's or vendor's RFP response warrants the protest. Typically, protesting an intent to award a contract must be done with physical evidence and proof that a violation in the winning consultant's or vendor's RFP response was made. Contract protest hearings are typically conducted to address any protests and to make available to the public the results of the contract protest.

- **RFP Contract Award and Contract Negotiations Commence**—After the protest period expires, the purchasing organization can commence with contract negotiations leading up to an awarded contract.

- **RFP Contract Award Is Signed and Executed**—Upon completion of the contract negotiations, the awarded contract is signed between the purchasing organization and the consultant or vendor who was awarded the contract.

- **RFP Contract for Products and/or Services Commences**—After the contract is engaged, the consultant or vendor commences the risk and vulnerability assessment project with a kick-off meeting to introduce the project team players and the overall project approach that is to be taken for the organization. Interfacing, communicating, and working in conjunction with the organization's IT and IT security staff is typically required and must be planned during the project's kick-off meeting.

Procurement Best Practices

Procuring the services of an outside consulting firm or vendor to conduct an objective risk and vulnerability assessment is not an easy task. This is especially true if the assessment is to be intrusive or nonintrusive.

Many organizations desire a rigorous risk and vulnerability assessment that includes the use of tools to find and uncover risks, threats, and vulnerabilities on a production network. This type of intrusive assessment means that the assessor will utilize tools and monitor the IT infrastructure during production hours when tests will be conducted. Some organizations demand that a nonintrusive risk and vulnerability assessment be conducted given the sensitivity and nature of their production systems and environments. In most cases, risks, threats, and vulnerabilities can be identified through careful examination of the IT infrastructure physically, logically, and on-site at the organization's data center and facilities.

When purchasing the outside services of an objective, independent consultant or vendor company to conduct a risk and vulnerability assessment, consider these best practices:

- Make sure the consultant or vendor company does not sell or represent any hardware or software products. This may bias their assessment and recommendations. One way to eliminate any bias is to disqualify the consultant or vendor selected for the risk and vulnerability assessment from selling any hardware or software products that may be recommended for securing the organization's IT infrastructure and assets.

- Objectivity can best be obtained by hiring a consultant or vendor company that is independent and that does not resell or represent any products of any kind. Many organizations make it an RFP mandatory minimum requirement that the consulting firm be only a consulting firm and not a reseller of products and services.

- Obtain and check at least three past performance references from the consultant or vendor company and ask them how their risk and vulnerability assessment project was using the consultant or vendor company.

- Define the Statement of Work's tasks and deliverables very succinctly and specifically within the RFP document itself. This way the purchasing organization knows exactly what it is buying and what it wants from the risk and vulnerability assessment.

- Define and map the goals and objectives for conducting the risk and vulnerability assessment to the organization's business drivers. This will ensure that the results of the risk and vulnerability assessment can be used to build a business case for enhancing the security of the IT infrastructure throughout the organization.

- Ask the consultant or vendors in the RFP response section to describe their understanding of the project, their approach to conducting the risk and vulnerability assessment, and how much time and resource support from the organization they are going to need to fulfill the tasks and deliverables. The consultants or vendor's response to these questions will clearly identify whether the consultant or vendor understands the situation and how they will approach the project. If the consultant or vendor company requires a significant amount of the organization's IT and IT security resources, that may not fall favorably with the RFP evaluation, especially if there is minimal IT and IT security staff. Obviously, the purchasing organization has to make a resource commitment for this type of project to be pursued. Risk and vulnerability assessments require extensive interviewing of personnel, collection and review of IT infrastructure, and asset documentation; access to systems and assets throughout the IT infrastructure must either be granted or performed by the organization's IT staff in the presence of the consultant or vendor company conducting the risk and vulnerability assessment service.

- Create and define the selection criteria and RFP evaluation point system up front, especially if there is no need to do so in a nonpublic procurement procedure. This is important to do so that objectivity in the evaluation of the RFP is methodical and unbiased.

- Ask the consultant or vendor for a 100% performance guarantee for the tasks and deliverables associated with the risk and vulnerability assessment service. This is important to obtain if you quite simply don't trust the consultant or vendor company. There are some consultants and vendor companies that will provide a 100% performance guarantee. It is not a guarantee for repayment, but rather a guarantee that the consulting firm or vendor company will redo any task or deliverable at its cost if the organization is not completely satisfied with the deliverable.

- Obtain the resumes of the actual people on the risk and vulnerability assessment project team. These individuals should be proficient in the IT systems and environment that is to be assessed. They should have proper training and professional certifications in the information security field, such as CISSP or GIAC, and the technical writing and documentation deliverables of these individuals should be reviewed. It does not hurt to ask the consultant or vendor company for writing samples to review as part of the evaluation.

- Negotiate favorable rates and delay payments to the consultant or vendor company until project deliverables are submitted and accepted. Delaying payments upon delivery and acceptance of the project's deliverables minimizes any potential problems or risk that the consultant or vendor company did not perform to the organization's satisfaction

- Implement a fixed-fee, not-to-exceed maximum contract value for the tasks and deliverables as stated in the LOU, RFQ, RFP, or SoW. This protects the organization from any unknowns or outside-the-scope-of-work issues that may arise. Typically, the consultant or vendor company must submit a Change in Scope Acceptance form that describes any new tasks or deliverables that are required after the project commences. This Change in Scope Acceptance form protects both the consultant or vendor company and the organization from any project unknowns, overages, or unauthorized hours for tasks and deliverables that are not officially approved.

- Specify the desired format and sections of the project deliverables in the LOU, RFQ, RFP, or SOW. For example, always ask for an Executive Summary, Project Approach Section, Summary of Findings, Assessment, and Recommendations. This will assist in the communication and delivery of the recommendations to the organization's executive management team. This will allow the organization to pull from the deliverables information and data needed to create executive management presentations and reports to make sound business decisions.

In summary, dealing with consultants and vendor companies can be a tedious and unpleasant experience, especially if you are being sold something, rather than finding a solutions partner. For risk and vulnerability assessments, use of independent or small consulting firms may provide you with the necessary technical and security expertise at a much lower cost. Use of a large consulting firm or vendor company may not be the most cost-effective, but may provide more experience and project references.

The personality of the organization should match the personality of the consultant or vendor company in that the consultant's or vendor's understanding of the project, approach to the project, and style for working with the organization are also factors to consider when selecting an outside consultant or vendor company. The most important evaluation element to consider for hiring an outside consultant or vendor company is how that consultant or vendor reiterates the understanding of the project and their approach for handling the risk and vulnerability assessment.

The consultant's or vendor's ability to articulate this as well as map the project's tasks and deliverables to their approach to the project should be evaluated carefully for relevance to the organization's ultimate project goals and objectives. This is the most important criteria to review and evaluate when selecting an outside consultant or vendor company to perform a risk and vulnerability assessment.

E

SIRT Team Report Format Template

This appendix provides a sample template for a SIRT Team Incident Report. This template outlines the information, data, and procedures for documenting a security breach or incident so that accurate information can be collected for each security breach or incident that is identified by the organization. Note that this is an example and each organization should modify this template and/or have their legal counsel and IT security managers provide additional input into the SIRT Team Incident Report.

SIRT Incident Report

The SIRT Team is responsible for timely and accurate documentation of every step in the security incident investigation. This documentation can best be organized using the following sample SIRT Team Incident Report Format.

SECURITY INCIDENT RESPONSE REPORT FORMAT

Report Date:_____   Report Time:_____

Trouble Ticket #:_____   Reported By:_____

Incident Severity Definition:_____

(Note: Critical and major incidents require paging the SIRT Team Leader immediately.)

A. Incident Response Data Collection

This portion of the security incident documentation is concerned with documenting the "when" and "what" for the particular incident. Critical and Major security breaches or incidents will require SIRT Team Leader involvement.

1. State the date and time when the incident was first discovered.

2. State who first discovered the incident.

    Name:_____   Organization:_____

    Email:_____   Phone:_____

3. State how the incident was discovered and describe any symptoms or abnormalities that were identified.

4. Describe the security incident and any immediate threats that it poses and classify the Security Incident as Critical, Major, or Minor based on its Incident Severity Definition as defined by the organization.

5. Did the security incident involve unauthorized access to a production system (for example, web server, LAN application server, network device, or mainframe-based system)? If yes, state the data-classification level that was compromised based on the custodian's data classification definition.

6. Specify the systems, servers, applications, and data that may have been compromised during the security incident.

7. Specify the hardware, software, applications, and other systems that were involved in the security incident. Provide as much detail as possible and obtain a copy of the system's log or audit files of all systems affected (for example, IDS/IPS, routers, switches, hubs, servers, systems, and so on).

8. Determine whether the security incident was conducted internally or externally to the IT infrastructure. Provide detail and supporting evidence to confirm.

B. Incident Response Forensics

This portion of the security incident documentation is concerned with documenting the "where," "why," and "what" for the particular incident. Critical and Major incidents will require SIRT Leader involvement in an effort to capture data and information that may be used as evidence in a court of law if a violation of a law, mandate, or regulation occurred.

1. Identify the source IP address or source IP network that the security incident came from, if possible. By examining the source IP address of the IP packets that the security incident originated from, information about the source of the attack may be provided.

2. For the systems and applications that are being compromised (real-time) or that were compromised, the SIRT Team Leader must make the following decisions:

    A. If the security incident is occurring in real-time, the SIRT Team Leader may decide to monitor the security incident rather than remove the system from the production environment to capture more data and determine the source of the perpetrator. This must be done under careful scrutiny to monitor the system access and maintain the integrity of the system's log files.

    B. For non-real-time security incidents, the SIRT Team Leader may decide to remove the system from the production environment in an effort to preserve and document the affected systems and any unauthorized manipulation or violations of the organization's policies.

3. Preserving in its original, compromised state the audit and log files for all systems, application, data manipulation or loss, and other pertinent damage that may have occurred is critical. Under the guidance of the SIRT Team Leader, document the steps and actions that were taken, such as the following:

    A. What actions were taken to preserve the affected systems, applications, and data?

B. What actions were taken to preserve the affected system log files? Specify whether these were tampered with or left in their original condition.

C. What other information about unauthorized access, systems compromised, and violations of the organization's security policies were identified? Identify and document all known violations.

D. Which systems in any of the seven areas of information security responsibility were taken offline in an effort to preserve the affected systems, applications, and data?

E. For enterprisewide systems and applications that were compromised, which services and processes were removed from the production network environment?

F. Which systems and servers were physically or logically disconnected from the production network environment?

G. For systems and servers that were compromised via a User or System Administrative level account, isolate the login ID and password that was compromised and delete or make an immediate change to the login ID and password.

H. Systems, resources, and data that have been compromised should be taken offline so that a thorough investigation of the affected systems and data can be conducted to assess any damage or tainting of data. This may require the system, resource, or data to be recovered as per the organization's backup and recovery procedures.

I. Prepare the Security Incident Response Report and keep all information and the details of the investigation confidential between the SIRT and the organization's executive management (CEO, CIO, CSO) prior to informing any other party. The SIRT Leader will decide who needs to be informed of this security incident based on the nature of the incident.

The purpose of a SIRT is to carry out the procedures and guidelines for an appropriate response to a security breach or incident for the organization. This appropriate response is part of an overall data and information collection task so that forensic data and evidence can be analyzed and evidence can be used in a court of law if criminal charges are warranted. In many cases, the organization must assess whether it wants to file criminal charges should the perpetrator who violated the organization's IT infrastructure and assets be found. This would become public domain information and would be part of the public record, which some organizations prefer not to do.

Tip

Proper data and information collection techniques must be followed and the integrity of collected data and information pertaining to a security breach or incident must be maintained in accordance with local, state, provincial, and federal law enforcement guidelines. Organizations should contact their legal counsel to define guidelines pertaining to the collection of forensic data used for security breaches or incident investigations if this data or physical evidence is to be used in a criminal case.

Index

exposure

defined, 66

factors, 66, 72

Extensible Authentication Protocol (EAP), 29

external attackers, 108

F

false acceptance rate (FAR), 29, 34

false rejection rate (FRR), 29, 34

FAR (false acceptance rate), 29, 34

Federal Information Security Management Act. *See* **FISMA**

FIN scans, 167

final reports

analysis sections, 198-199, 249

analysis, preparing for, 189-190

conclusions sections, 202, 250

contents, recommended, 196

executive summary sections, 197, 248

findings sections of, 200-201

impact rating, 191

importance of, 189

introduction sections, 197, 249

major goals of, 196

methodology statements, 197-198

notice sections, 196, 248

OICMs in, 198

options, offering, 200

pictures in, 197

policy control, 190, 193-194

probability scales, 192

purpose of, 195

ranking findings, 190-195

raw risk, 199

recommendations sections, 250

risk scores, 190-195, 199

SCMs in, 198

sections of, 196, 247-248

security baseline recommendations, 202

solution formulation approaches, 189

statement of work sections, 197-198, 249

summary, 203-204

team involvement, 189

templates for, 247-250

test results appendices, 250

writing quality issues, 196

financial institutions security law. *See* **GLBA**

financial losses due to attacks, 55

financial records

confidentiality laws, 45

information-gathering with, 166

findings sections of final reports, 200-201

fingers, 135. *See also* **OS fingerprinting**

FIPS 140-1 & 2 URL, 235

firewalls

defined, 16

deny-all recommended, 86

FISMA (Federal Information Security Management Act)

information assurance (IA) programs, 48

purpose of, 37, 48

reporting requirements, 49

risk assessment requirements, 48

forensic analysis plans, 60

forms (templates for assessments). *See* **security assessment forms**

risk management basis, 210-212

sample elements of, 215-216

staff training, 216

standards defined, 210

technical standards defined, 210

terminology for, 209-210

threat and vulnerability policies, 210

threat management, 216

vulnerability management, 216

ITSEC (Information Technology Security Evaluation Criteria), 10, 17, 148

J – K – L

job searches, 166

John the Ripper, 178, 239

kickoff meetings

defined, 106

key issues to discuss during, 91-93

Kismet, 175

labeling systems, documentation review of, 150

LAN areas, 217-219

LAN-to-WAN areas, 217, 220

LANguard, 182

legal issues

accounting. See Sarbanes-Oxley Act

compliance as cause of vulnerability assessments, 13

criminal breach guidelines for data collection, 263

current risk assessment laws, list of, 37

financial record confidentiality, 45

mandates, 62

medical data. See HIPAA; HIPPA

privacy laws, 45

regulatory documents, 103

scope definition, 89

security law. See Sarbanes-Oxley Act

U.S. Code 1029, 45

letters of understanding (LOUs), 252

level I assessments

account management, 145

categories of policy control, table of, 139

COBIT, 154

common policy problems, 151-153

communication security, 149

defined, 8, 106

document review process. See reviewing documentation

education training and awareness, 151

guidelines for, 152

identification and authentication, 145

interviewing process, 154-156

ISO 17799, 153

labeling systems, 150

maintenance documentation, 147

malicious code protection category, 147

management controls, 141-144

media controls, 149-150

networking connectivity, 148

operational controls, 149-151

personal security, 150

physical security, 150

RFC 2196, 154

scoping phase policy review, 141

security auditing, 147

session controls, 146

system assurance, 147-148

requests for information, 252

requests for proposals, 253-258

requests for quotations, 253

requirements creation, RFP, 255

resources required by consultants, 259

resumes of individuals, 259

selection criteria creation, 251

statements of work, 253, 258

steps in, 254-258

terminology, 252-253

productivity losses, 55

program crackers, 110

project management scope definition, 89-90

proportionality, 10

Public Company Accounting Oversight Board (PCAOB), 49

public information, 22

public key encryption, 31

publicly traded corporations security law. *See* **Sarbanes-Oxley Act**

Q – R

qualitative risk assessments

advantages of, 75

analysis, 62

best practices, 76

criticality assessments. *See* OICMs; SCMs

data classification standards for, 74

definition of qualitative assessments, 106

purpose of, 74

sample scenario, 74-75

team membership, 74

valuations, 70

quantitative risk assessments

advantages of, 75

ALE calculation step, 73-74

Annualized Loss Expectancy, 76

Annualized Rate of Occurrence (ARO), 76

ARO calculation step, 73

asset identification, 71

assets value determination, 75

best practices, 75-76

data needed for, 71

defined, 71

exposure factor scaling, 76

exposure factor valuation, 72

Single Loss Expectancy, 76

single loss expectancy calculation, 72-73

steps in, 71

threat likelihood, 71

valuations, 70

RAIDs (redundant arrays of inexpensive disks), 35

Rainbow Series, DoD

system assurance aspect of, 148

URLs for, 236

RainbowCrack technique, 177, 240

rate limiting network traffic, 116

raw risk

calculating, 192-193

components of, 190

defined, 205

impact rating, 191

presentation of, 199

probability scales, 192

rankings matrices, 192

RFC 2196, 154

roles and responsibilities, 142–143

scheduling implementation, 152

security auditing, 147

security auditors, 143

session controls, 146

system assurance, 147–148

technical controls, 144–149

testing, 152

users, 142

RFC 2196

purpose of, 161

reviewing documentation, 154

RFIs (requests for information), 252

RFPs (requests for proposals)

award announcements, 257

bid document creation, 255

bidders conferences, 256

contract completion, 257

defined, 253

due dates for, 256

evaluation completion, 257

evaluation methodology, 254

format development, 254

importance of, 254

instructions for, 255

intent to submit response, submitting, 256

mandatory minimum requirements reviews, 256

objective of, 254

protest periods, 257

public announcements of, 255

requirements creation, 255

team assembly, 254

RFQs (requests for quotations), 253

Rijndael, 21, 33

risk

acceptance, 17

application systems as assets, 38

analysis. *See* risk analysis

assessments. *See* risk assessments

avoidance, 17

backup systems as assets, 39

defined, 17, 38

documentation as assets, 39

elements of, 38

intellectual property as assets, 39

management. *See* risk management

methodologies. *See* risk assessment methodologies

mitigation, 17

network systems as assets, 38

operating systems as assets, 38

scoring. *See* risk scores

security systems as assets, 39

server systems as assets, 39

telecommunication systems as assets, 38

threats as causes of, 39–40

transference, 17

vulnerability component of, 40

workstations as assets, 38

risk analysis

attacker use of, 122–123

defined, 66

life cycle of, 69

risk assessment methodologies

asset valuation approach, 69–70

bottom-up approach, 77–78

defense-in-depth approach, 67–68

hybrid approach, 78–79

identification, 53

ISO 17799, 79–80

RBAC (role-based access control), 30, 35

remote access areas, 219

systems/applications areas, 221

WAN areas, 220

workstation areas, 218

S

safeguards, 66

SAINT, 181

sample final reports, 247-250

SANS, 239

SARA, 182

Sarbanes-Oxley Act

authentication issues, 50

certification of internal controls, 51

COBIT, 50

Control Environment, 51

COSO, 50

management structures requirements, 51

monitoring requirements, 50-51

network security, 50

oversight of, 49

PCAOB, 49

physical security, 50

purpose of, 49

risk assessment requirements, 51

scope of, 37

Section 302, 51

Section 404, 51

security policies, 50

segregation of duties, 50

user account management, 50

Sasser worm, 114

SATAN (Security Administrator Tool for Analyzing Networks), 163

scanning tools

banner grabbing, 170

inverse SYN cookies, 169, 186

network discovery, 167

Nmap, 168

OS identification, 167, 170

port scanning, 167

reconnaissance tools, 124-128

Scanrand, 169

stateless scanning, 169

steps for using, 167

SuperScan, 169

TCP scan techniques, 167

THC-Amap, 170

URLs for tools, 170

Xprobe2, 170

Scanrand, 169, 239

scarcity-based social engineering, 32

scheduling issues

key points for, 6-7

timeline construction, 14-15

SCMs (systems criticality matrices), 101, 106, 198, 245

scope

administrative information for, 88

breaches in security as drivers, 87

business reasons for, 85

compliance as driver for, 87

creep, 93-94, 106

critical systems identification, 92

defining for assessments, overview of, 85-86

driving events for defining, 86-88

due diligence as driver, 86

importance of, 85

information request forms, 88-89

key personnel identification, 92

U

X – Y – Z